D0392150

Praise for *It's Earnings That Count*

"Well-written, intellectually sound, "accessible" to those who take the time to understand, and a poke in the eye to those who abused our capitalistic system and those (pros) who let them get away with it."

—John C. Bogle, founder and former CEO, The Vanguard Group

"In a single, easy to use index, Hewitt Heiserman captures the essence of growth and value—a most insightful approach to stock picking."

—Charles W. Mulford, co-author, The Financial Numbers Game, director, DuPree Financial Analysis Lab and professor of Accounting, Georgia Institute of Technology

"Clear and engaging, Heiserman shows how to easily evaluate a growth company's investment potential for both conservative and aggressive investors. The result? The 'cautiously greedy' investor wins."

—Tom Jacobs, senior analyst, The Motley Fool

"Heiserman's unique and thorough analysis not only provides methods for avoiding companies with suspect earnings, but also uncovering the true gems that are able to grow well into the future."

—Timothy M. Mulligan, J.D., LL.M., CPA., CEO, Forensic Advisors, Inc.

"Hewitt Heiserman's innovative financial analysis technique goes a long way towards providing an investor with an extra edge in identifying the growth stocks of tomorrow without being unduly exposed to excessive investment risk today."

—Thornton L. Oglove, founder, Quality of Earnings Report

"This book lays the groundwork for becoming a successful long-term investor."

—Mark Sellers, equities strategist & portfolio manager, Morningstar, Inc.

"As an avid reader of investment books, I recommend this book wholeheartedly."

—*Arne Alsin, Real Money.com and The Turnaround Fund*

"In a clear, sound and practical way, Heiserman provides an investment road map that enhances the odds of your becoming a successful long-term investor."

—*Robert L. Rodriguez, chief executive officer, First Pacific Advisors and two-time recipient of Morningstar Mutual Fund's Manager of the Year*

"You really do have to understand 'earnings' if you are to succeed long term in investing."

—*Jim Rogers, author, Adventure Capitalist* and *Investment Biker*

"Heiserman shows investors how to uncover Wall Street earnings quackery and frauds. A must read."

—*Kenneth Lee, author, Trouncing the Dow*

"Like a professional athlete, Hewitt Heiserman Jr. brings intensity and brainpower to the world of investing. You need the graduate school that *It's Earnings That Count* can provide. Buy the book and do your homework."

—*John D. Spooner, director-investments SmithBarney Citgroup and author of Confessions of a Stockbroker, Sex and Money,* and *Do You Want to Make Money or Would You Rather Fool Around?*

"Great addition to the literature! Hewitt Heiserman has crafted an easy read, basic tutorial on avoiding the most common mistakes caused by accounting phony baloney-combined with some age old investment wisdom. Mandatory for the intermediate investor!"

—*Kenneth L. Fisher, CEO of Fisher Investments Inc. and Forbes' "Portfolio Strategy" columnist*

IT'S EARNINGS THAT COUNT

IT'S EARNINGS THAT COUNT

Finding Stocks with Earnings Power for Long-Term Profits

HEWITT HEISERMAN JR.

McGraw-Hill

New York Chicago San Francisco Lisbon London Madrid
Mexico City Milan New Delhi San Juan Seoul
Singapore Sydney Toronto

The McGraw-Hill Companies

Library of Congress Cataloging-in-Publication Data

Heiserman, Hewitt Jr.
It's earnings that count : finding stocks with earnings power for long-term profits / by Hewitt Heiserman, Jr.
p. cm.
ISBN 0-07-142323-0 (hardcover : alk. paper)
1. Stocks. 2. Financial statements. 3. Investment analysis. 4.Portfolio management. I. Title.

HG4661.H44 2003
332.63'2042—dc21 2003013491

1 2 3 4 5 6 7 8 9 0 DOC/DOC 0 9 8 7 6 5 4 3

ISBN 0-07-142323-0

Printed and bound by RR Donnelley.

This book was printed on recycled, acid-free paper containing a minimum of 50% recycled, de-inked fiber.

To Dad

A kind and generous man.

CONTENTS

FOREWORD

A HISTORIC BUBBLE INFLATES

It is only a matter of time until the Great Stock Market Bubble of 1998–2000 takes its proper place, at least metaphorically, in a new edition of *Extraordinary Popular Delusions and the Madness of Crowds*, the classic 1841 compilation of market manias by Charles Mackay. But we already know many of its causes.

Surely the idea that a "New Era" lay before us was one of them. We were entering the Information Age, happily coincident with Y2K and the new millennium. And quantum advances in computer technology, plummeting prices for microchips, and the World Wide Web combined to present tangible evidence that our global society was at the threshold of radical change.

"This time *is* different" was the rallying cry. The stock market headed upward, almost unremittingly, as investors enthusiastically jumped aboard the bull market bandwagon. From the start of 1998 until the peak was reached in March of 2000, the Nasdaq composite index—largely "new economy" stocks—soared by 220 percent, and even its stodgy "old economy" counterpart—the New York Stock Exchange Index—returned 40 percent.

A NEW GILDED AGE

The Great Wall Street Selling Machine was quick to sense, then join, and then promote the idea that a new Gilded Age was at hand. Indeed, fostered by vigorous promotion of existing growth stocks and even more vigorous promotion (often in the guise of "investment research") of initial public offerings, a new Gilded Age *was* at hand. But not for investors. Rather, those who reaped billions—likely hundreds of billions—of dollars from the Great Bubble were the financial tycoons, the investment bankers, the money managers, the Internet pioneers, and the entrepreneurs, who created new concepts and new companies as fast as the public would accept them.

It was a Gilded Age, too, for corporate executives. The multiplicity of flaws in our executive compensation system—stock options that rewarded managers for transitory increases in the price of the stock rather than durable enhancement in the intrinsic value of the corporation; the absence of a cost-of-capital hurdle; no requirement, God forbid, that executives actually *hold* the shares acquired through exercise; burying the true costs of options by not characterizing them as corporate expenses—lured our business establishment into turning the classic model of capitalism upside down. That move from the traditional system of *owners'* capitalism into a new system of *managers'* capitalism would gradually erode the moral and ethical standards on which capitalism had traditionally been based. Not only did corporate directors fail to place shareholder interests above management interests, but even the owners of corporate America looked on without knowing, or at least without caring, that it was in fact *their* ox that was being gored.

At the fulcrum of the forces that drove stock prices onward and upward was the improper reporting of corporate earnings. In explaining soaring stock prices, stock market participants came to seek rationalization over reason. The "new economy," it was said, requires new accounting principles; corporate earnings could be not only "managed," but managed from each quarter to the next; *pro forma* earnings were more important than earnings determined under generally accepted accounting principles. Yet, amazingly, much of this foolishness took place with the eyes, not just of novice individual investors, but also of experienced institutional investors, wide open.

THE HAPPY CONSPIRACY

Why didn't someone do something or say something? In part, because investors were loving the ride. "Everybody" was getting rich. But shouldn't we have known better? Of course. And didn't we realize that the great bull market was destined to end badly? Again, yes. Indeed, two years before the collapse of Enron, I warned about earnings management. In a speech entitled "The Silence of the Funds," delivered before the New York Society of Security Analysts on October 20, 1999, I felt like a stranger in a foreign land when I stood up and spoke these words:

Today, we live in a world of managed earnings. While it is corporate executives who do the managing, they do so with at least the tacit approval of corporate directors and auditors, and with the enthusiastic endorsement of institutional investors with short-term time horizons, even speculators and arbitrageurs, rather than in response to the demands of long-term investors. Like it or not, corporate strategy and financial accounting alike focus on meeting the earnings expectations of "the Street" quarter after quarter. The desideratum is steady annual earnings growth—manage it to at least the 12 percent level, if you can—and at all costs avoid falling short of the earnings expectations at which the corporation has hinted, or whispered, or "ballparked" before the year began. If all else fails, obscure the real results by merging, taking a big one-time write-off, and relying on pooling-of-interest accounting. All of this creative financial engineering apparently serves to inflate stock prices, to enrich managers, and to deliver to institutional investors what they want.

But if the stock market is to be the arbiter of value, it will do its job best, in my judgment, if it sets its valuations based on punctiliously accurate corporate financial reporting and a focus on the long-term prospects of the corporations it values. However, the market's direction seems quite the opposite. For while the accounting practices of America's corporations may well be the envy of the world, our nation's financial environment has become permeated with the concept of managed earnings. The accepted idea is to smooth reported earnings, often by aiding security analysts to establish earnings expectations for the year, and then, each quarter, reporting earnings that "meet expectations," or, better yet, "exceed expectations." It is an illusory world that ignores the normal ups and downs of business revenues and expenses, a world in which "negative earnings surprises" are to be avoided at all costs…

…with huge restructuring changes, creative acquisition accounting, "cookie jar" reserves, excessive "immaterial" items, and premature recognition of revenue, earnings management has gone too far. As SEC chairman Arthur Levitt has said, "almost everyone in the financial community shares responsibility [with corporate management] for fostering this climate." It is, in a perverse sense, a happy conspiracy. But I believe that no corporation can manage its earnings forever, and that managed earnings misrepresent the inherently cyclical nature of business. Even as we begin to take for granted that fluctuating earnings are steady and

ever-growing, we ought to recognize that, somewhere down the road, there lies a day of reckoning that will not be pleasant.

THE DAY OF RECKONING ARRIVES

Only a brief six months later, the inevitable day of reckoning arrived. On March 24, 2000, the great bull market drew to its inevitable close. Since the huge advance in stock prices was unsustainable (using the inspired phraseology of economist Herb Stein), it couldn't be sustained. The aftermath has hardly been pleasant. From the market's peak in March 2000 to the low (so far, at least) in early October 2002, the Nasdaq Index tumbled by 75 percent, and the NYSE Index fell 33 percent. Today, as I write these words, both have recovered smartly from their lows but remain near their pre-bubble levels of late 1997. But brutal damage has been done to investors, to our capitalistic system, and to our society.

The bad behavior of business has rewarded the winners—the executives who cashed in their shares, the IPO entrepreneurs, the Wall Street firms who sold the IPOs to the public, and the mutual fund managers who attracted nearly one trillion (!) dollars of the public's assets, largely in aggressive, risky funds that were focused on the new economy, nearly 500 of them organized solely to capitalize on the market madness as it reached its zenith.

The bad behavior of business has also penalized the losers. *Not* the long-term investors who saw their portfolios rise from reasonable valuations to absurd valuations, only to revert once again to reasonable levels. The real damage was done to short-term stockholders, including millions of public investors lured into the mania by clever marketers or by their own greed or ignorance, as well as, ironically, corporations that repurchased their own shares to avoid the dilution from the shares they issued under excessively generous option plans. While the final returns, as it were, are not yet in, it is fair to say that we have witnessed a massive transfer of wealth, largely *to* those who knew what was truly going on in corporate financial statements, *from* those who either didn't know or, worse, didn't care.

It is my duty to acknowledge that too many mutual fund managers fall into this latter group. By its lackadaisical approach to investment analysis, this industry bears considerable responsibility for the boom and subsequent bust in the stock market. Way back in 1968, Columbia Law School Professor Louis Lowenstein observed that fund managers "exhibit a persistent emphasis on momentary stock prices. The subtleties and nuances of a particular business utterly escape them." Since then, things have proceeded to get even worse. Annual mutual fund portfolio turnover, about 15 percent during the 1950s, had risen to 40 percent by the late 1960s. But that was only the beginning. Last year, the average turnover of the average fund was 110 percent, the culmination of our transition from an *own-a-stock* industry to a *rent-a-stock* industry. Indeed, when Oscar Wilde described the cynic as one "who knows the price of everything but the value of nothing," he could have as easily been describing today's mutual fund manager.

IT'S EARNINGS THAT COUNT

Returning the stock market to a solid footing will require mutual funds and other institutional shareholders to abandon their present focus on short-term speculation based on momentary stock prices and return to their traditional focus on long-term investing based on intrinsic corporate values. And since the value of a corporation depends—as it does, as it must, and as it always will—on the discounted value of its future cash flows, it follows that corporate earnings must be presented fairly, accurately, and dependably. It is here that this fine book by Hewitt Heiserman enters the field of play.

It's Earnings That Count is a title well chosen. Of course it's earnings that count! One need only look at the chart on page xvi comparing total stock market returns over the past 130 years with the returns created by corporate earnings growth and dividend yields to see the truth of that statement. While in the short run stock prices may vastly depart from these investment fundamentals, in the long run investment returns are all about earnings and dividends. Dividends, of course, are real. On the other hand, given the remarkably wide parameters of Generally Accounted Accounting Principles (GAAP), earnings have become whatever management wants them to be.

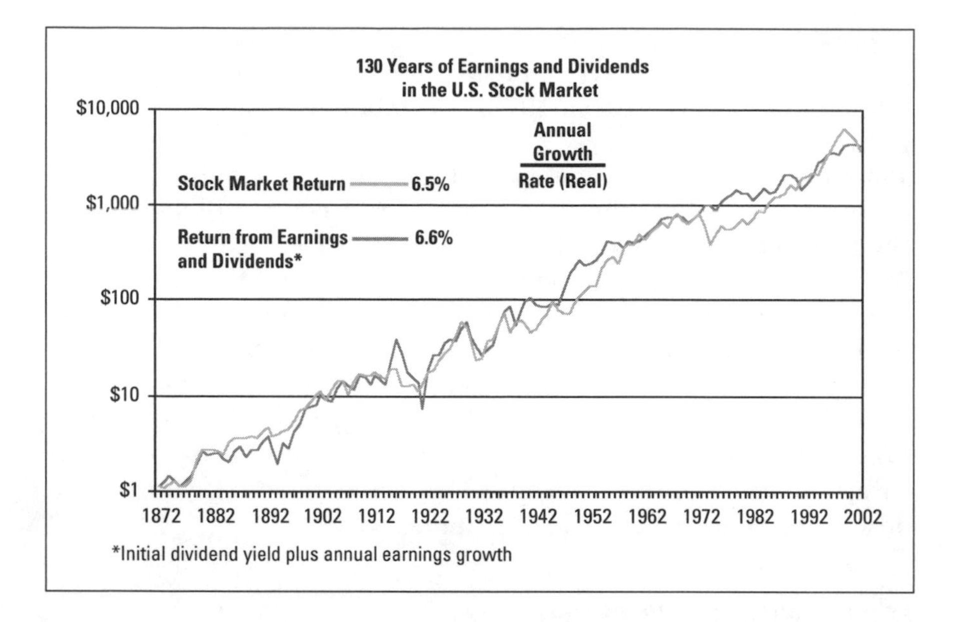

When earnings can't be managed to meet management's projections, just change the terminology. Move the focus from *reported* earnings to *operating* earnings, so that the write-offs of all those earlier foolish capital expenditures and unwise mergers are ignored. If that doesn't do the trick, report pro forma earnings that *exclude* all those "bad" experiences that are said to be nonrecurring and *include* all those "good" revenues, often both nonrecurring and undisclosed. And when operating earnings and pro forma earnings aren't good enough to meet the market's demands, report *fraudulent* earnings. Just "cook the books," and in the post-Enron environment, we've already seen far too many cases of fraud. We can only hope that the cheats receive tough jail sentences in hard penitentiaries for the crimes they have committed. But we should not forget that they have betrayed capitalism as well.

In the rules-based environment of GAAP, it has proven impossible for the *defense*—the public accountants and the directors, even if they are not co-opted by management, and the regulators, struggling with limited resources—to keep up with the wily *offense* so often waged by the CEO and his *eminence grise*, the chief financial officer. When they control the numbers, the press releases, and the organization itself, they have the *opportunity* to report what they will. Too often our flawed system of executive compensation system gives them the *motive* to push those accounting "principles" to their very limit. And when opportunity and motive meet, don't be surprised when things go badly awry in financial statements.

Simply put, the fact is that our accounting principles are broad enough to drive a truck through. And even if U.S. business were to move, as many thoughtful observers have suggested, from today's *rules-based* system to the kind of *principles-based* system that exists in Great Britain, ample room will remain for maneuver designed to produce the best-looking results. One improvement that might be useful would be to have the corporation report *two* sets of earnings, one using the most favorable interpretations (in terms of enhancing earnings)—presumably close to what is reported today—and another using the *least* favorable interpretations (that is, if the tax rate were to rise to 90 percent, how *little* earnings could a company report?).

MEASURE THRICE, CUT ONCE

Even if that idea one day finds acceptance (an unlikely event!), Hewitt Heiserman's concept of creating two alternative earnings statements makes consummate good sense. One is a *defensive* income statement that reveals the extent to which a company depends on outside sources of capital. The other is an *enterprising* income statement that reveals the company's return relative to its total capital base, including stockholders' equity. (Both can be constructed through information publicly available in corporate annual reports and 10-K and 10-Q reports to the U.S. Securities and Exchange Commission.)

The author properly credits others for these two concepts. But by combining them in his simple "Earnings Power Chart" methodology, he presents these two statements in a manner that is accessible to any serious investor who is willing to undertake the modest amount of analysis required. (In *The Intelligent Investor*, Benjamin Graham defines such an investor as the "enterprising" investor, and the "defensive" investor as one who entrusts others with the responsibility for the stewardship of his assets. Heiserman's terminology, while using a different context, provides a refreshing echo of Graham's value-driven approach to stock selection.)

Do we really need *three* earnings statements? I don't see why not. And when you read the author's thoughtful case for these two supplements to the existing GAAP statement, I believe you'll agree that they combine to make a sensible, logical case for intelligent stock selection. An ancient rule for the carpenter advises, "measure twice, cut once." Since investors have much more at stake than a single piece of lumber when they select a stock, surely it makes good sense to evaluate a company's earnings in all *three* dimensions—"*Measure thrice, cut once.*"

One can only marvel that this fine book was produced by a mere intelligent investor rather than an academic or an MBA-trained, experienced security analyst. Yet with so much of the investment world now focused on marketing rather than management, we shouldn't be surprised. Wall Street is, as it always has been, a powerful (and, truth be told, necessary) machine designed to sell securities. And mutual fund managers have greater incentives to increase assets under management than to produce superior records. (After all, *all* managers have the ability to bring in money; only a small minority have the ability—or luck—to beat the market.) Those who were beneficiaries of the "happy conspiracy" that I described earlier had good reason not to point out that the reported earnings "clothes" of the stock market "emperor," when they existed at all, left much to the imagination.

A PERSONAL NOTE

I must confess that I surprised myself when I agreed to write a foreword to this book on how analyzing earnings statements can improve stock selections. But this book is about much more than earnings quality. It is a wonderful catalog of what went wrong in corporate America, a theme with which I've been deeply concerned for the better part of a decade. The book also implicitly raises the question of what other institutional investors within the financial system could have been thinking as the market madness went on. In that sense, *It's Earnings That Count* is a sort of poke-in-the eye both to those corporate leaders who abused our capitalistic system and to those financial pros who let them get away with it.

I want to be clear that my endorsement is not inconsistent with my philosophy as a dyed-in-the-wool "indexer"—a believer that since stock selection is not only a loser's game but an expensive one, the best strategy for accumulation of equity capital is to own the entire stock market. And I reaffirm my view that buying a share in every company in America at minimal cost through an all-stock-market index fund, and holding it for Warren Buffett's favorite holding period—*forever*—is the surest route to long-term investment success.

Nonetheless, for better or worse, nearly all investors love the challenge of matching wits with the market, and no matter what I advise, most investors are probably going to pick at least a stock or two. Using the principles in this book should give those investors a fighting chance to win the game—truly an awesome challenge. The author candidly and humbly acknowledges that he shares my view that "beating the market is hard," and agrees with my own oft-stated philosophy that an all-stock-market index fund or other widely diversified stock portfolio should represent 95 percent of an investor's equity assets. I endorse his advice that you follow his principles with no more than 5 percent of your equity assets during the first few years that you use them. If they work for you, "then maybe you double your bet, to 10 percent."[1]

Good luck!

John C. Bogle
Founder and former CEO, The Vanguard Group

About John C. Bogle

Mr. Bogle has worked in the investment management field since graduating magna cum laude from Princeton University in 1951 with a degree in Economics. In 1974 he created The Vanguard Group, Inc., which today has $600 billion in assets. The Vanguard 500 Index Fund, the first of its kind, was conceived by Mr. Bogle in 1975. In 1999 he received the Woodrow Wilson Award from Princeton University for "distinguished achievement in the Nation's service." That same year Fortune named Mr. Bogle one of the investment industry's four "Giants of the 20th Century." He is the author of four books, including *Bogle on Mutual Funds: New Perspectives for the Intelligent Investo*r, a best-seller since its publication in 1993. Mr. Bogle remains at Vanguard as president of the Bogle Financial Markets Research Center, where he continues to speak forcefully on the behalf of individual investors. Mr. Bogle is also chairman of the National Constitution Center, in Philadelphia, Pennsylvania.

ACKNOWLEDGMENTS

First I want to thank John C. Bogle, who I've admired from afar for many years, for writing this book's foreword.

Thanks, as well, to Warren E. Buffett, Philip Fisher, the late Benjamin Graham, Jim Rogers, and John Train, from whom I have learned so much.

William H. Apfel, Ph.D., Katherine W. Bantleon, Debbie Bosanek, Robert J. Bradfield III, Esq., Anna Burke, John K. Cameron, L. John Constable, Tony Crescenzi, Joseph I. Diamond, Esq., Alan Farley of HardRightEdge.com, W. John Flamish, Paul Gambal, Ann Grimes, Thomas A. and Betsy Grimes, Cheryl Holland, Mark Holloway of Holloway Investment Advisors, the staff of the Horn Library at Babson College, Jeffrey S. Johnsen, Frank Jolley, Irving Kahn, Jeffrey S. Katz, Caroline G. Lawlor, Kevin P. Laughlin, Kenneth W. Lee, John K. Leister, Fr. Craig J. Lister, Patsy McGregor, Jeffrey C. Macklis, Andrew S. Milgram, John S. Milgram, Thomas B. Milgram, the Rev. Harry S. Mills, Doerthe Obert, Betsy Wenzel, Marguerite Whitley May, John F. O'Reilly, Matt Richey, Dr. and Mrs. Carl R. Peterson, Suzette Peterson, Michele Piersiak, James D. Robins, John P. Schenk, Florence and the late Judge Nathan A. Schwartz, Fraser P. Seitel, Peter J. and Laura Seoane, Andy Simmons, the Rev. Sheldon M. Smith, Richard W. Snowden, Judge John C. Stevens III, Henderson Supplee III, Joshua C. Thompson, Whitney Tilson of Tilson Capital Partners, G. Darwin Toll, Jr., Neil and Kristin Trueblood, Jeffrey J. Upton, Esq., Patricia Upton, Pauline O. Walker, Derek P. B. Warden, A. Churchill Young IV and Cynthia A. Zickel of The Haverford Trust Company, all helped me out along the way.

Thanks, as well, to my friends at TheStreet.com, including Mike Anderson, James J. Cramer, Christopher Edmonds, Michael Goodman, Herb Greenberg, Doug Kass, David Morrow, Christopher Nichols, and Helaine Tishberg. I am especially indebted to Michelle Zangara, editor of TheStreet's award-winning RealMoney.com website.

Patricia Crisafulli of Chicago, Illinois, Luna Shyr of New York, New York, and John Simon of Portsmouth, New Hampshire, all burned the midnight oil to get this manuscript shipshape.

I want to thank my terrific editor, Kelli Christiansen, at McGraw-Hill's Professional Book Group. Daina Penikas, editing supervisor at McGraw-Hill, also made things easy for me.

Arne Alsin, CPA, J.D., of Alsin Capital Management, Inc., Jeffrey F. Brotman, Esq., John Del Vecchio, CFA, of David W. Tice & Associates, Brian Gilmartin, CFA, of Trinity Asset Management, Mark Haefele, PhD, of Sonic Capital, Thomas C. Jacobs, Esq. of The Motley Fool, Susan Lakatos, CFA, CFP, of TheStreet.com's Street Insight, John Linder, CPA, MAC, and David Segelov, CFA, each made valuable suggestions to improve this book.

Thanks, as well, to my teachers and coaches at The Haverford School, including Donald G. Brownlow, the late Neil Buckley, Edward R. Hallowell, and Daniel J. McWilliams, and to my professors at Kenyon College, including Roy T. Wortman.

I am especially grateful to William C. and Laura T. Buck, the late Gerry W. and Margaretta S. Cox, Gerry W. and Audrey R. Cox, Jr., my brother David S. Heiserman, my sister Margaretta H. Himes, my mother Mary C. C. Heiserman, Betty and the late Robert B. Heiserman, Jr., Douglas L. Hoffmann, Joseph B. and Margaretta C. Milgram, Jr., and Nathan A. Schwartz, Jr., Esq.

Of course, I couldn't have written this book without the support of my smart, loving, and patient wife Laura. This was a team effort from day one. Thank you, Laura...and Benjamin, too!

INTRODUCTION

In the winter of 1994 the New York Society of Security Analysts celebrated the one hundredth birthday of Benjamin Graham, the father of security analysis. Graham had died 18 years earlier, in 1976, but several of his friends, colleagues, former students, and admirers attended the event.

The highlight of the occasion was a question-and-answer session with three successful investors who had known Graham well. Irving Kahn, founder of Kahn Brothers & Co., Inc., and Warren Buffett, who had been a student of Graham's at Columbia University, as well as Walter Schloss, had all worked with Graham at one time or another. Buffett, who has been famous for owning just a few stocks at a time, asked by a guest toward the end of the session whether he was comfortable owning such a concentrated portfolio, replied that he'd be "even more comfortable if it were smaller because that would mean that I would like those securities even that much more. And there aren't that many wonderful businesses." Buffett paused, then blurted out: "A lot of great fortunes in the world have been made by owning a single wonderful business. If you understand the business, you don't need to own very many of them." [1]

Buffett is right, of course. You can prosper handsomely by finding the right company and investing in its success for long-term profits. Microsoft Corporation is just one of the many success stories from the last decade. But how do you find that single wonderful business?

Many investors look for stocks of companies that keep making more and more money every year—a growth stock, in other words. If you own one Microsoft in your lifetime, the capital gains can bail you out of a lot of bad stock picks plus leave you with extra cash for the future.

Unfortunately, growth investing is tricky for three reasons.

First, growth stocks tend to be expensive because investors' optimism about a company's bright future often pushes the stock price beyond its true worth. Should these expectations change for the worse, the stock collapses under its own vertiginous weight. Look at Microsoft: After years of rapid growth in the 1990s its market value dropped by two-thirds in 2000.

Second, many promising growth companies get eclipsed when a competitor comes out with a better product. So these firms that once had so much potential become like meteors in the sky, burning brightly for a time and then flickering out because they can't adapt to changes in consumer preferences.

Third, a firm that appears to be profitable on its income statements, in the way that accountants define profits might, in fact, have low earnings quality. That's not to say that its earnings are misstated or inflated or that there is any evidence of fraud (although it's always a possibility). Instead, net income, without breaking a single law or accounting rule, can, upon close examination, prove to be less than it appears.

How can an investor determine earnings quality? That's where this book can help. Although I address the first two points—of valuation and competitive advantage—the main objective of *It's Earnings That Count* is to help you with point number three. Specifically, we will learn that the income statement in every annual report, 10-K and 10-Q has four substantive limitations. As a result, a company may be profitable in the traditional sense of the word but not have authentic earnings power. My advice is that you build two alternate income statements, a defensive income statement and an enterprising income statement.

- The defensive income statement reveals the degree to which a company depends on outside sources of capital and, in the extreme, the risk of going bankrupt. The defensive income statement matches the mindset of the defensive investor, for whom not losing money is paramount. (Think commercial banker.)
- The enterprising income statement assesses the return generated by all of a company's sources of capital, including stockholders' equity. The enterprising income statement appeals to the enterprising investor who wants to find a big opportunity before everyone else. (Think venture capitalist.)

Albeit valuable, even these two alternate perspectives have their own limitations. The defensive income statement is too defensive for the enterprising investor, the enterprising income statement too enterprising for the defensive investor. What I do in this book is convene a meeting of these two mindsets.

Enter the Earnings Power Chart, which is a visual representation of a company's defensive and enterprising income statements. As you will learn, the chart plots defensive and enterprising profits (or losses) as coordinates along an *X* and *Y* axis. The push and pull of these sometimes opposing forces determines which of the four boxes the company is situated in. As you would expect, the best companies (but not necessarily the best stocks) are situated in the upper-right box, the Earnings Power Box. These companies are profitable on both a defensive and enterprising basis. If the company is really special, it will also be moving in an upper-right direction. Microsoft is one of these companies, as we see in Figure I.1. Companies like Microsoft I call "Earnings Power Staircase" companies because the pattern of steady improvement year after year resembles the profile of a staircase. Not only do these companies get bigger, *they get better*.

The Earnings Power Chart synthesizes ideas popularized in *Cash Flow and Securities Analysis* by Kenneth Hackel and Joshua Livnat and *The Quest for Value* by Bennett Stewart. The defensive income statement introduced by Hackel and Livnat (which they call "free cash flow") fixes two substantive limitations of the traditional (or "accrual" because it is based upon accrual accounting) income statement. Meanwhile, the enterprising income statement promoted by Stewart (which he calls Economic Valued Added, or EVA) fixes the other two significant limitations of the accrual income statement.

Taken together, the defensive and enterprising income statements give you a clearer picture of a firm's earnings quality. And since pictures have a higher emotional valence than numbers or words, this two-dimensional view of a company's financial results will help you make the right decision when it comes time to decide whether to buy, sell or hold.

My goal here is to present the concepts of the defensive and enterprising income statements in a way that is accessible to anyone who wants to improve their investment results. This book assumes nothing on your part except a willingness to learn. Yes, you will learn a few things about accounting and finance, but the math is fourth-grade easy—just addition and subtraction and occasional multiplication and division. Of course, as in learning any new skill, effort on your part is required

What you will see throughout this book is that choosing the right investment is really a process of elimination. A minority of the thousands of publicly traded companies in which you could conceivably invest have authentic earnings power and even in this select group fewer still will qualify as an Earnings Power Staircase company. If you are a long-term cautiously greedy investor looking for that single wonderful business, most companies are not worth touching; your focus must be on identifying firms that have the potential to be great growth stocks for the

Figure I.1

Microsoft's Earnings Power Chart, 1990–1999

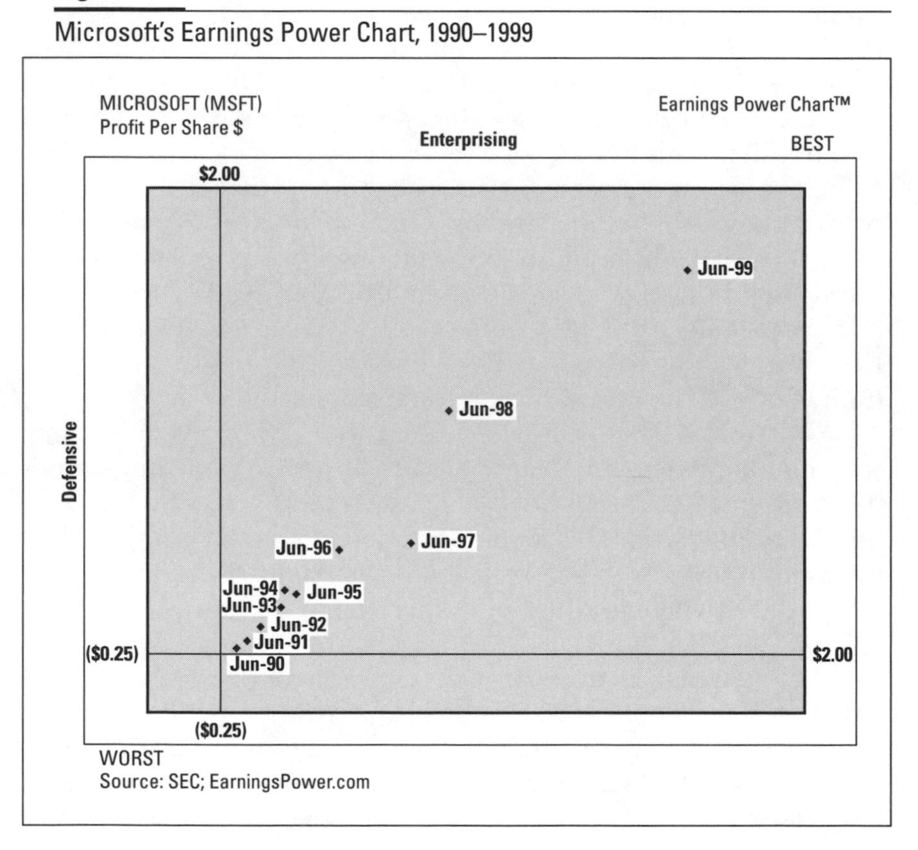

next several years without exposing you and your portfolio to excessive risk.

As we learn how to build an Earnings Power Chart, we will look at the results of one particular company: The Wm. Wrigley Jr. Company. Wrigley is an excellent case study because most people have tried their products (mostly chewing gum) at one time or another. Also, Wrigley's financial statements are comprehensible to the beginning investor. We will also use the Earnings Power Chart to examine many other noteworthy companies from the last several years, including Cisco Systems, Dell Computer, Enron Corporation, Lucent Technologies, and WorldCom.

In Chapter 1 we look at three obstacles confronting the growth investor, including that a company may appear profitable in the traditional sense of the word even though its earnings quality is poor. In Chapter 2 we look at Wrigley's 2002 results in order to give the reader a short course on how to read a financial statement.

In Chapter 3 we explore what it means to be a defensive investor, intent on guarding against risks, and an enterprising investor eager to identify promising opportunities. We also examine the components of the defensive and enterprising income statements, specifically, how they fix the four substantive limitations of the accrual ledger. At this point, so that you make the best use of your time, we introduce in Chapter 4 the five-minute test. This is the bar over which any company must pass to warrant further study. We show, in Chapter 5, how to construct a defensive income statement and, in Chapter 6, how to build an enterprising income statement.

We use these alternate income statements to plot, in Chapter 7, an Earnings Power Chart for Wrigley. We will also look at several companies that cost investors time or money to see if the Earnings Power Chart was a better leading indicator of stock prices than the accrual P&L. (Short answer: It was.)

In Chapter 8, we look at Wrigley, WorldCom, Lucent, and Enron. Each of these companies was profitable in the accrual sense of the word but only one possessed authentic earnings power as we use the term in this book. The other three companies had defensive losses, enterprising losses, or a combination of both.

In Chapter 9 we look at three Earnings Power Staircase companies: Microsoft, Apollo Group, and Paychex. If you find a company with a similar chart, you'll probably want to become a part-owner. Two of the most talked-about companies in recent years, Cisco Systems and Dell Computer, are examined in Chapter 10.

Chapter 11 introduces two simple but powerful ratios that complement the Earnings Power Chart. How to determine whether management's interests are aligned with those of stockholders is explored in Chapter 12. In Chapter 13 we enter "Graham's classroom" to summarize the main points of this book. Since the Earnings Power Chart was inspired by a line from Graham's *The Intelligent Investor*, it seems a fitting way to wrap up everything we've explored thus far. Chapter 14 ticks off several topics that are important to all investors, whether or not you choose to use the earnings power methodology.

By the end of this book you will learn five ways to use the Earnings Power Chart to improve your investment results. These are:

1. A source of new investment ideas (either through a long or short position);
2. A report card on your current portfolio (are your companies getting stronger or are they weakening?);
3. A litmus test of management candor (did they say it was a good year even though the company moved in a lower-left direction?);
4. A check on how your company's competitors are doing (if a competitor is having trouble, then your company may be next);
5. A check on how your company's customers are doing (if a customer is having trouble, then your company may be next).

Now, let's get going.

CHAPTER 1

Obstacles for the Growth Investor

All investors share a common aspiration: to own a stock that makes a *difference*. After all, just imagine what your life would be like today if you had bought $10,000 worth of Microsoft Corporation at the beginning of 1990. A decade later those same shares would have been worth $966,000. Imagine indeed.

So, how do you find your own Microsoft?

There are, of course, many ways to prosper handsomely on Wall Street, just as there are many ways to *lose* money in the stock market. Venerable investment strategies include net-net, sum-of-the-parts, turnaround, spin-off, cyclical, short selling, liquidation, corporate restructuring, merger arbitrage, and operating leverage.

Perhaps the most popular strategy, though, is to buy shares of a "growth" company. A growth company, as the term is commonly understood, is a business whose earnings keep growing as the years roll by. These tend to be the companies that you hear so much about.

During the 1990s Microsoft was a growth company, as its earnings per share (EPS) climbed from $0.03 to $0.70. Investors noticed what was happening out in Redmond, Washington, and bid shares of Bill Gates's company up 4,150 percent, to $45.10 as of fiscal 1999 (see Table 1.1), from a split-adjusted $1.06. Along the way there were 72 stock splits. Microsoft has since fallen from its highs for reasons we will address later, but it has made many long-term owners wealthy.

It's an extraordinary achievement when a company generates consistent earnings gains every year over a long stretch, especially if the growth rate is as steep as Microsoft's circa 1990-1999. So if you are lucky or prescient enough to own such a corporate masterpiece, then congratulations. Here are some of the benefits—pecuniary and otherwise—that you will enjoy.

1. *Generate substantial wealth.* Depending on the number of shares you buy and when, the capital gains from a growth company can help you buy a larger home, pay for a child's college education, care for a loved one, retire a few years early to a place where it's always sunny, or make a generous bequest to a needy institution. In 1961, Donald and Mildred Othmer followed the lead of Mildred's mother and sister and put $50,000 into a partnership run by Warren Buffett, an old family friend from their hometown of Omaha. The childless couple lived quiet, unpreten-

Table 1.1

Microsoft Corporation: A Decade of Extraordinary Achievement

Fiscal Year	EPS	Stock
1990	$0.03	$1.06
1991	$0.05	$1.42
1992	$0.08	$2.19
1993	$0.10	$2.25
1994	$0.12	$3.22
1995	$0.15	$5.65
1996	$0.21	$7.51
1997	$0.33	$15.80
1998	$0.45	$27.10
1999	$0.70	$45.10

Source: Value Line, www.bigcharts.com. Stock prices as of fiscal year ending 6/30.

tious lives. Upon their deaths their combined estates were worth $800 million and nearly everything went to charity.

2. *Contribute to a stronger economy.* When you own a growth company you are financing a business that makes products or provides services that people want or need. In turn, these kinds of businesses provide jobs, take an active role in community affairs, and pay taxes that fund essential services like national defense, healthcare, and education.

3. *Psychological.* Being a part-owner of a flourishing endeavor is deeply satisfying, similar to the feeling you get from watching a tree you plant in your backyard grow. Many growth investors take pride in owning shares of a company for a long time.

4. *Reduce frictional costs.* It's expensive to constantly buy and sell stocks due to the friction caused by the dealer spread and commissions. The spread is the difference between the bid (selling) and ask (asking) price. It averages about 5 cents per share for the typical New York Stock Exchange–listed company. The commission, the price you pay your broker to buy or sell a stock, adds another 3 cents per share to the friction. Combined, this amounts to a total frictional cost of 8 cents per share.

To illustrate the high cost of friction, let's look at The Gap. According to its profile in Yahoo! Finance's Web page, in early 2003 The Gap had 889 million shares outstanding and average daily trading volume was 6.14 million shares. With 252 trading days per year, that puts the San Francisco-based clothing retailer's annualized trading volume at about 1.5 billion shares. If we assume the frictional cost to be 8 cents per share, as cited above, the total frictional cost to all participants is $124 million. That's how much investors are paying in spreads and commissions to buy and sell The Gap over one year's time. To put this into context, for the fiscal year ending February 1, 2003, The Gap earned $477 million. Thus, investors incurred $0.26 in frictional costs for every dollar of Gap earnings. What a waste, because that doesn't even include the cost to buy the stock!

5. *Defer capital gains taxes.* The more you buy and sell stocks, the more you'll pay in capital gains taxes (assuming, of course, that your stock goes up). Capital gains taxes make it harder to grow a nest egg, whether you buy stocks or invest in mutual funds. But when you are a growth investor, you do not have to pay any tax on your capital gains until you sell your stock. Thus, the amount that you would pay in taxes can build on itself creating brand new profits, some of which will be yours. Keep capital gains taxes to a minimum and you will accumulate wealth faster than if you keep writing checks to Uncle Sam.

Here's an illustration that shows the benefit of deferring capital gains taxes as far into the future as possible. In 1950 Walter O'Malley bought the Brooklyn Dodgers major league baseball team for $700,000. Forty-eight years later, in 1997, O'Malley's heirs sold the team to Rupert Murdoch's News Corporation for a reported $350 million. That works out to a pretax compound annual return of 13.8 percent. Assuming a long-term capital gains tax rate of 20 percent, we can assume that the O'Malley heirs paid $70 million in taxes and pocketed the other $280 million.

Now let's suppose that another family, the O'Sullivans, had bought the Dodgers back in 1950. The O'Sullivans earned the same 13.8 percent annual return as the O'Malleys. And just like the O'Malleys, the O'Sullivans moved the team to Los Angeles in 1957 and won four World Series titles. In fact, the O'Sullivans did everything the O'Malleys did with one vital exception: They sold the team at the end of each season and paid and deducted from their profits 20 percent for capital gains taxes. Then the next day they repurchased the team. The O'Sullivans repeated this process every year until they sold the team one final time. After taxes, the frenetic O'Sullivans netted $108 million, well below the $280 million after-tax gain that the patient O'Malleys realized from their buy-and-hold strategy.

How did the O'Malleys keep so much more money than the O'Sullivans? By paying their taxes *once* rather than every year. So even after the O'Malleys paid a $70 million tax bill in 1997 they wound up with 2.6 times more money than the O'Sullivans.

It seems so easy: All you have to do to succeed on Wall Street is buy shares of a company like Microsoft and then sell when its earnings growth starts to wane. In fact, growth investing is tricky.

As a result, if you don't know what you are doing you can lose lots of money—fast, too. One reason why growth investors lose money is they buy at the wrong time, like after a long run when everyone else wants a piece of the action and the stock is priced for perfection. Also, many growth companies attract competition, which can erode a business's favorable position. Last, just because a company is profitable and earnings are rising does not mean that it possesses authentic earnings power.

Let's look at how a premium valuation, loss of competitive advantage, and poor earnings quality make growth investing so challenging.

VALUATION: THE NEXT MICROSOFT WILL BE EXPENSIVE

Growth companies tend to be expensive. Why? Because we all want to own "the next Microsoft." As a result, every year that a company shows improvement emboldens us to pay a little higher multiple for a dollar's worth of earnings. If a company can maintain its earnings growth rate, fine. But what happens all-to-often is that a firm's price-earnings ratio gets bid up so high that investors extrapolate a future that may not come to pass. If, then, the company stumbles and earnings fall (this happens all the time), the stock gets hammered and the crowd moves on to the next high-octane story.

That growth companies do not always make the best stocks is supported by a study cited in *Contrarian Investment Strategies* by David Dreman. According to Dreman, Francis Nicholson, then with the Provident National Bank in Philadelphia, analyzed 189 "blue chip" companies in 18 industries over the 25 years between 1937 and 1962. Nicholson divided the stocks into five equal groups solely according to their price to earnings (P/E) ranking for periods of one to seven years.[1] Recasting the quintiles annually on the basis of new price-earnings ratios resulted in the stocks most out of favor (that is, the lowest price-earnings ratios) showing a much higher annual rate of appreciation than the popular growth stocks (the highest price-earnings ratios). Subsequent research upholds Nicholson's findings that a bundle of cheap stocks that no one wants will outperform a collection of expensive stocks that the crowd is passionate about.

Recent events also show how popular stocks can cost investors (especially the late arrivals!) a king's ransom. As we see in Table 1.2, Cisco Systems in mid-1999 had a price-earnings ratio of 184x. That means buyers of the San Jose, California-based firm were paying $184 for every dollar of earnings. With such a high multiple there's little protection on the downside in case something goes wrong. Well, as so often happens, something did go wrong; in early 2001 demand for Cisco's Internet servers and routers plunged, catching management by surprise and resulting in a $2.5 billion inventory write-off. The stock, which traded over $80 a share in 2000, eventually fell below $10.

COMPETITION IS THE ENEMY OF A PROFITABLE FIRM

Owning a growth company is like marriage: It requires a long-term commitment. If you buy-and-hold the right growth company, you can make a lot of money. But if you buy-and-hold the *wrong* growth company, it will cost you time or money or both. Stock market history tells us that for every Microsoft there are dozens of other businesses that will fade in the stretch or be left

Table 1.2

Stock-Price Chart of Former Highflier Companies

	mid-1999		August 2003	
Stock Company	Price	Price-Earnings ratio	Stock Price	% decline from mid-1999
Cisco Systems	$34	184×	$18	−47%
EMC Corporation	$30	119×	$11	−63%
Enron Corporation	$40	44×	$0.05	−99%
Lucent Technologies	$50	101×	$2	−96%
Microsoft Corporation	$48	82×	$26	−46%
Sun Microsystems	$20	125×	$4	−80%
S&P 500 Index	1,400		1,000	−29%
Tyco International Ltd.	$45	61×	$20	−56%
WorldCom Inc.	$50	68×	$0.05	−99%

Source: Morningstar, www.bigcharts.com

at the gate. In 1990, for example, you could have bought Microsoft, but you could have also bought Kaypro, Digital, Wang, Commodore, Burroughs, Olivetti, and Apricot.

The fierce, grinding nature of capitalism makes it tough for a growth company to stay ahead of the pack. In a free-market economy, capital flows to the highest prospective returns. But too much capital in an industry spurs competition, which leads to price wars. The trouble with price wars is that if a growth company marks down its inventory, but can't cut overhead, profits fall hard. Another problem with competition is that other firms come out with newer technology. That means your company gets stuck trying to sell yesterday's hot product. In time, a business that has enjoyed a competitive advantage will struggle to differentiate itself. In the mid-1990s Iomega enjoyed rapid earnings growth, and its stock went from a couple of dollars a share to $137. But then demand for its Zip drive tapered off, and its profits wilted. Iomega is still in computer storage business, but 2002 earnings were 30 percent of what they were back in 1997. Shares of the former high-flyer recently traded for about $12.

Even companies that operate in seemingly mundane businesses can lose their way. In the late 1960s, Converse's famed Chuck Taylor All Star sneaker enjoyed a nearly 90 percent market share of the basketball shoe business. But the company eventually succumbed to better technology, relentless marketing, more efficient distribution networks, and cheap overseas labor from competitors like Nike. By 2001, things got so bad for Converse that it filed for bankruptcy. Ironically, Nike later paid $305 million to buy Converse because its canvas sneakers were back in vogue.

POOR EARNINGS QUALITY

The third obstacle to making big money with growth stocks is poor earnings quality. Just because a company is profitable in the traditional sense of the word does not mean that it possesses authentic earnings power. Why? Because the accrual income statement found in every annual and quarterly report has four substantive limitations.

1. *Omission of investment in fixed capital.* Fixed capital investments in plant, property, and equipment are not recorded in their entirety but depreciated over time.
2. *Omission of investment in working capital.* Year-to-year changes in working capital (basically, receivables and inventory less accounts payable and accrued expenses) are not accounted for on the income statement.
3. *Intangible growth-producing initiatives are immediately expensed.* Outlays for research and development and advertising, which pay off over time, are written off in the year incurred.
4. *Stockholders' equity is considered free.* Earnings that have been reinvested back in the business (rather than paid to stockholders in the form of dividends) are not treated as an expense.

These limitations can disguise a company's true financial health. As a result, a perceived growth company can suddenly fall on hard times and may even go bankrupt. Enron Corporation is a case in point. In the decade leading up to its spectacular demise, the energy trader's per-share earnings rose like a plane at takeoff: $0.22, $0.51, $0.61, $0.63, $0.85, $0.97, $1.08, $0.16, $1.01, $1.10, $1.12.[2] Yes, 1997 was an aberration, but Enron recovered the following year. Unfortunately, in 2000, the company skidded off the runway and into bankruptcy court. In a scant 14 months the stock went from $90 to pennies a share.

A question, then: is there a way to distinguish between companies like Microsoft that have high-quality earnings growth from companies like Enron that have low-quality earnings growth?

The answer is yes, there is a way to pick between the gold and iron pyrite. But to do so requires that you think about a firm's performance from the perspective of the defensive investor who wants to avoid committing serious mistakes or losses, as well as the enterprising investor who wants to own companies that are both sound and more attractive than the average. As we will learn in this book, a model I developed called the Earnings Power Chart uses a "defensive" income statement to fix limitations #s 1 and 2 of the accrual income statement, and an "enterprising" income statement to fix limitations #s 3 and 4. What's more, the Earnings Power Chart enables you to see with your own eyes the quality of a company's earnings—or lack thereof. (For examples, see Chapter 7.) Crucially, this two-axis chart incorporates not only a company's income statement, but also other important financial statements like the balance sheet, statement of cash flow, and footnotes. The net result? You are able to peer into the future a little further than everyone else. And that slight advantage is often the difference between stock market success and failure.

To learn more about the Earnings Power Chart, let's take a closer look in Chapter 2 at the accrual income statement.

How to Read the Accrual Income Statement

The language of financial statements, like that for any new subject, might seem intimidating at first. Still, you can't hope to do well picking stocks if you're financially illiterate. It's like riding a bicycle with your eyes closed. You won't get very far and you'll probably get hurt in the process. This chapter will help you learn how to "read the numbers" even if you don't have any prior experience.

A financial statement consists of an income statement, balance sheet, statement of retained earnings, statement of cash flows, and footnotes. They all tie together, much like the assembly in a fine Swiss watch.

All public companies in the United States must prepare their financial statements using so-called accrual accounting. Under the rules of accrual accounting a sale is recorded when a product is delivered or a service rendered and an expense is recorded when a resource is used up or an obligation incurred, which is not necessarily when cash is exchanged.

Example: Suppose you buy a one-year subscription to *National Geographic*. You send in a check for $30, which immediately increases the magazine's cash balance by $30. But when it prepares a quarterly income statement, only $7.50 is booked as revenue. What happens to the other $22.50? It gets spread over the three remaining quarters. This way current sales are matched with current expenses and future sales are matched with future expenses. The same applies to expenses. The cost of a new printing press is depreciated (expensed) over its useful life rather than entirely in the year acquired.

The rules of accrual accounting follow Generally Accepted Accounting Principles, or GAAP for short. Think of GAAP as *According to Hoyle* for corporate America. GAAP, in turn, is set by the Financial Accounting Standards Board (FASB), a group of accountants deputized by the Securities and Exchange Commission, to make binding pronouncements on these kinds of matters. The SEC reports to Congress.

Let's go through each of the documents you'll find in a company's financial statement.

DOCUMENTS IN A FINANCIAL STATEMENT

To introduce the different reports you'll encounter in a financial statement, we'll look at the Wm. Wrigley Jr. Company for the fiscal year ending December 31, 2002. Copies of Wrigley's income statement, balance sheet, statement of cash flow, and statement of stockholder' equity are found at the end of this chapter. Wrigley's has produced, marketed, and distributed chewing gum and other confectionery products since 1891. Today, Wrigley has plants in 12 countries, does business in more than 150 countries, and employs 10,000 people worldwide. Some of Wrigley's best-known brands include Juicy Fruit, Doublemint, Big Red, and Wrigley's Spearmint. In 2000, the company began selling a type of gum to treat heartburn.

The Wm. Wrigley Jr. Company

The Wrigley Company was founded in 1891 by William Wrigley Jr., the son of a soap maker. Initially, Wrigley sold scouring soap. When baking powder proved to be more popular than soap, the young entrepreneur switched to baking powder. The following year Wrigley got the idea of offering two packs of gum with each can of baking powder. The success of that offer led him to decide that chewing gum was the product with the greater potential. His first two chewing gum brands were Lotta and Vassar. Juicy Fruit gum came next in 1893. Wrigley's Spearmint was introduced later the same year.

Wrigley has been a family business from the start. Founder William Wrigley Jr. was followed by son Philip K. Wrigley. His son, William Wrigley, led the company for 38 years until his death in 1999. William Wrigley Jr. is the firm's current president and Chief Executive Officer (CEO).

Headquartered in Chicago, Illinois, the Wrigley Building is one of America's most famous office towers. Its architectural shape is patterned after the Seville Cathedral's Giralda Tower in Spain, while the ornamental design is adapted from the French Renaissance style. At night, the terra-cotta cladding gleams, making the Wrigley Building a symbol of Chicago in many motion pictures and television programs. The giant two-story clock in the south tower has four dials, each 19 feet, 7 inches in diameter. Because of its multiple dials and height above street level, people coming from all directions use the clock to check the time.

And what of Wrigley Field, home of baseball's hapless Chicago Cubs? The estate of Philip K. Wrigley was one of 800 stockholders that owned the team until its sale in 1981 to the Tribune Company. With its purchase of the ball club, the Tribune received an option to buy Wrigley Field. Three months after the sale of the club, the Tribune exercised that option. The stadium's name, however, remained intact, as did the ivy covering the outfield walls.[1]

Income Statement

The income statement tells you whether the company made or lost money during the period being reported. It's also called the profit-and-loss statement, or P&L for short.

Revenues are what a firm collects for selling its goods or services. Expenses are the resources consumed to generate revenue. Accrual profit (that is, net income), what remains after deducting expenses from revenue, is the proverbial "bottom line."

Thus:

Accrual profit (net income) = Revenue − Expenses

In 2002 Wrigley's accrual profit was approximately $402 million, reflecting revenues of $2.7 billion and expenses of $2.3 billion.

Balance Sheet

The balance sheet shows a company's financial position on a particular day, for example, December 31, 2002. There is no such thing as a balance sheet for 2002. Assets always equal liabilities plus stockholders' equity. Thus:

Assets = Liabilities + Stockholders' equity

Assets include liquid assets such as cash and marketable securities; working capital assets such as receivables and inventory; fixed capital assets such as land, buildings, and equipment; and intangible assets such as goodwill. By convention, assets are listed in descending order of liquidity.

There are two types of liabilities. Spontaneous liabilities are those incurred in the normal course of business (for example, accounts payable, wages payable, accrued expenses, and accrued taxes). The other type of liability, debt, includes working capital lines of credit, the current portion of long-term debt, long-term debt, and capital leases. Debt liabilities are the result of contracts that can run more than one hundred pages in length and contain, among other things, information on interest rates, repayment schedules, and types of collateral.

Stockholders' equity, the third major component of the balance sheet, is simply assets minus liabilities. As accounting professors tell their students every September, stockholders' equity is not a pot of cash with which you can buy pizza and beer. Instead, it's like a family's net worth: it's what remains after subtracting credit card debt, car loans, mortgage, and so forth from the value of your checking account, savings, stocks, retirement funds, home, cars, silver flatware, and other possessions.

This analogy works to a point. With a personal financial statement assets are listed at current market value, whereas companies, under GAAP, report assets at their purchase price, less accumulated depreciation. Thus, you might see your home, for example, appreciate as the years pass, but a building owned by a company lose value.

On December 31, 2002, Wrigley had $2.1 billion of assets, nearly $600 million of liabilities, and $1.5 billion of stockholders' equity. It's always a good sign when stockholders' equity is greater than a firm's liabilities, as is the case here. Normally, a positive net worth means the company has been profitable over the years.

How Does a Company Finance Itself?

All companies are financed with a mixture of debt and equity capital. Both come at a price.

To employ debt, management must show lenders (for example, banks and bondholders) that the borrowed funds will be repaid on time, with interest. Debt bears an explicit and legally binding rate of interest and is reported in the income statement as an expense just like raw materials, electricity, wages, and landscaping.

The other primary source of capital is a firm's corporate net worth, that is, stockholders' equity. This represents a firm's accrual profits (net income) from prior years less any dividends. If you own shares of a company, some of that equity is yours. You're happy to have management reinvest a portion of the firm's earnings back into the business every year so long as it earns a satisfactory return on that investment. If, however, the return is below your expectations, then you may decide to sell your ownership interest. Should enough other stockholders reach the same decision, a firm's stock price will tumble. The longer a firm's stock price remains at a depressed level, the harder it becomes to stay competitive.

Statement of Retained Earnings

The statement of retained earnings, also known as the statement of stockholders' equity, shows how much the stockholders' equity account in the balance sheet changed during the year or quarter. If the company made money, this statement shows how much of the accrual profit was reinvested back into the business and how much was distributed to stockholders via dividends or share buybacks.

Wrigley began 2002 with about $1.3 billion of stockholders' equity and ended the year with $1.5 billion of corporate net worth. The biggest lift to stockholders' equity was the $402 million of net income, the biggest reduction was a payment of $185 million in dividends.

Statement of Cash Flows

The statement of cash flows shows a firm's sources and uses of cash. Like the balance sheet, the statement of cash flow is divided into three major components: operating activities, investing activities, and financing activities.

Operating activities begins with net income, shows noncash charges such as depreciation and amortization, and ends with changes in working capital assets and liabilities (principally, receivables, inventory, payables, and accrued expenses).

Investing activities shows how much money was spent buying fixed assets such as factories and trucks that generate revenue. You'll also find the cash outlay for any acquisitions in this section.

Financing activities shows changes in a firm's capital structure, including loan advances and paydowns, the issuance or repurchase of common stock, and dividend payments.

If all this seems too confusing, just remember that in the statement of cash flows positive numbers are *sources* of cash (resulting in an increase) and negative numbers are *uses* of cash (a decrease).

In 2002 Wrigley generated $374 million of cash from operating activities, consumed $208 million in investing activities, and used another $198 million in financing activities. Given this net $29 million use of cash, Wrigley ended 2002 with $279 million of cash and equivalents, down from $307 million at the beginning of the year.

Footnotes

The footnotes are where management explains what accounting policies were used to prepare the financial statements. For example, when does the company book a sale? How is inventory valued? What's the useful life of the fixed capital? These are important things to know.

COMPONENTS OF THE ACCRUAL INCOME STATEMENT

The income statement receives the lion's share of attention by most investors. Throughout this book I refer the income statement found in the financial statements as the "accrual" income statement to distinguish it from the defensive and enterprising income statements, which we'll discuss later. Income statements can vary somewhat in the details they list, but what follows are comments on some items that are commonly featured.

Definition: "Accrual Profits"

The income statement found in every company's annual report, 10-K, and 10-Q is an accrual income statement. The word *accrual* is used because these statements follow the rules of accrual accounting as well as to distinguish them from defensive and enterprising income statements. Accrual profits, then, are the same thing as net income as determined by GAAP.

The first line on the accrual income statement is sales or revenue. Technically, revenue is a broader term since it includes nonoperating items such as interest income and royalty payments as well as funds generated directly by the sale of a product or service. In 2002 Wrigley's net sales totaled $2.7 billion.

Cost of goods sold, or cost of sales, represents the direct costs of producing a finished good, principally raw materials, labor, and shipping and handling. Service businesses such as advertising agencies and engineering consultancies use the term cost of services. Wrigley's cost of sales for 2002 was about $1.2 billion.

Selling, general and administrative (SG&A) is a catch-all for the indirect costs of producing a good or providing a service (for example, rent, electricity, office supplies, the CPA audit fee, fire insurance, and salaries for switchboard operators). A euphemism for SG&A is "overhead." Wrigley's selling, general and administrative costs amounted to $1 billion in 2002.

Moving down the page we see $9 million of investment income, $11 million in other expenses, and $182 million in income taxes.

Finally, we arrive at net income (or loss). A company that has made money is said to have been "in the black," a company that has suffered a loss is said to be "in the red." Profits and earnings are the same as net income. Wrigley was safely in the black, earning $401 million in fiscal year 2002, as mentioned earlier.

Net income is used to calculate earnings per share (EPS), net profit margin, the price-earnings ratio (P/E), and return on equity (ROE). It is also the E in EBITDA (earnings before interest, taxes, depreciation and amortization), which many investors use as a yardstick for corporate performance.

To calculate earnings per share, just divide net income by shares outstanding. A company with a complex capital structure will have two sets of EPS figures: basic and diluted. Always use the diluted number, which reflects the watering down that will occur if convertible securities, stock options, and warrants are converted into common stock. Wrigley had $1.78 in diluted earnings per share for 2002.

A Glossary of SEC Filings

All public companies report detailed financial results to the SEC once a year using Form 10-K. This report is audited by an independent accountant and is due 90 days after the close of the fiscal year. The 10-K includes information about a firm's markets, products, competition, and employees as well as its financial statements. It also lists the names of directors and top executives as well as any individual or group that owns more than 5 percent of the stock. Be sure to read the management discussion and analysis that addresses firm performance for the year.

The government does not require companies to file an annual report, although one is mandated by many corporate bylaws. The annual report contains much of the same information as the 10-K as well as the letter to stockholders from the chief executive officer.

A quarterly report called a 10-Q must be filed within 45 days of the close of the first, second, and third quarters. These reports contain financial statements, but without much of the detail found in the 10-K. The 10-Q is not audited by an independent accounting firm. As a result, a company can show smooth sailing in the first three quarters, then, after the fourth quarter, the accountants come in and reverse many of the earlier assumptions, which can mean lower earnings for the year than previously reported.

Form 8-K covers unusual occurrences or corporate changes that might affect a firm's operations and earnings (for example, a takeover attempt, a big contract, the sale of a subsidiary, auditor changes, the resignation of a board member, bankruptcy). These reports are due within 15 days of the event, except in the case of auditor changes, which must be reported within five days.

A Form 144 is used by insiders to register whenever they buy or sell stock.

DEF 14A, better known as the proxy statement, has important information that you won't find anywhere else. For example, the proxy will tell you about management's background, any relationships the company or its officers might have with customers, executive compensation (including stock options), and how much the auditor is paid for consulting services.

Once a year a company closes its books. Wrigley, like most firms, uses a December 31 fiscal year. Many retailers, though, end the bookkeeping year in late January or early February to include holiday sales and make it easier to take inventory. Microsoft uses a June 30 fiscal year.

The accrual income statement, as outlined in Chapter 1, has four major limitations that might distort the quality of a firm's earnings. On top of that, many companies in the last several years have, despite being required to submit financial statements using GAAP, calculated profits in idiosyncratic ways, among them, cash earnings, EBITDA, operating earnings, fully diluted earnings, and consolidated earnings. Press releases issued by companies to put their results in the best possible light have practically created a new accounting system.

The most sulfurous variation on accrual profits, "pro forma" earnings, enables companies to present their results in press releases and other venues any way they please. Keep in mind, however, that they are still required to submit to the SEC financial statements that conform to GAAP, not pro forma results.

Pro forma is a Latin expression meaning "as if." Originally, pro forma was used when, say, a company lost a factory in a hurricane and recorded a one-time loss. Under pro forma earnings, the gain would be excluded to show what the company's operations would have looked like as if the one-time loss had never occurred. But things spiraled out of control in the bull market of the late 1990s as fast-growing companies tried to exempt acquisition-related charges, unusual losses, and a bevy of other costs that might have obscured their growth. For example, pro forma earnings typically exclude write-downs and restructuring charges as nonrecurring when, in fact, shutting down plants is a normal part of business. Essentially, companies tried to exclude expenses that they aren't supposed to exclude.

To its credit, the accrual income statement, despite its four major limitations, is at least calculated uniformly, which is why we have accounting standards in the first place.

That's a brief overview of the accrual income statement, a source of a great deal of important information, albeit constrained by some significant limitations. To correct these shortcomings, we look at the traditional ledger from different perspectives that enable us to view companies' financial reports with greater accuracy and confidence.

WRIGLEY'S FINANCIAL STATEMENT

Wrigley's financial statement for the year ending December 31, 2002 starts on the next page.

CONSOLIDATED STATEMENT OF EARNINGS

In thousands of dollars except per share amounts

	2002	2001	2000
EARNINGS			
Net sales	$ **2,746,318**	2,401,419	2,126,114
Cost of sales	**1,150,215**	997,054	904,266
Gross profit	**1,596,103**	1,404,365	1,221,848
Selling, general and administrative expense	**1,011,029**	891,009	758,605
Operating income	**585,074**	513,356	463,243
Investment income	**8,918**	18,553	19,185
Other expense	**(10,571)**	(4,543)	(3,116)
Earnings before income taxes	**583,421**	527,366	479,312
Income taxes	**181,896**	164,380	150,370
Net earnings	$ **401,525**	362,986	328,942
PER SHARE AMOUNTS			
Net earnings per share of Common Stock (basic and diluted)	$ **1.78**	1.61	1.45
Dividends paid per share of Common Stock	**.805**	.745	.701

CONSOLIDATED BALANCE SHEET

In thousands of dollars

	2002	2001
ASSETS		
Current assets:		
Cash and cash equivalents	$ 279,276	307,785
Short-term investments, at amortized cost	25,621	25,450
Accounts receivable		
(less allowance for doubtful accounts: 2002-$5,850; 2001-$7,712)	312,919	239,885
Inventories:		
Finished goods	88,583	75,693
Raw materials and supplies	232,613	203,288
	321,196	278,981
Other current assets	47,720	46,896
Deferred income taxes - current	19,560	14,846
Total current assets	1,006,292	913,843
Marketable equity securities, at fair value	19,411	25,300
Deferred charges and other assets	213,483	124,666

Deferred income taxes - noncurrent	33,000	29,605
Property, plant and equipment, at cost:		
Land	48,968	39,933
Buildings and building equipment	393,780	359,109
Machinery and equipment	1,049,001	857,054
	1,491,749	1,256,096
Less accumulated depreciation	655,639	571,717
Net property, plant and equipment	836,110	684,379
TOTAL ASSETS	$ 2,108,296	1,777,793

In thousands of dollars and shares

	2002	2001
LIABILITIES AND STOCKHOLDERS' EQUITY		
Current liabilities:		
Accounts payable	$ **97,705**	91,397
Accrued expenses	**172,137**	128,264
Dividends payable	**46,137**	42,741
Income and other taxes payable	**66,893**	68,467
Deferred income taxes — current	**3,215**	1,455
Total current liabilities:	**386,087**	332,324
Deferred income taxes — noncurrent	**70,589**	46,430
Other noncurrent liabilities	**129,044**	122,842
Stockholders' equity:		
Preferred Stock — no par value Authorized: 20,000 shares Issued: None		
Common Stock — no par value		
Common Stock Authorized: 400,000 shares Issued: 2002 - 190,898 shares; 2001 - 189,800 shares	**12,719**	12,646
Class B Common Stock — convertible		

	2002	2001
Authorized: 80,000 shares Issued and outstanding: 2002 - 41,543 shares; 2001 - 42,641 shares	**2,777**	2,850
Additional paid-in capital	**4,209**	1,153
Retained earnings	**1,902,990**	1,684,337
Common Stock in treasury, at cost (2002 - 7,335 shares; 2001 - 7,491 shares)	**(297,156)**	(289,799)
Accumulated other comprehensive income:		
Foreign currency translation adjustment	**(112,303)**	(149,310)
Gain (loss) on derivative contracts	**(853)**	46
Unrealized holding gains on marketable equity securities	**10,193**	14,274
	(102,963)	(134,990)
Total stockholders' equity	**1,522,576**	1,276,197
TOTAL LIABILITIES AND STOCKHOLDERS' EQUITY	**$ 2,108,296**	1,777,793

CONSOLIDATED STATEMENT OF CASH FLOWS

In thousands of dollars

	2002	2001	2000
OPERATING ACTIVITIES			
Net earnings	**$ 401,525**	362,986	328,942
Adjustments to reconcile net earnings to net cash provided by operating activities:			
Depreciation	**85,568**	68,326	57,880
Loss on sales of property, plant and equipment	**1,014**	2,910	778
(Increase) Decrease in:			
Accounts receivable	**(55,288)**	(53,162)	(18,483)
Inventories	**(31,858)**	(29,487)	(2,812)
Other current assets	**1,304**	(8,079)	199
Deferred charges and other assets	**(78,585)**	(15,852)	30,408
Increase (Decrease) in:			
Accounts payable	**756**	20,537	12,988
Accrued expenses	**33,416**	16,360	18,015
Income and other taxes payable	**(3,715)**	9,565	14,670
Deferred income taxes	**19,082**	5,570	2,546
Other noncurrent liabilities	**1,216**	10,817	3,152

Net cash provided by operating activities		**374,435**	390,491	448,283
INVESTING ACTIVITIES				
Additions to property, plant and equipment		**(216,872)**	(181,760)	(125,068)
Proceeds from property retirements		**5,017**	2,376	1,128
Purchases of short-term investments		**(41,177)**	(24,448)	(125,728)
Maturities of short-term investments		**44,858**	26,835	115,007
Net cash used in investing activities		**(208,174)**	(176,997)	(134,661)
FINANCING ACTIVITIES				
Dividends paid		**(181,232)**	(167,922)	(159,138)
Common Stock purchased, net		**(16,402)**	(34,173)	(131,765)
Net cash used in financing activities		**(197,634)**	(202,095)	(290,903)
Effect of exchange rate changes on cash and cash equivalents		**2,864**	(4,213)	(10,506)
Net increase (decrease) in cash and cash equivalents		**(28,509)**	7,186	12,213
Cash and cash equivalents at beginning of year		**307,785**	300,599	288,386
Cash and cash equivalents at end of year	$	**279,276**	307,785	300,599
SUPPLEMENTAL CASH FLOW INFORMATION				
Income taxes paid	$	**173,010**	146,858	136,311
Interest paid	$	**1,636**	1,101	749
Interest and dividends received	$	**8,974**	18,570	19,243

CONSOLIDATED STATEMENT OF STOCKHOLDERS' EQUITY

In thousands of dollars and shares

	Common Shares Outstanding	Common Stock	Class B Common Stock	Additional Paid-in Capital	Retained Earnings	Common Stock In Treasury	Other Comprehensive Income	Stock-holders' Equity
BALANCE DECEMBER 31, 1999	183,764	$ 12,481	3,015	273	1,322,137	(125,712)	(73,419)	1,138,775
Net earnings					328,942			328,942
Other comprehensive income:								
Foreign currency translation adjustments							(36,095)	(36,095)
Unrealized holding loss on marketable equity securities, net of $5,166 tax							(9,500)	(9,500)
Total comprehensive income								283,347
Dividends to shareholders					(158,532)			(158,532)
Treasury share purchases	(3,535)					(131,765)		(131,765)
Stock awards granted	67			73		999		1,072
Conversion from Class B Common to Common	1,155	77	(77)					—
BALANCE DECEMBER 31, 2000	181,451	$ 12,558	2,938	346	1,492,547	(256,478)	(119,014)	1,132,897
Net earnings					362,986			362,986
Other comprehensive income:								
Foreign currency translation adjustments							(12,945)	(12,945)
Unrealized holding loss on marketable equity securities, net of $1,655 tax							(3,077)	(3,077)

Gain on derivative contracts, net of $21 tax							46	46
Total comprehensive income								347,010
Dividends to shareholders					(171,196)			(171,196)
Treasury share purchases	(744)					(36,432)		(36,432)
Options exercised and stock awards granted	170			807		3,111		3,918
Conversion from Class B Common to Common	1,432	88	(88)					—
BALANCE DECEMBER 31, 2001	182,309	$ 12,646	2,850	1,153	1,684,337	(289,799)	(134,990)	1,276,197
Net earnings					401,525			401,525
Other comprehensive income:								
Foreign currency translation adjustments							37,007	37,007
Unrealized holding loss on marketable equity securities, net of $2,150 tax							(4,081)	(4,081)
Loss on derivative contracts, net of $363 tax							(899)	(899)
Total comprehensive income								433,552
Dividends to shareholders					(184,628)			(184,628)
Treasury share purchases	(527)					(27,759)		(27,759)
Options exercised and stock awards granted	633			1,676		20,402		22,078
Tax benefit related to stock options exercised				1,380				1,380
Conversion from Class B Common to Common	1,098	73	(73)					
ESOP tax benefit					1,756			1,756
BALANCE DECEMBER 31, 2002	**183,513**	**$ 12,719**	**2,777**	**4,209**	**1,902,990**	**(297,156)**	**(102,963)**	**1,522,576**

CHAPTER 3

Opposing Personalities

If there is a willing buyer and seller for every transaction, what causes a stock to go up or down in price? The answer, of course, is the natural law of supply and demand. When there are more buyers than sellers, excess demand pushes a stock's price upward. In some instances, such as the debut of a hot initial public offering, a stock can double or more in price on the first day of trading due to feverish demand. If, on the other hand, there are more sellers than buyers, a stock's price will fall. This unfortunate circumstance often happens to companies whose earnings per share fall short of the consensus forecast.

We might say, then, that stock prices are set at the margin between the caution of the defensive investor, who frets about losing money, and the greediness of the enterprising investor, who wants to snap up the next great opportunity before everyone else. Benjamin Graham introduced these two personality types in *The Intelligent Investor* (1973). The chief aim of the defensive investor, Graham explains, is to "avoid committing serious mistakes or losses," while the primary objective of the enterprising investor is to own companies "that are both sound and more attractive than the average."[1] Combining these two viewpoints is to be cautiously greedy, the attribute of every successful investor.

Unfortunately, the challenge is to employ a cautiously greedy outlook using traditional accounting. As we briefly mentioned in Chapter 1, due to its four major limitations, the accrual income statement is not well suited to meeting the needs of either the defensive or enterprising investor (let alone a combination of the two).

From the defensive investor's perspective, the following are problems with the accrual income statement:

1. The omission of fixed capital
2. The omission of working capital

Although investment in fixed and working capital are uses of cash, they are not accounted for as such in the accrual income statement. As a result, a firm might appear to be financially stronger than it actually is.

From the enterprising investor's perspective the following are problems with the accrual income statement:

1. Intangible growth-producing initiatives are expensed in the year incurred.
2. Stockholders' equity is considered free.

Expensing intangibles like R&D and advertising penalizes forward-thinking companies that are laying the foundation for higher future sales and earnings. As for stockholders' equity, because no charge is recorded for its use, a company might appear more profitable than it really is.

Hence, the need for two alternate income statements, the defensive and the enterprising, to meet the needs of these two investment point of views.

Benjamin Graham (1894–1976)

Benjamin Graham is the father of security analysis. He was born in London in 1894 and moved with his family to New York City the following year. Graham's father, who represented the family chinaware firm, Grossbaum & Sons, believed that America offered greater opportunity than England. (The family changed its name to Graham during World War I.) When Graham was but nine years old a series of tragedies beset the family: His father died, the family business failed, and his mother lost half her money in a margin account.

Graham was a gifted student, though, and he graduated Phi Beta Kappa and second in his class from Columbia University in 1914. Graham then got a job on Wall Street, and within several years he was making $600,000 a year as a partner with Newburger, Henderson & Loeb.

Itching to run his own shop, Graham struck out on his own in 1926, forming an investment partnership which he managed in return for a share of the profits. During the first year he was joined by Jerome Newman, the brother of a friend, with whom he worked throughout the rest of his business career.

The Benjamin Graham Joint Account got off to a promising start. Then came the Great Crash of 1929. The fund was down 20 percent. Graham, however, was convinced that the worst was over, so he borrowed on margin and plunged back into the market. It was a horrific decision, and by 1932 the fund had lost 70 percent of its asset value. Graham was wiped out, forcing the family to leave its park-view duplex in the Beresford for a small rear apartment in the nearby El Dorado, where space was going empty. His wife, a dance teacher, went back to work. Graham was ready to quit the securities industry, but one of Newman's relatives put up $75,000, enough to enable the firm to survive. When Graham's epic *Security Analysis* was published in 1934, he had gone five straight years without a paycheck.

Chastened, Graham and Newman resolved never to lose money again. Over the next 20 years their partnership specialized in buying stocks of companies that were cheap in relation to their assets or earnings. The results were favorable. In *The Money Masters*, John Train estimates that Graham-Newman earned an average return of 21 percent a year for the next two decades. The partnership was terminated in 1950.

Train theorizes that Graham's success as an investor was knowing how to say no. "One of his assistants in Graham-Newman has described to me ruefully what it was like proposing a list of carefully selected and researched opportunities for Graham's consideration, only to have him find something substantive to object to in every one. He felt no compulsion to invest at all unless everything was in his favor."

In *The Intelligent Investor*, Graham compresses his investment philosophy into three just words—"margin of safety." If you are going to buy a firm's stock, Graham argues, then make sure there is a gap between the purchase price and what you believe the company is worth. The bigger the gap, the better.

In 1928 Graham began to teaching a class on investing at Columbia University. "Though generally reserved," Roger Lowenstein writes in *Buffett: The Making of an American Capitalist*, "he had an almost parental fondness for his students." Still, Graham was no pushover when it came to handing out grades. Indeed, 22 years would pass before Graham awarded his first A+. The recipient? Warren E. Buffett of Omaha, Nebraska. In time, Buffett would chisel his own mark on Wall Street, turning a $100 grubstake into a $30 billion fortune.

In 1934 David Dodd used Graham's class notes as the basis for the 658-page *Security Analysis*, which has been revised four times since. First editions of this text have sold for more than $10,000 and in 2000 a signed copy fetched $20,000, close to a record for a work of twentieth-century nonfiction.

In the early 1960s, Graham helped shape the Chartered Financial Analyst test.

Just before his eightieth birthday Graham confided to a friend that he hoped every day to do "something foolish, something creative, and something generous." He died in 1976 at his second home in Aix-en-Provence in the south of France.[2]

THE DEFENSIVE INVESTOR

The most ruinous mistake you can make as a buyer of common stocks is to own a company that goes bankrupt. For this reason, the defensive investor judges the quality of a firm's accrual profit on the basis of its ability to self-fund. This is a measure of self-reliance, that is, whether a company produces from ongoing operations more cash than it consumes. If a company earns a defensive profit, it means that it is able to finance its growth with internally funds, and therefore doesn't need to raise outside capital by borrowing money from banks or selling additional shares of stock. Being able to self-fund, a company can stand on its own two feet can watch its cash balance accumulate or, if it chooses, deploy the cash to build new factories, acquire a competitor, launch a new ad campaign, form a strategic alliance, pay down debt, repurchase stock, or raise the dividend. All of these activities are positive developments for stockholders.

Companies with defensive losses, meaning their ongoing operations consume more cash than they produce, can still be viable. However, lenders and owners must be willing to put new money into the business to subsidize the cash deficits. Also, until the company generates defensive profits, it is living on borrowed time. If, at some point, the capital markets tire of the losses and decide to withdrawl their financing, the company will run out of cash and be forced into bankruptcy. Even if bankruptcy is averted, the company's inability to self-fund is stressful for a firm's executives, employees, suppliers, customers, lenders, and stockholders. This, in turn, puts a company at a competitive disadvantage vis-à-vis the other companies in its industry.

To put it in human terms, think about a firm's inability to self-fund in the context of your own life. What would you do if your bank told you to repay the outstanding balance on your mortgage by the end of the month? Without cash, you would face tough decisions. Would you deplete your savings account or retirement funds? Sell assets like your coin collection, perhaps at a distressed price? Borrow money from another mortgage company? Or perhaps take an advance on your credit card? There are no good choices here.

The same pressure exists for companies. If a lender gets nervous and asks for the loan to be repaid (known as "calling the loan") management has four choices: spend down the cash balance in its checking account; sell assets such as buildings or subsidiaries; borrow more money from another lender; or sell additional shares of stock. These actions enable management to raise extra cash but at a cost. To determine whether a company is able to self-fund (generating defensive profits), use the defensive income statement. As we will learn in Chapter 5, the defensive income statement solves two of the limitations of the accrual income statement. Specifically, it accounts for fixed and working capital, dollar-for-dollar, in the year incurred. A company that makes money after these two adjustments has made a defensive profit. For the defensive investor, having a positive outcome on a defensive income statement translates into peace of mind.

THE ENTERPRISING INVESTOR

At the opposite end of the spectrum, personality-wise, is the enterprising investor. To this investor, the test of a promising company is its ability to create value.

What do we mean by the term "create value"? A safety engineer creates value by ensuring that cranes are operated properly so that no one gets hurt, a hotel concierge by making guests' visits so pleasant that they return again and again, a truck driver by getting the arugula to the restaurant without freezer damage.

Companies create value, at least in the financial sense of the word, when the return on capital is greater than the cost of that same resource. To determine whether a firm is creating value we use what's called an enterprising income statement. Like the defensive income statement, it starts with, but addresses two other limitations of, the accrual ledger.

First, intangibles are converted from operating expenses to capital expenses. Thus, if a firm spends $100 million on R&D and you believe the expected useful life is five years, then in the enterprising income statement $20 million is expensed this year, with the remaining $80 million charged over the next four years. This adjustment fulfills a mandate of accrual accounting, namely, to match current sales with current expenses and future sales with future expenses. In contrast, in the accrual income statement the entire $100 million outlay is immediately deducted even though the benefits to the firm may last for several years.

Second, the opportunity cost of stockholders' equity (the portion of company profits that is reinvested into the business) is expensed even though it is a noncash charge. As we will learn in Chapter 6, only if management earns a profit after the owners deduct their opportunity cost can a firm be said to have created value. The higher the enterprising profit, the better.

And what if the company has an enterprising loss? It is not necessarily headed for bankruptcy court. There are many companies that have enterprising losses and yet stay in business. On the other hand, if a company racks up several years' worth of subpar returns then stockholders will liquidate their holdings and go elsewhere in search of better returns. If there are too many sellers and not enough buyers, the only direction for the stock is down.

Granted, enterprising profit is a theoretical profit. It's what a company would earn if the accounting playing field were level so that distinctions between intangibles and fixed capital spending and between debt and stockholders' equity were eliminated. Still, companies with enterprising profits create value and make good use of their owners' time, while businesses with enterprising losses destroy value and squander wealth. Life is too precious and your time is too valuable to waste on the latter. Tempis fugit.

Asking whether one alternate income statement is better than the other is a bit like asking whether your car's gas pedal is more important than the brake. They are *both* useful, but for different reasons. The defensive income statement tells you whether a company can self-fund (and not go deeper into debt or dilute current stockholders, for example); the enterprising income statement reveals whether the business is creating value (and not wasting its owners' time). This distinction is important: The two are not the same, yet both are essential to generate authentic earnings power. A brief summary of the defensive and enterprising income statements is found in Table 3.1.

Critics might challenge some of the assumptions in the defensive and enterprising income statements (see Chapters 5 and 6). Of course, there are several assumptions in the accrual income statement. For example, when is a sale recorded? Is the bad debt reserve realistic? What is the value of inventory? What is the useful life of fixed capital? What is the assumed rate of

Table 3.1

Two Alternate Gauges of Profitability

	Defensive	Enterprising
Personality	Avoid committing serious mistakes or losses	Own companies more attractive than average
Income statement	"Defensive"	"Enterprising"
Adjustments:		
#1. Fixed capital	Expenses dollar-for-dollar in the year incurred	n/a
#2. Working capital	Expenses dollar-for-dollar in the year incurred	n/a
#3. Intangibles	Expenses dollar-for-dollar in the year incurred	Converts from an operating expense to a capital asset, and then depreciates over an appropriate number of years
#4. Stockholders' equity	Free	Expenses at investor's estimated opportunity cost

return for the employee pension fund? The point is, despite the assumptions in the two alternate income statements, use them to your advantage. After all, the more data points you can collect on a firm's earnings quality, the better.

The Earnings Power 'Spreadsheet'

If you know how to use an electronic spreadsheet (such as Excel), you can create a template for the defensive and enterprising income statements.

That way on the template you just enter the data you need from the accrual income statement, balance sheet, statement of cash flows, and footnotes and let the computer do all the tiresome calculations. When we get to the earnings power ratios in Chapter 11, you can also set up your spreadsheet to calculate the debt repayment period and return on greenest dollar. By letting the computer do the hard work, you'll have more time to spend on the other things that are important to you and your family.

To recap, the accrual income statement has four major limitations that can be fixed by using two alternate approaches to calculating income, namely, the defensive and enterprising income statements. We use the defensive income statement to see whether a company can self-fund, and an enterprising income statement to check if it is creating value. Thus, a proposition: A company has authentic earnings power when it has both defensive and enterprising profits.

$$\begin{aligned}\text{Earnings power} &= \text{Defensive profits} + \text{Enterprising profits}\\ &= \text{Self-fund} + \text{Create value}\end{aligned}$$

If you are a growth investor, make sure the companies you own are able to self-fund and create value. These are the best companies to own over long periods. The worst companies, on the other hand, have defensive and enterprising losses (even if they have accrual profits). If you own one of these companies, bid it adieu tout de suite.

So, does Wrigley possess authentic earnings power? We begin answering this question in Chapter 4.

The Five-Minute Test

The Earnings Power Chart is a powerful visual tool to check whether a growth company has authentic earnings power. But you don't want to spend lots of time with every Tom, Dick, and Harry stock tip that comes your way.

Enter the five-minute test, a rough-mesh screen to help you sift out the obvious losers in order to focus your analytical efforts exclusively on the highest-probability winners. Only those companies that still look promising after this analysis (which, with practice, should take about five minutes) are worth submitting to the more thorough scrutiny described in Chapters 5 and 6.

To get started, you'll need the candidate company's latest annual report or 10-K. To get either document, call the Investor Relations department and ask for an investor packet. (Be sure to jot down the person's name and telephone number so that if you don't receive the reports in a few weeks you'll know whom to call. You'd be surprised at how often people forget to send you the information because they have lost your name and address.) Many companies post their financial statements on their Web sites, which you can download and print. You can also find 10-Ks (but not annual reports) at the Securities and Exchange Commission's Web site (www.sec.gov). Go to the heading "Filings and

Forms" and double-click on "Search for Company Filings." Although the SEC's site is free, many of the filings do not fit on the page when you hit the "print" button on your computer. For a nominal fee, you can get from www.edgaronline.com the SEC filings without the annoying formatting problems. Edgaronline will even notify you by email when a company submits a new 10-K, 10-Q, proxy, 8-K or other important filing to the SEC.

Many commercial Web sites, including Multex, Yahoo!, and Morningstar, also maintain, on a quarterly and annual basis, income statements, balance sheets, and statements of cash flows for thousands of companies. A word of caution about getting financial data from secondhand sources is that you are relying on someone else's work. Thus, if someone mistypes a number, you won't know it unless you double-check against the firm's 10-K or 10-Q. These kinds of mistakes happen.

Let's walk through the five-minute test with Wrigley. Again, we'll use its financial statements for the fiscal year ending December 31, 2002. There are a total of nine tests.

TEST ITEM 1. AUDITOR'S OPINION

By law, public companies must have their year-end financial statements audited by a certified public accountant. So check for the "going concern" letter in the annual report or 10-K. (10-Qs are not audited.) If the company doesn't get a clean bill of health from its accountant, discard it from your pile of candidates and move on to the next idea.

On page 24 of Wrigley's 2002 annual report we find a letter from independent auditor Ernst & Young LLP explaining to the stockholders and board of directors that Wrigley's financial statements have been audited in accordance with auditing standards generally accepted in the United States of America:

> "In our opinion, the financial statements referred to above present fairly, in all material respects, the financial position of the Company at December 31, 2002 and 2001, and the consolidated results of their operations and their cash flows for each of the three years in the period ended December 31, 2002, in conformity with accounting principles generally accepted in the United States."[1]

Bingo! That's the language you want to see…that Wrigley's financial statements *present fairly* and are *in conformity* with GAAP.

Alas, you can't let your guard down even if a company receives a going concern letter. In many of the largest public bankruptcies in recent years there was no advance warning from the independent auditors that trouble was brewing. Moreover, just because a company gets a thumbs up does not mean, ipso facto, that it can self-fund and create value.

TEST ITEM 2. LAWSUITS

Next, examine the footnotes under legal proceedings for evidence of lawsuits that could mortally wound the company. Practically all companies are defendants in lawsuits. That's just the way things are today. What you're looking for are legal torpedoes, court cases that, if lost, could inflict serious harm or even put the company out of business.

Sometimes management will dismiss these problems with a chuckle and wave of the hand, insisting that they will have "no material effect" on business. (What would you expect them to say?) Accept these words at your peril. Instead, consider what the lawsuit alleges. Is the company's flagship product a dud? That's a bad sign. Class action lawsuits are more ominous. If you don't understand the full ramifications of a lawsuit, don't go any further.

Wrigley's 2002 annual report makes no mention of any lawsuits. This is a good sign.

And what about Microsoft? You will recall that back in 1997 the United States Justice Department attempted to divide the software maker into separate pieces, on the grounds that it had become a monopoly. If the government prevailed in court, who knew what the effect would have been Microsoft. Thus, if you follow this checklist to a T, then perhaps you might have moved on to the next stock idea. And if you owned Microsoft at that time, you may have decided to sell at least some of your shares. In 2001, the government withdrew its case, which put an end to the break-up scheme.

TEST ITEM 3. UNUSUAL LOSSES

Many companies provide, somewhere in their annual report or 10-K, a summary of operations for the last 5 or 10 years. This snapshot typically includes highlights from the income statement, balance sheet, and statement of cash flows, as well as such other pertinent information like the number of employees, new store openings, or stock prices.

What you're looking for is whether, and how often, the company reported an unusual loss in the last several years. Unusual losses can include bad debt, worthless inventory, machinery that's outlived its useful life, and severance payments to laid-off workers. You should be suspicious of a firm's earnings quality if it has a history of unusual losses.

In Motorola's 2002 annual report there is a line for reorganizing the business. In 2000 these charges totaled $596 million; in 2001 it was $1.9 billion; and in 2002 the figure was $1.8 billion. Given Motorola's recent results, how can you have any confidence that there won't be more unusual losses in the years ahead?

Wrigley's income statement has no unusual losses or restatements in the last three years. That's what we want to see.

TEST ITEM 4. EARNINGS RESTATEMENTS

More troubling than an unusual loss is an earnings restatement. A restatement is when results previously verified by the independent auditor are later deemed bad. In a column for *MSN Money*, Victor Niederhoffer and Laurel Kenner point out that almost every major financial disaster of the last few years—Adelphia Communications, Dynegy, Enron, Global Crossing, Lucent Technologies, MicroStrategy, Rite Aid, Sunbeam (now American Household), WorldCom Group—has been preceded or precipitated by an earnings restatement.[2] Therefore, be sure the company that interests you hasn't restated in the last several years.

So which companies are least likely to restate? Niederhoffer and Kenner cite a study that companies with independent audit committees, that is, no executive members, that meet more than twice a year are the least likely to restate earnings.

Wrigley has not restated its financials in the last several years. Also, according to the 2002 proxy, Wrigley's audit committee met five times in 2002. The committee has four members, each a non-employee, independent director. These are all positive factors.

TEST ITEM 5. INTANGIBLES ASSETS RATIO

Noted value investor Michael Price tells the story that shortly after he began his career at Mutual Fund Shares Fund, Max Heine asked him to look at the F&M Schaefer Brewing Company: "I'll never forget looking at the balance sheet and seeing a +/– $40 million net worth and $40 million in 'intangibles'." I said to Max, 'It looks cheap. It's trading for well below its net worth.... A classic value stock!' Max said, 'Look closer.' I looked in the notes and at the financial statements, but they didn't reveal where the intangibles figure came from. I called Schaefer's treasurer and said, 'I'm looking at your balance sheet. Tell me, what does the $40 million of intangibles relate to?' He replied, 'Don't you know our jingle, *Schaefer is the one beer to have when you're having more than one?*'"[3]

As Price alludes to, intangible assets must be viewed skeptically. That's because if management decides at some later point that the intangible is somehow impaired, the asset will have to be written off, which reduces stockholders' equity. You don't want to see a firm reduce its corporate net worth, because this may lead to adverse debt ratios and possible violation of loan covenants with banks and other lenders.

The most common type of intangible asset is goodwill. This represents the amount of the purchase price that is in excess of an acquired firm's net assets. It often constitutes a significant percentage of the assets of a firm that is a serial acquirer and is overpaying for its deals.

The situation at AOL Time Warner illustrates the risk of buying stocks of companies with lots of goodwill. On December 31, 2001, the media giant had $209 billion of assets, including goodwill and other intangible assets valued at $128 billion from the merger between America Online and Time Warner at the beginning of 2000.

$$\text{Intangible assets ratio} = \frac{\text{Goodwill} + \text{Other intangibles}}{\text{Total assets}}$$

$$= \frac{\$128{,}338 \text{ million}}{\$208{,}559 \text{ million}}$$

$$= 62\%$$

As calculated, 62 percent of AOL Time Warner's assets at year-end 2001 consisted of goodwill and other intangibles. For me, an intangible assets ratio over 20 percent is a red flag. That's because management might be overpaying for the acquisition or acquisitions that gave rise to the goodwill. Also, if a company gets into financial straights and needs to raise cash fast, it may not be able to sell its goodwill assets as quickly (and at the desired price) as tangible assets such as inventories or warehouses.

In AOL Time Warner's case, much of this $128 billion asset was written off over the next several months, so much, in fact, that a year later, on December 31, 2002, the goodwill line on the balance sheet had shrunk to $37 billion. AOL Time Warner's stock, which sold for about $60 at the time of the merger, now goes for $15.

There aren't any intangibles on Wrigley's balance sheet, so this is a good sign.

A variation on the intangibles assets ratio is to subtract goodwill and other intangibles from stockholders' equity. What remains is a firm's tangible book value. If this figure is negative, drop the company like a hot coal and move on to the next one. Companies with negative tangible book value lack the balance-sheet muscle to protect themselves in a recession or from better-financed competitors.

TEST ITEM 6. DEBT-TO-EQUITY RATIO

You will want to determine a prospective investment's debt-to-equity ratio to avoid getting mixed up with companies that are at risk of going bankrupt for financial reasons. This ratio is equal to the sum of all interest-bearing debt divided by stockholders' equity. The lower the ratio, the higher a firm's credit-worthiness.

For the purposes of the five-minute test, debt includes working capital lines of credit, short-term debt, the current portion of long-term debt, long-term debt, and capital leases. All this information is found on the liability side of the balance sheet.

Consider cable television provider Adelphia Communications Corporation of Coudersport, Pennsylvania. It is the sixth-largest cable television provider in the United States, which, through various subsidiaries, provides cable television and local telephone service to customers in 29 states and Puerto Rico. On December 31, 2000, the company had approximately $13 billion of debt and $4.2 billion of stockholders' equity.

$$\text{Debt-to-equity ratio} = \frac{\text{Debt}}{\text{Stockholders' equity}}$$

$$= \frac{\$12.603 \text{ billion}}{\$4.150 \text{ billion}}$$

$$= 304\%$$

As calculated, Adelphia's debt-to-equity ratio was 304 percent, meaning that it employed about three dollars of debt for every dollar's worth of corporate net worth. With so many stocks to buy, it's puzzling why anyone would want to own shares of a company with such a leveraged capital structure. And yet in mid-2001 the cable operator had a market value of $5.4 billion. (A firm's market value is equal to its stock price times shares outstanding.) As they say, beauty is in the eye of the beholder.

So what became of Adelphia? The following year, in 2002, the Securities and Exchange Commission charged founder John J. Rigas, his three sons, and two senior executives with "one of the most extensive financial frauds ever to take place at a public company." In its complaint, the SEC alleged that Adelphia, at the direction of the individual defendants, "fraudulently excluded billions of dollars in liabilities from its consolidated financial statements by hiding them in off-balance sheet affiliates; falsified operations statistics and inflated Adelphia's earnings to meet Wall Street's expectations; and concealed rampant self-dealing by the Rigas Family, including the undisclosed use of corporate funds for Rigas Family stock purchases and the acquisition of luxury condominiums in New York and elsewhere." The stock, which traded over $80 in 1999, today is worthless.[4]

I avoid companies with debt-to-equity ratios over 75 percent, as companies with authentic earnings power don't need lots of debt to finance their growth. In Wrigley's case, its balance sheet shows nary a speck of debt, another good sign.

TEST ITEM 7. REVENUE GROWTH

Successful companies make products or provide services that people want or need. Therefore it's important, crucial even, to pay attention to top-line revenue growth. Revenue growth is the only way to get bigger over time. To be sure, many companies with flat or declining revenues might show earnings gains for a time. But these boosts usually come from cost cutting, a ploy that has a limited life. A company can cut costs just so far, but it can increase revenue indefinitely.

In 2002 Wrigley's net sales totaled $2.746 billion, versus net sales of $1.937 billion in 1997. Thus, its five-year growth rate is 42 percent, an impressive performance for a company that's been around for more than a century.

$$\text{Five-year revenue growth} = \frac{\$2.746 \text{ billion} - \$1.937 \text{ billion}}{\$1.937 \text{ billion}} \times 100$$

$$= \frac{\$0.809 \text{ billion}}{\$1.937 \text{ billion}} \times 100$$

$$= 42\%$$

Of course, this cursory examination doesn't reveal the *source* of Wrigley's revenue growth. Is it due to an increase in units sold? Price increases? Acquisitions? The best revenue growth is from an increase in units sold, because this means customers want or need a firm's products or services. Next best is price increases. The lowest-quality revenue growth is from acquisitions. If a company makes lots of acquisitions, it's hard to know what a firm's organic (internal) growth is. To learn how much, if any, revenue gain is due to acquisitions, read the notes to the financial statements. Wrigley has not made any major acquisitions, which is favorable.

If you are looking for one of Warren Buffett's "single wonderful businesses," stick with companies that have high-quality revenue growth. As a minimum, you should look for growth in the topline of at least 30 percent over the last five years.

Read the Notes to Financial Statements

As just about everywhere in life, you have to read the fine print to understand a document's importance. All U.S. publicly traded company's quarterly (10-Q) and annual (10-K) reports filed with the SEC contain tables and explanations. Pay special attention to the "Notes to (sometimes "Consolidated") Financial Statements. If the company wants to hide some bad news, the notes section is a good place to do it. Companies know that many investors don't like to read the notes because the words and numbers are in small print, and because there aren't any pictures.

TEST ITEM 8. STOCK–BASED COMPENSATION RATIO

One of the hot-button issues in recent years is whether to count stock options awarded to executives and other employees as an expense. Employee stock options are not a cash cost like raw materials or rent, and do not have a market price because they cannot be sold. But many investors view options as a hidden expense that overstates a firm's profitability. Also, when employees exercise their options, those extra shares increase share count, which dilutes existing stockholders' claims on a firm's net assets and future earnings power. Of course, management can repurchase the stock to keep a lid on share count, but that use of cash reduces the amount of money available for other growth-producing initiatives like building a new distribution center or paying down debt.

For these and other reasons, you may want to avoid companies whose stock-based compensation is more than 15 percent of accrual profits. To illustrate, let's look at eBay, the Internet auction site that was inspired by a Pez dispenser and that hawks everything from applesauce labels to zoetropes. According to eBay's 2002 10-K, its stock-based compensation amounted to almost $193 million. Accrual profits, meanwhile, totaled about $250 million. As we see below, eBay's stock-based compensation equaled 77 percent of its 2002 accrual profits.

Stock-based compensation % accrual profits

$$= \frac{\text{Stock-based compensation}}{\text{Accrual profits}}$$

$$= \frac{\$192.902 \text{ million}}{\$249.891 \text{ million}}$$

$$= 77\%$$

eBay is a great company, and has also been a hot stock of late (up 1,200 percent over the last five years). Still, it's troubling to see such a high ratio of stock-based compensation to accrual profits. This ratio suggests that the bulk of eBay's earnings (which belong to the stockholders) are being transferred to employees. Of course, no one will complain as long as the stock maintains its torrid ascent.

What about Wrigley? The footnotes in its financial statements show that accrual profits in 2002 were $401.5 million before the effects of stock-based compensation, and $390 million after deducting the costs. Therefore, the imputed cost of options was $11.4 million. Using the $401.5 million figure as our denominator, Wrigley's stock—based compensation was only 3 percent of 2002 accrual profits. That's a good sign.

Stock-based compensation % accrual profits

$$= \frac{\text{Stock-based compensation}}{\text{Accrual profits}}$$

$$= \frac{\$11.4 \text{ million}}{\$401.5 \text{ million}}$$

$$= 3\%$$

TEST ITEM 9. SHORT RATIO

Most investors buy a stock hoping that it will go up in price. In the argot of Wall Street, this is called as "going long." But a handful of investors take the opposite tack; they look to profit by finding companies whose stock price is set to fall. This strategy is called "short selling." As a rule, short sellers are a skeptical lot. They have to be, because it is more dangerous to short a stock than it is to go long. (When you short a stock your potential gain is limited to 100 percent, while your potential loss is infinite.) So unless you really know what you are doing, avoid companies with high short interest.

How can you determine whether short sellers are betting on a firm's demise? The easiest way is to look at the percentage of the float that is sold short. The float is the number of shares that freely trade in the market. The higher the percentage, the more confident short sellers are that the company is on the brink of a collapse.

According to its profile page on Yahoo! Finance, on April 17, 2003, Wrigley had 4.21 million shares sold short. The float was 163 million shares. Therefore 2.6 percent of Wrigley's float was sold short:

$$\begin{aligned}\%\ \text{Shares sold short} &= \frac{\text{Shares short}}{\text{Float}} \\ &= \frac{4.21\ \text{million}}{163.0\ \text{million}} \\ &= 2.6\%\end{aligned}$$

If more than 15 percent of a company's float are sold short, find out why. At the very least, that should give you pause. With less than 3 percent of its shares sold short, Wrigley passes this test with flying colors.

A REVIEW OF WRIGLEY'S PERFORMANCE

Let's review Wrigley's performance using the results from our five-minute test. It has a clean auditor's opinion, there don't appear to be any serious lawsuits, no unusual losses in the last three years, no restatements, the intangibles assets ratio is zero, the debt-to-equity ratio is zero, revenue growth is 42 percent over the last five years, stock-based compensation is 3 percent of accrual profits, and the short ratio is about 3 percent. Wrigley is the model of probity. Our findings are summarized in Table 4.1

One question you may ask is whether a company has to do well on all of our tests to be considered for further study using the Earnings Power Chart methodology? Or will a majority do?

Just as some opinions are more valuable than others, some tests are more important than others. An unfavorable auditor's opinion is a deal breaker, as are lawsuits that suggest there's something defective or injurious about the firm's product or service. While repeated unusual losses aren't the end of the world, it may mean that management doesn't know what it is doing.

There's no reason to spend lots of time with companies that have earnings restatements, negative stockholders' equity, a leveraged balance sheet (indicated through the debt-to-equity ratio), or high short ratios.

As for lethargic revenue growth, determine the cause. If it's because customers no longer want or need a firm's products or services, why would you want to be a part-owner?

If nothing objectionable turns up, go ahead and build the defensive and enterprising income statements, as described in the Chapters 5 and 6.

This list is not comprehensive by any means. As your analytical skills improve, you may want to add or subtract from it. The point is to devise a way to quickly dispense with companies that don't deserve your full attention.

Table 4.1

The Five-Minute Test: Wrigley 2002

Criteria	Benchmark	Wrigley
1. Auditor's opinion	Clean opinion	Clean opinion
2. Lawsuits	No material lawsuits	No material lawsuits
3. Unusual losses	No more than one in last three years	None in the last three years
4. Earnings restatements	No restatements	None
5. Intangibles assets ratio	Intangibles less than 20% of total assets	0%
6. Debt-equity ratio	Less than 75%	0%
7. Revenue growth	At least 30% over the last five years	42%
8. Stock-based compensation ratio	Less than 15%	3%
9. Short ratio	Less than 15% of the float sold short	3%

Source: Company reports, EarningsPower.com

CHAPTER 5

The Defensive Income Statement

The chief aim of the defensive investor, it will be recalled, is to avoid committing serious mistakes or losses. For the defensive investor, the most serious mistake is the permanent loss of capital that comes from owning a company that goes bankrupt. To avoid such unpleasantness, the defensive investor turns to the defensive income statement to check whether a company can self-fund. When a company can self-fund, it is able to finance its growth by producing more cash from ongoing operations than it consumes. Crucially, because the accrual income statement does not expense investment in fixed and working capital, it is, in many cases, a poor gauge of self-sufficiency. Simply put, the accrual income statement is not defensive enough for the defensive investor.

In this chapter we examine what it means for a company to make an investment in fixed and working capital. Then we build a defensive income statement for our protagonist, the William Wrigley Company. The results from the defensive income statement give us one of the two coordinates we need to build an Earnings Power Chart. The other coordinate, enterprising profit (loss), is the subject of Chapter 6.

OMISSION OF INVESTMENT IN FIXED CAPITAL

A company invests in fixed capital when it buys long-lived assets like trucks, buildings, lathes, telephone networks, desks, and filing cabinets. The value of these purchases is added to, or capitalized as an asset on, the balance sheet. On the accrual income statement, the cost of newly acquired assets aren't immediately expensed; instead, the purchases are written-off over time via depreciation. The logic of depreciating rather than expensing the cost of fixed capital is because these types of assets wear out gradually rather than just in the year they were bought.

In 2002 Wrigley spent $216.9 million on additions to property, plant, and equipment. Its depreciation charge, meanwhile, was $85.6 million. Thus, Wrigley made a $131.3 million investment in fixed capital. This use of cash is an expense in the defensive income statement.

Capital spending	$(216.9) million
Less: Depreciation	85.6 million
Investment in fixed capital	$(131.3) million

Wrigley's investment in fixed capital raises three important points.

First, Wrigley's ratio of capital spending to depreciation is 2.5-to-1. This means in 2002 Wrigley spent $2.50 on new plant, property and equipment for every dollar's worth of depreciation. The higher the ratio of capital spending to depreciation, the more the accrual income statement overstates a firm's cash-generating ability.

Second, while stockholders hope that Wrigley's $131.3 million cash outlay will generate higher future sales and earnings, there are no guarantees. Home Depot is a case in point. This was one of the great growth stocks of the last quarter-century, rewarding stockholders with a 12,000 percent gain—before dividends—from 1985 to 2000. A key ingredient in the home-improvement chain's rapid expansion was the building of all those new stores that you see when you drive around town. At last count Home Depot had 1,500 stores in four countries, versus four stores in Atlanta, Georgia, in 1979.

Recently, however, Wall Street has soured on Home Depot partly due to concerns of overexpansion. In my corner of New England, for example, we have three Home Depot stores within a seven-mile radius of our home. It's conceivable that these stores may be cannibalizing each other. If true, then some of Home Depot's capital spending is a waste of stockholder capital.

Third, for better or worse, the statement of cash flow does not distinguish between maintenance capital spending and discretionary capital spending. Maintenance capital spending is the amount needed to oil the machinery and give the walls a fresh coat of paint. Discretionary capital spending is money spent to produce incremental revenue over the next several years.

In Wrigley's case, I suspect most of its $216.9 million of capital spending is discretionary. Why? Because its depreciation charge is so low, only $85.6 million. Often, a firm's maintenance capital spending is equal to, or slightly more than, its depreciation. If we assume Wrigley's maintenance capital spending is, say, 125 percent of its depreciation (an educated guess, nothing more), then $107 million is maintenance ($85.6 million x 1.25) and the other $109.9 million is discretionary ($216.9 million - $107 million).

Many experienced investors exclude discretionary capital spending from the defensive income statement to avoid penalizing companies that are investing for future growth. However, since we will be using two income statements, I prefer to take the cautious route here and expense everything. (In the enterprising P&L capital spending is an indirect expense.) To me, it's all a use of cash. Also, you never know if discretionary spending will pan out. Better safe than sorry.

Look at Enron Corporation. In 2000 the flamboyant energy trader spent $4.4 billion on capital spending, well above its depreciation charge of $855 million. Chances are, a large portion of the $4.4 billion of capital spending was discretionary. But what good did that investment do for the stockholders? Within a year's time Enron filed for bankruptcy.

Capital spending	$4.410 billion
Less Depreciation	$0.855 million
Investment in fixed capital	$3.555 billion

To sum things up, if you are a defensive investor, better to err on the side of caution and expense all capital spending—maintenance and discretionary—in the year incurred. For one thing, it is a use of cash. Also, who knows whether the outlays will generate higher future sales and earnings. For these reasons, I recommend that you also expense the cash cost of any acquisitions that a firm may make. This outlay is treated as a separate line item in the investing section of the statement of cash flows.

OMISSION OF INVESTMENT IN WORKING CAPITAL

Working capital assets include accounts receivable, inventory, and other current assets such as prepaid insurance premiums. Working capital liabilities include accrued expenses and other current, non-interest-bearing liabilities. The net of these two items is a firm's working capital position—or working capital, for short. When working capital increases from one year to the next, a firm has made an investment in working capital. This, too, is a use of cash that does not appear on the accrual income statement.

As we see in Table 5.1, on December 31, 2001, Wrigley's working capital assets were valued at $565.8 million and its working capital liabilities at $330.9 million, resulting in a working capital position of $234.9 million. One year later, on December 31, 2002, Wrigley's working capital assets were $681.8 million and its working capital liabilities $382.9 million, resulting in a working capital position of $299 million. Thus, in 2002 Wrigley made a $64.1 million investment in working capital.

Eventually, when a firm makes an investment in working capital no charge is recorded on the accrual income statement. Why? Because according to GAAP this incremental change in a firm's balance sheet is an investment.

Semantics aside, the net increase in a firm's working capital is a use of cash. Moreover, if a company makes a large investment in working capital that may be a harbinger of trouble. In January 2000, to cite just one prominent example, Lucent Technologies' stock fell sharply after management announced that

Table 5.1

Wrigley's Investment in Working Capital, 2002 (in thousands)

	12/31/01	12/31/02
Receivables	$239,885	$370,976
Inventory	278,981	503,291
Other current assets	46,896	91,608
Total	$565,762	$681,835
Payables	$ 91,397	$97,705
Accrued expenses	128,264	172,137
Accrued expenses	42,741	46,137
Income taxes payable	2,568	66,893
Total	$330,869	$382,872
Working capital	$234,893	$298,963
Investment working capital	n/a	$ 64,070

Source: Company reports; EarningsPower.com

its fiscal first-quarter results would fall well short of expectations. The news caught Wall Street flat-footed, but had you watched Lucent's investment in working capital shoot up for the fiscal year ending September 30, 1999, you would have seen the signs. (Lucent's 10-K was filed with the SEC on December 21, 1999; management announced the first-quarter shortfall in early January 2000.) As we see in Table 5.2, for the fiscal year ending September 30, 1999, Lucent invested approximately $6 billion in working capital, triple the $2 billion investment in fiscal 1998 and a six-fold increase from two years earlier.

Investment in working capital is fine provided management can collect its receivables and sell the inventory quickly and at full price. Think of receivables as revenue that a firm hasn't been paid for, inventory as potential revenue. If receivables or inventories grow faster than payables or accrued expenses, find out why. If a firm isn't collecting receivables fast enough, it might be a sign of channel stuffing (selling to companies that already have more product than they need), or perhaps its customers are unhappy with its product or service and are refusing to pay. For companies that sell products with

Table 5.2

Lucent Technologies' Investment in Working Capital, Fiscal 1997-1999

	9/30/97	9/30/98	9/30/99
Receivables	$5,373	$ 6,939	$10,439
Inventory	2,926	3,081	5,048
Prepaid expenses and other	1,519	1,750	3,046
Total	$9,818	$11,770	$18,533
Payables	$1,931	$ 2,040	$2,878
Accrued expenses	2,417	2,698	2,437
Other current liabilities	3,852	3,459	3,599
Total	$8,200	$ 8,197	$8,914
Working capital	$1,618	$ 3,573	$9,619
Investment working capital	$1,045	$ 1,955	$6,046

Source: Company reports; EarningsPower.com

rapidly changing technology, inventory buildup is particularly vexing because it may mean the firm is falling behind its competitors and customers no longer want or need what the firm has to sell.

In recent years, Dell Computer has managed its working capital spectacularly. Dell's revenue in 2002 was $31 billion, up from $890 million in 1992 (see Table 5.3). That's impressive enough. But now look at what happened to its working capital position over this period...it *declined*. This is a bravura performance and is a benchmark against which all other companies should be compared.

How did Dell achieve rapid growth in revenue while also making a negative investment in working capital? It did so by having vendors carry raw materials (a type of inventory) up to the last minute, and requiring customers to pay for their computers upfront. If you find a company that can grow rapidly while make little, if any, investment in working capital, you may have found the next Dell. We take a closer look at Dell in Chapter 10.

Table 5.3

Dell Computer's Working Capital, 1992–2002 (in millions)

Year	Revenue	Working capital assets	Working capital liabilities	Working capital
1992	$ 890	$357	$230	$128
1993	$2,014	$757	$494	$264
1994	$2,873	$711	$538	$173
1995	$3,475	$943	$751	$192
1996	$5,296	$1,311	$939	$372
1997	$7,759	$1,395	$1,658	$(263)
1998	$12,327	$2,068	$2,697	$(629)
1999	$18,243	$3,158	$3,695	$(537)
2000	$25,265	$3,549	$5,192	$(1,643)
2001	$31,888	$4,053	$6,543	$(2,490)
2002	$31,168	$3,963	$7,519	$(3,556)

Source: Company reports; EarningsPower.com

Working Capital Red Flags

If a company makes a large investment in working capital, is it due to an increase in receivables? Inventory? Or, a combination of the two?

Investment in working capital due to rapid growth in receivables almost always means trouble. Common reasons for receivables growing faster than sales include management granting generous payment terms in an effort to prevent customers from switching to a rival; poor collection efforts; customers being in financial straits and unable to pay their bills; or customers being unhappy with the product or service and waiting for problems to be resolved before paying for their bills.

Investment in working capital due to growth in inventory is more difficult to interpret. There are good increases in inventory; a toy manufacturer, for example, might accumulate inventory during the summer to get ready for the all-important Christmas selling season (at which point inventory should drop sharply). Also, a company that is about to launch a new product is likely to have lots of inventory on hand in the months leading up to the debut.

But permanently high (and rising) inventory levels can also mean that production is outpacing sales (which increases storage costs) or that consumer preferences are changing (a sign the company is falling behind the technology curve.) Whatever the cause, to move inventory the company will eventually have to cut prices. An inventory yard-sale reduces a firm's profit margin and cuts into per-share earnings.

Now let's put it all together and create a defensive income statement for Wrigley for 2002:

1. Revenue: $2,746.3 million.
2. Cost of sales: $1,150.2 million.
3. Selling, general & administrative: $1,011 million.
4. Other expense: $10.6 million.
5. Investment income: This $8.9 million gain is omitted from the defensive income statement because it is a nonoperating item. Wrigley's business is selling gum to customers around the world, not making money on its investments.
6. Investment in fixed capital: $131.3 million.
7. Investment in working capital. $64.1 million.
8. Intangible growth-producing initiatives. Not applicable.
9. Interest expense: Being debt-free, Wrigley has no interest expense.
10. Taxes. You can use the amount shown on the accrual income statement if you like. A more sophisticated approach, which I prefer, takes into account balance sheet changes in net deferred taxes (see the end of this chapter). This method results in a tax bite of $164.1 million.

As we see in Table 5.4, Wrigley's 2002 accrual profits of $401.5 million, or $1.78 per share, compare with defensive profits of $215 million, or $0.95 per share. So congratulations to Wrigley, which can self-fund its growth.

Table 5.4

Types of Profits: Wrigley. For the year ending December 31, 2002 (thousands, except per-share)

Income statement	Accrual	Defensive
Revenue	$2,746,318	$2,746,318
Cost of sales	1,150,215	1,150,215
Selling, marketing and admin.	1,011,029	1,011,029
Other expense	10,571	10,571
Investment income	(8,918)	n/a
(Intangibles reversal)	n/a	n/a
Investment fixed capital (#1)	n/a	131,304
Investment working capital (#2)	n/a	64,070
Intangibles (advertising) (#3)	n/a	n/a
Interest expense (#4)	n/a	n/a
Taxes	181,896	164,086
Total expenses	$2,344,793	$2,531,275
Profit	$401,525	$215,043
Profit per share (225,575 shares)	$1.78	$0.95

Source: Company reports; EarningsPower.com

Defensive Profit in 30 Seconds

Once you get the hang of things it will take only a few minutes to build a defensive income statement. However, a quick way to determine whether a company can self-fund is to subtract capital spending and acquisitions from operating cash flow. All three numbers are found in the statement of cash flows. Be sure to also subtract from operating cash flow nonoperating sources of cash like the tax benefit from stock-based compensation.

In Wrigley's case, cash provided by operating activities totaled $374 million, cash used in investing activities $208 million. The net of these two amounts is $166 million, indicating that Wrigley is profitable on a defensive basis. We note that the "30-second" approach yields a lower profit figure than the defensive income statement. This discrepancy is because the defensive income statement does not expense changes in deferred charges and other assets, which in Wrigley's case totaled $79 million in 2002. The key thing here is that both approaches tell us that Wrigley is able to self-fund.

For better or for worse, the defensive income statement is stringent. ("Tough love" is the term my dear father would use.) Indeed, it will discourage you from buying stocks of companies that will make other investors lots of money. But the defensive income statement will also prevent you from committing what Ben Graham termed "serious mistakes or losses." Owning a company that goes bankrupt for a lack of cash is a serious mistake. Just ask anyone who owned Enron Corporation.

I also want to point out that the defensive income statement can be manipulated. If, for example, management wants to maximize its defensive profits, it can skimp on property upkeep, forgoing maintenance on its truck fleet, or delay replacement of a leaky warehouse roof. Thus, if a firm's defensive profits for a given year or two look high in relation to the last, say, five years, then management might be milking the business, that is, not adequately investing for future growth. If this seems to be the case, look at the capital spending–depreciation ratios and working capital trends of other companies in the same industry to determine what is normal. You don't want to buy a company that's mortgaging its future for short-term gains.

To sum up, the defensive income statement corrects two limitations of the accrual income statement, the omission of investments in fixed and working capital. That still leaves us with the other two limitations: the expensing of intangibles and stockholders' equity is free. To correct these, we create in Chapter 6 the enterprising income statement.

Exercise

DEFENSIVE TAXES

In the defensive income statement, taxes equal the provision for taxes (see accrual income statement) plus the investment in net deferred tax assets.

As calculated in Table 5.5, Wrigley in 2002 made a $(17.8) million investment in net deferred taxes assets. All else being equal, a negative investment in net deferred tax assets is a good thing because it is a source of cash.

Now that we know Wrigley's investment in net deferred tax assets, we are ready to calculate its defensive taxes for 2002.

Table 5.5

Wrigley's Investment in Net Deferred Tax Assets, 2000

	12/31/01	12/31/02
Deferred Tax Assets		
Current deferred taxes	$14,846	$19,560
Deferred taxes	29,605	33,000
Total	$44,451	$52,560
Deferred Tax Liabilities		
Current deferred taxes	$1,455	$3,215
Deferred income taxes	46,430	70,589
Total	$47,885	$73,804
Net deferred tax assets	$(3,434)	$(21,244)
Investment in net deferred tax assets		$(17,810)

Source: Company reports; EarningsPower.com

This is equal the sum of a firm's accrual taxes and its investment in net deferred tax assets. As shown below, Wrigley's defensive taxes in 2002 was $164.1 million, somewhat less than the amount reported on the accrual income statement.

Accrual taxes	$181.896 million
Plus: Investment in net deferred tax assets	(17.810) million
Defensive taxes	$164.086 million

CHAPTER 6

The Enterprising Income Statement

The primary objective of the enterprising investor, once again, is to own companies that are both sound and more attractive than the average. For the enterprising investor, companies that are both sound and more attractive than the average are those that create value. To find such companies, the enterprising investor turns to the enterprising income statement. When a company creates value, it produces a return on capital that is greater than the cost of that same resource. Crucially, because the accrual income statement expenses intangibles and treats stockholders' equity as a source of cost-free financing, it is often a poor indicator of value creation. Simply put, the accrual income statement is not enterprising enough for the enterprising investor.

In this chapter we make the case for treating as assets outlays for research and development and advertising, and why stockholders' equity should be expensed even though it is a noncash charge. Then we build an enterprising income statement for the William Wrigley Company, using the per-share figure to give the second of the two coordinates we need to build an Earnings Power Chart. Wrigley is looking good in the five-minute test and the defensive income statement. But does it create value? Let's find out.

EXPENSING OF INTANGIBLES

The nation's economy has changed over the last 50 years. Half a century ago, our biggest companies extracted coal from the earth and forged I-beams in blast furnaces. Today, the prime creators of wealth for many firms are brands, patents, teamwork, customer service, licensing agreements, imagination, distribution routes, intellectual property, innovative technology, and reputation. All of these are "intangible growth-producing initiatives," or intangibles for short.

No one really disputes the value of intangibles. Under the rules of accrual accounting, however, they are expenses—even if the payoff is realized over many years.

Why, when it comes to intangibles, do accountants deviate from their basic policy of matching current sales with current expenses and future sales with future expenses? Why in the accrual income statement are bricks assets and brains expenses? Here are four reasons.

First, self-preservation. Since accountants are more likely to be sued for overstating than for understating earnings (and assets), it's in their best interest to err on the side of caution. Thus, intangibles are expensed in full when incurred rather than at some later date, even if most of the benefits will be booked down the road.

Second, intangibles are a use of cash. Every dollar a firm spends on R&D or advertising is a dollar less that is available to pay down debt, increase the dividend, or repurchase stock.

Third, if a company needs a few more pennies to meet Wall Street's quarterly expectations, management might be tempted to include with R&D a portion of operating expenses, say, rent on a research facility. When a company converts an operating expense to a capital asset, the effect is to reduce the current period's expenses and increase bottom-line earnings. (Of course, that capital asset will eventually make its way back onto the income statement as an expense.)

Fourth, there's no guarantee that intangibles will generate increases in future sales and earnings. Xerox is a case in point. As others have asked, has any other company in the history of technology done less with more than Xerox? Adjusted for splits, the stock price of this company whose researchers have created, among other things, the first personal computer, color copying, and laser printers, is lower today than in 1970.

Still, expensing intangibles, as the accrual and defensive income statements do, penalizes companies in mind-based industries for investing for future growth. In 2001 Pfizer invested $4.8 billion, or 15 percent of revenues, in the search for the next generations of Zithromax, Zoloft, Celebrex, and Viagra. What's more, according to its annual report for that year, Pfizer had more than 160 projects in development and several hundred projects in research. The benefits of these R&D efforts might not be seen for years, but under the rules of accrual accounting Pfizer must expense the $4.8 billion all at once.

Ironically, had Pfizer spent that $4.8 billion on, say, 160,000 trucks each costing $30,000, it could have depreciated the outlay over, say, five years. That Pfizer's long-term outlook is better served by investing in R&D than investing in a truck fleet isn't reflected in its accrual income statement.

Advertising is another important intangible. It builds market share and enables companies to charge higher prices for their products and/or services. To illustrate, fill in the blanks in the list below with the first company you think of that's associated with the product on the left:

Soft drink ____________

Chocolate ____________

Sneaker ____________

Family entertainment ____________

Blue jeans ____________

Motorcycle ____________

You probably answered, in descending order, Coca-Cola, Hershey Foods, Nike, Walt Disney, Levi's, and Harley-Davidson, which just goes to show the power of advertising. (Being a Philadelphia native, I'd be remiss not to mention a comment by John Wanamaker, the famous nineteenth century retailing magnate. Wanamaker, whose flagship store was for years a landmark in the City of Brotherly Love, once rued: "I know half the money I spend on advertising is wasted, I just don't know which half.")

Because the enterprising investor seeks companies that are sound and more attractive than the average, the enterprising income statement converts R&D and advertising from operating expenses to capital assets. This fulfills a key goal of accrual accounting, namely, to match current sales with current expenses and future sales with future expenses. The adjustment also rewards companies that are investing for future growth.

To convert an intangible from an operating expense to a capital asset, you begin by estimating its useful life. Clearly, this is an educated guess. You might use as a guide Table 6.1. The estimates are for well-established, Fortune 500-type companies that have been around for awhile, as well as for younger companies that don't have a track record. Naturally, many companies you study will fall between these extremes. Use your best judgment and don't lose any sleep over whether you picked the right

Table 6.1

Suggested Depreciation Periods for Common Types of Intangibles

Intangible	Company Profile	Depreciation Period
Research & Development	Fortune 500, profitable, positive net worth	10 years
	Start-up, unprofitable, negative net worth	3 years
Advertising	Fortune 500, profitable, positive net worth	5 years
	Start-up, profitable, negative net worth	2 years

depreciation period. The key point here is that the longer the depreciation period, the greater the amount of current intangible spending that is pushed into the future.

What about our case study, Wrigley? You won't find a line item for intangibles on its accrual income statement. However, if you look on page 31 of its 2002 annual report, you'll see advertising expense was $362.5 million in 2002, $328.3 million in 2001, and $308.4 million in 2000.

If we assume Wrigley's advertising has a useful life of three years, we divide $362.5 million by 3, resulting in an annual charge for the next three years of $120.8 million. Of course, when we calculate the enterprising cost of advertising for 2002, we must also add back the deferred costs from 2001 and 2000. As we see in Table 6.2, Wrigley's intangibles depreciation charge for 2002 totals $333.1 million (the sum of $120.8 million, $109.4 million, and $102.8 million). The faster the growth rate in intangibles spending, the bigger the gap between the enterprising cost of intangibles and the accrual (and defensive) cost.

Getting ahead of ourselves a bit, enterprising investors view net capitalized intangibles as a form of capital, just like debt, stockholders' equity, net deferred taxes, and capitalized operating leases. All else being equal, the less capital a firm

Table 6.2

How To Calculate Intangibles Depreciation (in thousands)

Year	2000	2001	2002
Current year-accrual	$308,446	$328,346	$362,548
Depreciation period	3	3	3
Year 1	$102,815	$109,449	$120,849
Year 2		$102,815	$109,449
Year 3	-	-	$102,815
Depreciation total			$333,113
Gross accrual expense	$308,446	$636,792	$999,340
Less accumulated depreciation	(102,815)	(315,079)	(648,193)
Net capitalized intangibles	$205,631	$321,713	$351,147

employs to produce a dollar's worth of earnings, the better. (A good analogy is your salary. The fewer hours a week you have to work to earn the same paycheck, the better.) For Wrigley, gross accrual expense for advertising at year-end 2002 is $999.3 million, accumulated depreciation is $648.2 million, and net capitalized intangible is $351.1 million.

America Online Capitalizes Its Intangibles

Capitalizing intangibles is a controversial topic. Consider the situation involving America Online Inc., which agreed to pay a $3.5 million penalty to settle SEC allegations that it improperly accounted for advertising and marketing costs in the mid-1990s.

According to the *Wall Street Journal*, the SEC alleged that AOL's use of an aggressive accounting method—counting subscriber advertising costs as assets—enabled it to report profits for six of eight quarters during fiscal 1995 and 1996. Had AOL properly booked the marketing costs of acquiring new customers, the Dulles, Virginia–based company would have lost money for those periods, claimed the SEC. [1]

Accounting rules generally don't permit companies to treat advertising costs as assets unless past performance indicates that revenue from new customers will exceed the costs. New online companies, such as AOL at the time, did not have a track record to demonstrate that they could recover advertising costs, according to the SEC, which maintained that AOL should not have used the accounting method "because the volatile and unstable nature of the Internet marketplace precluded reliable forecasts of future revenues."

With the Earnings Power Chart, AOL's advertising costs would be expensed in the defensive income statement because they are a use of cash and because you don't know whether the outlay will generate higher future sales and earnings. In the enterprising income statement, the advertising costs would be converted from an operating expense to a capital asset, and then depreciated over its estimated useful life (recognizing, of course, that forecasts are fallible). This gives you two scenarios: a worst case (defensive) and a best case (enterprising). When it comes to the stock market, the more data points you have, the better.

The key point here is that under GAAP, companies that make large intangible investments are, with but a few exceptions, precluded from expensing those outlays over their useful life. The enterprising income statement, in contrast to the accrual and defensive income statements, recognizes intangibles to be investments in future growth.

STOCKHOLDERS' EQUITY IS CONSIDERED FREE

Here's a quiz. Which would you rather own: a $10 million company that makes 15 percent on its capital or a $100 millioncompany that makes 5 percent? Think carefully.

According to Warren Buffett, the correct answer is the $10 million company, even though it makes less money overall. Buffett explained why in a conversation with Malcolm Chace, president of Berkshire Hathaway, the only surviving textile manufacturer of any size in New England. It was 1965, and Buffett had just bought controlling interest of Berkshire Hathaway, at about $8 per share. (In May 2003, an "A" share of Berkshire Hathaway sold for $72,600.) The future billionaire wanted to explain to his handpicked president what mattered most, so Buffett told Chace that he wasn't especially interested in how much yarn was produced, or even how much was sold. What Buffett really cared about was Berkshire's profit as a percentage of invested capital. Said Buffett: "I'd rather have a $10 million business making 15 percent than a $100 million business making 5 percent. I have other places I can put the money." [2]

Buffett's point was that as a business owner he had an opportunity cost. Not only could Buffett invest his partners' money in Berkshire Hathaway, he could buy shares in, say, American Express (in fact, he later did), U.S. Treasury obligations, commercial office space, a dry cleaner, or farmland. In short, Buffett had choices.

Like Buffett, you incur an opportunity cost when you become a part-owner of a company. Crucially, however, the accrual income statement doesn't tell you whether a firm's management is earning an adequate return on the wealth you and others have invested in the business. Why? Because stockholders' equity is free. There's no line on the accrual income statement for its cost, as is the case with debt capital. This omission is a problem because management can do a bad job of allocating your share of the firm's corporate net worth and you might not know any better.

That putting a dollar value on an investor's opportunity cost is an arbitrary exercise is one of the practical reasons stockholders' equity is considered free by the accrual income statement. Who would decide the cost of a firm's equity? The chief financial officer? The outside auditors? The Financial Accounting Standards Board? Federal Reserve chairman Alan Greenspan?

That said, equity capital is more expensive than debt. It has to be, because it is not a deductible expense as is debt. Also, if you assume the risks of ownership (that is, lousy performance at best, business failure at worst), you'll want a larger payoff than a lender. In the event of a bankruptcy, lenders are paid before owners.

To fix this limitation, we estimate the cost of stockholders' equity ourselves. We do this by erasing the distinction between debt and equity; all capital is treated the same. This lets us track a firm's performance although its capital structure may change from one year to the next, and also compare different companies that may have different proportions of debt to equity. Sound complicated? It's really not. Do this calculation a few times and it will become second-nature to you.

A Walk Downtown

Stroll down the sidewalk of any city and you're likely to pass a bank, restaurant, newsstand, telephone company, commercial printer, and a sporting goods store. Each of these businesses is financed with a mix of debt capital and equity capital. Debt takes the form of a working capital line of credit, term loan, or mortgage. Stockholders' equity is the firm's corporate net worth, that is, assets minus liabilities. Since the different businesses you will pass on your walk will likely have different capital structures (that is, proportions of debt to equity) a dollar of earnings, both on an accrual and defensive basis, for one business is not comparable to a dollar of earnings for another business. This, in turn, may distort common methods of valuation, including the price-earnings ratio.

One of the things that's unique about the enterprising income statement is that it introduces comparability; it enables you to put all businesses, regardless of size, on a level playing field and compare them as true economic equals. That's not the case with the accrual and defensive income statements, which treat stockholders' equity as a source of cost-free financing.

To treat debt and equity capital as equivalents, the first thing we do is calculate enterprising capital. Enterprising capital consists of debt and stockholders' equity as well as other items like net capitalized intangibles, the deferred tax liability, and capitalized operating leases. Think of enterprising capital as the amount of wealth that's been invested in a business to produce revenue and earnings. For the enterprising investor, the best companies produce high levels of earnings in relation to enterprising capital. The worst companies, in contrast, produce low levels of earnings.

As Table 6.3 shows, Wrigley's gross enterprising capital at year-end 2002 was $1.8 billion. After subtracting excess cash (which I assume for a company of Wrigley's stature is any amount over 2 percent of revenue), short-term investments, and marketable securities, we get net enterprising capital of $1.5 billion. Since a firm's enterprising capital will change throughout the year, use the two-year average figure in your calculations. For Wrigley, it works out to $1.3 billion.

A word of caution: Make sure a firm's excess cash is truly excess. Some companies have restrictions placed on them by banks and other lenders. If so, the cash may not available for corporate use.

After we estimate a firm's enterprising capital, the next step is to determine the weighted average cost of capital, or WACC. This is a single composite interest rate that reflects a firm's cost of capital irrespective of its proportion of debt to equity. To estimate Wrigley's WACC we fill in a chart similar to the one in Table 6.4.

Table 6.3

Wrigley's Capital and Equivalents (in thousands)

		12/31/01	12/31/02
Debt	Working capital line of credit	n/a	n/a
	Current portion long-term debt	n/a	n/a
	Long-term debt	n/a	n/a
	Total debt	n/a	n/a
Other	Other senior liabilities	122,842	129,044
Stockholders' equity	Total	1,276,197	1,522,576
Capital Equivalents	Deferred taxes	3,434	21,244
	Capitalized operating leases	n/a	56,406
	Net capitalized intangibles	116,082	29,435
Enterprising Capital	Gross	$1,518,555	$1,758,705
	Less: Excess cash	(259,757)	(224,350)
	Less: Short-term investments	(25,450)	(25,621)
	Less: Marketable securities	(25,300)	(19,411)
	Net	$1,208,048	$1,489,323
	Average 2 years		$1,348,686

Source: Company reports; EarningsPower.com

Table 6.4

Wrigley's WACC, December 31, 2002

1	2	3	4	5
Capital	Capital (Avg. 2 Years)	Weight	After-tax Rate	Wtd. Avg Rate
Debt	n/a	n/a	n/a	n/a
Stockholders' equity	$1,399,387	100%	11.8% *	11.8%
Total	$1,399,387	100%		11.8%

* Cost of equity estimate from Ibbotson Associates

Source: Company reports, EarningsPower.com

In column 2, the average (two years) of debt and equity is $1.4 billion. In column 3, divide the two types of capital by the total figure at the bottom of column 2. The total line must add up to 100 percent. Wrigley, of course, is financed entirely with stockholders' equity. In column 4, make note of the after-tax cost of debt and the cost of equity. The after-tax cost of debt is equal to the pretax cost of debt multiplied by 1 minus the marginal tax rate. To estimate the pretax cost of debt, divide interest expense on the accrual income statement by average debt for the last two years.

For the cost of equity figure we rely upon data provided courtesy of Ibbotson Associates, an authority on these matters (see Table 6.5). Ibbotson estimates the cost of equity for large, S&P 500–type companies has ranged from as high as 15.6 percent in 1990 to a low of 11.8 percent in 2002. To arrive at these figures Ibbotson takes the sum of the equity risk premium (using data going back to 1926) and the yield of the 30-year Treasury with 20 years remaining before maturity. The equity risk premium is your extra reward for owning a share of stock over what you would earn from a less risky asset, such as a U.S. Treasury.

Each line in column 5 in Table 6-4 is the product of columns 3 and 4. Add the two numbers in column 5 to get the composite rate, or WACC: 11.8 percent. That's our estimate of Wrigley's interest rate it must pay in order to finance the entire company, irrespective of the proportion of debt to stockholders' equity. The

Table 6.5

The Cost of Equity for all S&P 500-type Companies, 1990–2002

Date	COE (%)
12/31/90	15.6
12/31/91	14.7
12/31/92	14.6
12/31/93	13.7
12/31/94	15.0
12/31/95	13.4
12/31/96	14.2
12/31/97	13.8
12/31/98	13.4
12/31/99	14.9
12/31/00	13.4
12/31/01	13.2
12/31/02	11.8

Source: Ibbotson Associates

higher a firm's WACC, the higher its enterprising interest and lower its enterprising profits.

SinceWrigley employed $1.3 billion of enterprising capital in 2002 and its WACC was 11.8 percent, we estimate its interest expense to be $159.1 million:

$$\text{Enterprising interest} = \text{Enterprising capital} \times \text{WACC}$$
$$= \$1.348 \text{ billion} \times 11.8\%$$
$$= \$159.1 \text{ million}$$

Now let's put it all together and create an enterprising income statement for Wrigley for the year ended December 31, 2002.

1. Revenue: $2,746.3 million.
2. Cost of sales: $1,150.2 million.
3. Selling, general & administrative: $1,011 million.
4. Other expense: $10.571 million.
5. Investment income: This $8.9 million gain is omitted from the enterprising income statement because it's a nonoperating item.
6. Intangibles depreciation expense: $333.1 million, as calculated previously. Be sure to reverse the $362.5 million charge for advertising, which management includes in other operating expenses.
7. Enterprising interest expense: $159.1 million.
8. Imputed interest operating leases: Since capitalized operating leases are treated as a form of enterprising capital, reverse the imputed rent expense. Otherwise, we would bill Wrigley twice—and that wouldn't be fair. In 2002, interest on operating leases is estimated at $2.2 million. For more details, please see the exercise at the end of this chapter.
9. Taxes: $172.1 million. To learn how to calculate enterprising taxes, please see the exercise at the end of this chapter.

Table 6.6

Types of Profits: Wrigley. For the year ending December 31, 2002 (thousands except per-share)

Income Statement	Accrual	Enterprising
Revenue	$2,746,318	$2,746,318
Cost of sales	1,150,215	1,150,215
Selling, marketing and admin	1,011,029	1,011,029
Other expense	10,571	10,571
Investment income	(8,918)	n/a
(Intangibles reversal)	n/a	(362,548)
Investment fixed capital (#1)	n/a	n/a
Investment working capital (#2)	n/a	n/a
Intangibles (#3) (advertising)	n/a	333,113
Interest expense (#4)	n/a	159,145
Imputed interest operating leases	n/a	(2,256)
Taxes	181,896	172,057
Total expenses	$2,344,793	2,471,327
Profit	$401,525	$274,991
Per-share (225,575 shares)	$1.78	$1.22

Source: Company reports; EarningsPower.com

As we see in Table 6.6, Wrigley's accrual profits of $401.5 million, or $1.78 per share, compare with enterprising profits of $275 million, or $1.22 per share. This is encouraging news, because it means management created value. If you are an enterprising investor, you want to own companies that create value because that's a sign that the company is sound and more attractive than the average. Companies create value when they earn a high return on capital.

Enterprising Profits in 30 Seconds

Go to the accrual income statement and find earnings before interest and taxes, or EBIT. Take that number and divide by the sum of debt and stockholders' equity. That's your pretax return on capital. If the return is over 18 percent, the company probably has enterprising profits. In 2002, Wrigley's EBIT was $583 million. Meanwhile, it had no debt and $1.5 billion of stockholders' equity. Wrigley's pretax return on capital, therefore, is 38 percent, well above our minimum 18 percent threshold.

At this point, we have calculated both defensive and enterprising income statements. Each alternate P&L has strengths and weaknesses. We exploit their strengths and mitigate their weaknesses by combining them to get the basis of the Earnings Power Chart, the subject of Chapter 7.

Exercise

ENTERPRISING TAXES

To calculate enterprising taxes, we begin with defensive taxes and then add the interest tax benefit and intangibles tax benefit, and then subtract the nonoperating income tax benefit. As shown below, Wrigley's enterprising taxes in 2002 totaled $172.1 million.

Defensive taxes	$164.1 million
Interest tax benefit	0.8 million
Intangibles tax benefit	10.3 million
(Nonoperating income tax benefit)	(3.1) million
Enterprising taxes	$ 172.1 million

The first calculation is the interest tax benefit. This is the sum of a firm's accrual interest and the implied interest on operating leases, times the marginal tax rate. In 2002, Wrigley did not have any interest expense. It, did, however, employ operating

Table 6.7

How To Calculate Wrigley's Capitalized Operating Leases (figures in thousands)

	Future Value	Discount Rate (@8%)	Present Value
Year 1	$35,467	0.9259	$32,840
Year 2	$10,269	0.8573	$8,804
Year 3	$13,042	0.7938	$10,353
Year 4	$5,999	0.7350	$4,409
Capitalized operating leases			$56,406
Capitalized operating leases-average 2 years			$28,203

Source: Company reports; EarningsPower.com

leases. The data in Table 6.7 are from the footnotes at the end of Wrigley's 2002 annual report.

The present value of Wrigley's capitalized operating leases, using an 8.0 percent discount rate, is $56.4 million. Since the company didn't report any operating leases for 2001, the two-year average is $28.2 million. (I recommend using a two-year average, because one year's results might overstate the amount of operating leases the company had to work with.) At an interest rate of 8.0 percent, the estimated interest expense is $2.3 million, as the following calculation shows:

Capitalized operating leases, average 2 years	$28.2 million
Times: Implied interest rate	× 8.0%
Implied interest	$2.3 million

The next step is to calculate the interest tax benefit. This is the sum of accrual interest and the implied interest on operating leases, which we just estimated for Wrigley to be $2.3 million. At a 35 percent tax rate, its interest tax benefit is $790,000.

Interest (accrual plus implied operating leases)	$2.3 million
Times: Tax rate	× 35%
Interest tax benefit	$0.8 million

The intangibles tax benefit is equal to the difference between the accrual expense for intangibles and the enterprising expense:

Accrual intangibles	$362.5 million
Less: Enterprising intangibles	333.1 million
Net spending intangibles	$29.4 million

In 2002, the enterprising cost of intangibles (advertising) was $29.4 million less than the accrual cost. Assuming a 35 percent tax rate, the intangibles tax benefit was $10.3 million, as shown below:

Net spending intangibles	$29.4 million
Times: marginal tax rate	× 35%
Intangibles tax benefit	$10.3 million

Our third calculation is the nonoperating income tax benefit. Recall that in 2002 Wrigley had $8.9 million of interest income, which is excluded from the enterprising income statement because it is a nonoperating source of income. Since we are removing this gain, we want to deduct the additional taxes Wrigley paid on this income. As shown below, the additional taxes total $3.1 million:

Interest income	$8.9 million
Times: Marginal tax rate	× 35%
Nonoperating income tax benefit	$3.1 million

CHAPTER 7

The Earnings Power Chart

Many investors exhibit characteristics of both the defensive and enterprising personalities. They want the caution of the defensive investor who wants to avoid risk and the greed of the enterprising investor who seeks promising new opportunities. Being cautiously greedy is a foundation for successful investing.

To display the elements of the defensive and enterprising income statements, we use a visual tool called the Earnings Power Chart. Think of the Earnings Power Chart as a kind of investment compass that points you toward companies with the highest-quality earnings growth and away from those unable to self-fund and create value.

We begin by preparing a table of the accrual, defensive, and enterprising income statements, as shown in Table 7.1. Wrigley's 2002 accrual, defensive, and enterprising profits were $401.5 million, $215 million, and $275 million, respectively. With 225.6 million diluted shares outstanding, per-share accrual, defensive, and enterprising profits were $1.78, $0.95, and $1.22, respectively.

Having arrayed the figures from the three income statements, we're going to build two charts for Wrigley. The first, the Quality of Profits Chart (see Figure 7.1), plots these earnings

Table 7.1

Three Types of Profits: Wrigley. For the year ending December 31, 2002 (thousands except per share)

Income Statement	Accrual	Defensive	Enterprising
Revenue	$2,746,318	$2,746,318	$2,746,318
Cost of sales	1,150,215	1,150,215	1,150,215
Selling, marketing and admin	1,011,029	1,011,029	1,011,029
Other expense	10,571	10,571	10,571
Investment income	(8,918)	n/a	n/a
(Intangibles reversal)	n/a	n/a	(362,548)
Investment fixed capital (#1)	n/a	131,304	n/a
Investment working capital (#2)	n/a	64,070	n/a
Intangibles (#3) (advertising)	n/a	n/a	333,113
Interest expense (#4)	n/a	n/a	159,145
Imputed interest operating leases	n/a	n/a	(2,256)
Taxes	181,896	164,086	172,057
Total expenses	$2,344,793	$2,531,275	$2,471,327
Profit	$401,525	$215,043	$274,991
Per-share (225,575 shares)	$1.78	$0.95	$1.22

Source: Company reports, EarningsPower.com

figures graphically. You can create your own chart in just a few minutes with graph paper. If you know how to use the Chart Wizard function in Microsoft Excel, then build an electronic version.

The key thing to look for in the Quality of Profits Chart is how tightly or loosely a firm's defensive and enterprising profits (losses) correlate with accrual profits. If we compare more than one year, we also want to look at trends.

Ideally, you'll see a tight fit, that is, a close correlation between the two alternate earnings figures and the GAAP figure in the annual report and 10-K. If the fit is loose (that is, if there are accrual profits but defensive or enterprising losses or a big discrepancy between the different types of profits), that's trouble. Something is not right with the firm's earnings quality and you'll want to determine the cause.

If the problem is with the defensive income statement (meaning there's a defensive loss), perhaps the company is slow to collect receivables, its warehouses are stuffed with inventory

Figure 7.1

Wrigley's Quality of Profits, 2002

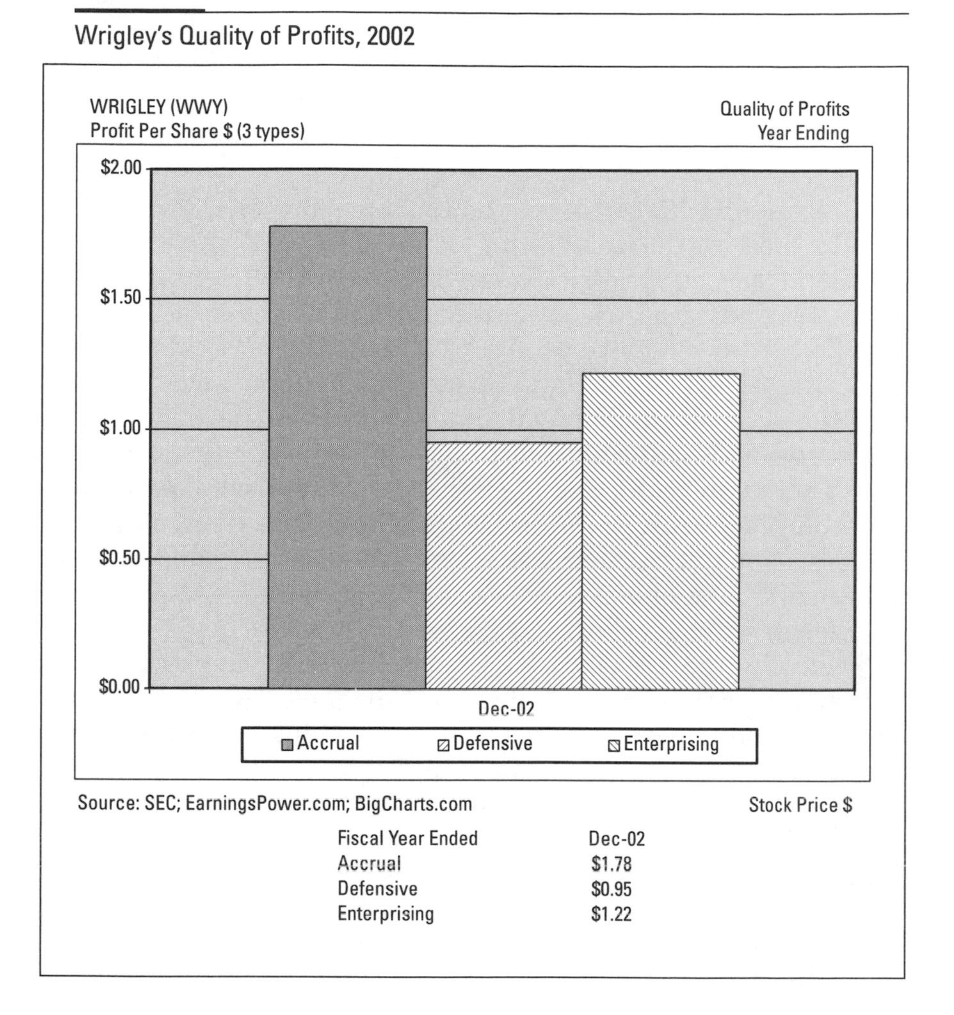

Fiscal Year Ended	Dec-02
Accrual	$1.78
Defensive	$0.95
Enterprising	$1.22

that won't sell, or it's in the midst of an aggressive capital spending program (which may or may not succeed). Whatever the case, you now have the analytical skills to find out.

If the enterprising income statement is the problem (meaning the bar representing enterprising income is negative) the company is earning a poor return on capital. Perhaps management overpaid for an acquisition or has too much working capital. These are questions you'll want to answer.

What does Wrigley's Quality of Profits Chart tell us? As we see, the company was profitable on an accrual basis and also had defensive and enterprising profits. This is a good sign.

EARNINGS POWER CHART

The next step is to construct the Earnings Power Chart. We do this by drawing horizontal and vertical axes and mark each off in equal increments (for example, 10 cents, 20 cents, and so forth, depending on the magnitude of the earnings per share). Next, plot the defensive profit (loss) along the vertical axis and the enterprising profit (loss) along the horizontal axis. Do not plot the accrual numbers; our interest here is the relationship between our two alternate earnings figures.

These two profit (loss) per-share amounts serve as coordinates on the Earnings Power Chart. The intersection, or origin, of these amounts (where the *X* and *Y* points connect on the chart) will be in one of four boxes formed by the *X* and *Y* axes. The result will be a chart like the one in Figure 7.2.

Ideally, the two per-share amounts will intersect in the chart's upper-right box, termed the Earnings Power Box. Companies situated here possess authentic earnings power, in other words, they are able to self-fund and create value. As we'll see later in this chapter, just because a company is profitable on an accrual basis does not mean that it can boast of authentic earnings power. Earnings power companies are the real blue chips of Wall Street.

The worst companies, in contrast, are situated in the lower-left box. These companies rely on external capital infusions and destroy value. Unless you have a compelling reason, stay away. The Earnings Power Chart is telling you something is wrong with the business or that it's not as profitable as it should be. One caveat to this rule is a lower-left box company that's in the midst of a turnaround. If the company gets its act together, the stock returns off the low can be dazzling. Christopher & Banks is a case in point. This retailer of women's clothing retailer is up 20-fold since the company emerged from bankruptcy in 1996.

Figure 7.2

Wrigley's Earnings Power Chart, 2002

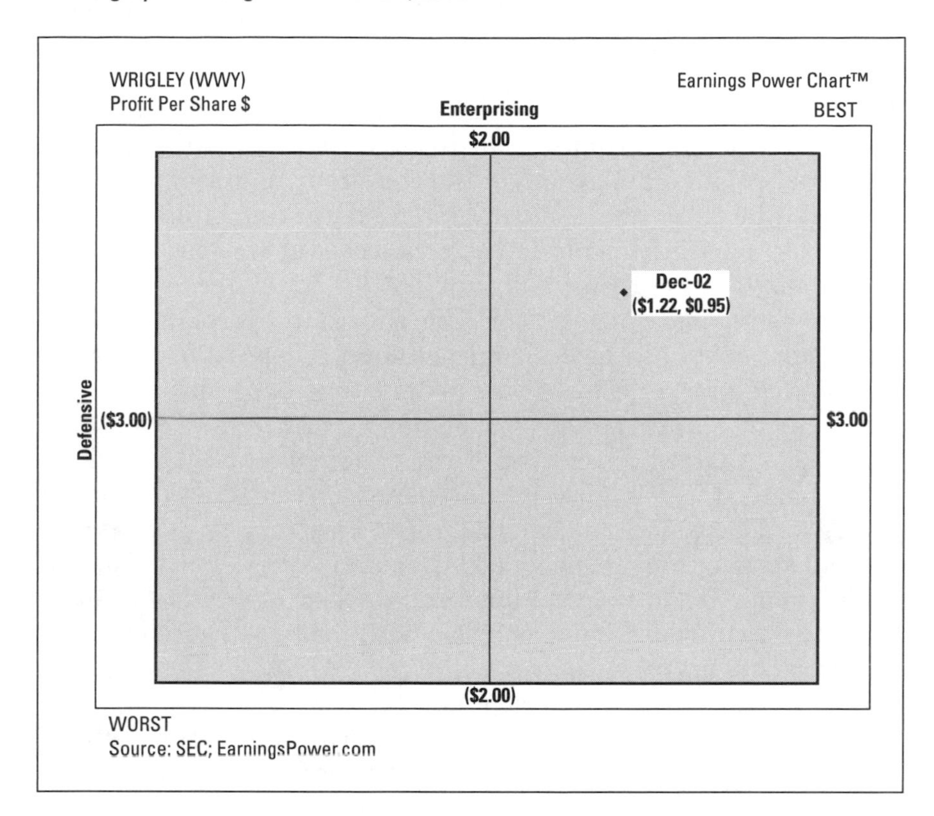

Here are signs that a turnaround candidate may be on the mend:

- New products or services are introduced
- Improved production efficiencies
- Increased sales
- A growing backlog of new orders
- Improved working capital management
- Closing of bad store locations
- A new management team
- Debt is reduced

Wrigley's placement in the Earnings Power Box confirms the quality of its accrual profits. What we don't know, however, is whether it's going to be another Microsoft, a topic that we will address later in Chapter 8.

There is an evocative scene in Robert Taylor's biography of W. C. Fields in which the grumpy comedian decides to organize a picnic for a party of four. Fields orders the chauffeur to "tune up the big Lincoln," the one with the silver-plated engine and built-in refrigerator. He unlocks from his liquor room a case of Lanson '28 Champagne, six bottles of Burgundy, six bottles of Sauternes, several bottles of gin, and a case of beer. Then he takes his companions to the Vendôme, a Los Angeles gourmet shop, where he buys caviar, pâté de foie gras, anchovies, smoked oysters, baby shrimps, crab meat, tinned lobster, potted chicken and turkey, several cheeses, a big bottle of Greek olives, and three or four jars of glazed fruit. Back home, Fields's cook has prepared an angel food cake, a devil's-food cake, and sandwiches (watercress, tongue, peanut butter and strawberry jam, chopped olives and nuts, deviled egg, and spiced ham). When the food has been packed in wicker hampers and the liquor loaded into the fridge with many extra ice buckets, Fields ushers his passengers into the car. "What we've missed," he deadpans, "we'll pick up on the road." [1]

If building the defensive and enterprising income statements has seemed a little like getting ready for a picnic with W. C. Fields, rest assured that the payoff is potentially considerably greater. But whereas Fields's concluding remark was meant to elicit laughs, we, in fact, do have a few things to pick up on the road. After exploring in Chapter 8 the characteristics of the archetypal companies that occupy each of the four boxes of the Earnings Power Chart, examining in Chapter 9 what makes a great stock for the long-term cautiously greedy investor, and considering in Chapter 10 two of the most celebrated stocks of the 1990s, we throw in a few garnishes. These are meant to ensure that the feast goes off without a hitch or, in our case, that your stock portfolio contains only the absolutely best prospects.

In Chapter 11 we present two earnings power ratios that gauge the degree to which a company is financially leveraged and its investment acumen with respect to the opportunities with which it is presented. Because ultimately these ratios are determined by the actions of corporate management, we offer in Chapter 12 a set of guidelines for evaluating a company's executive officers and directors. In Chapter 13 we emphasize the need to consider when you've found some candidate earnings power companies whether their earnings are likely to be sustainable and whether their valuation renders them suitable investment opportunities. In Chapter 14, we conclude with some ideas on where to find promising investment candidates, stocks to avoid, and other pointers that will make you a better investor and that don't pertain specifically to the Earnings Power Chart.

Now let's look at the charts to which all of this work to date was meant to get us. To avoid any ex post facto bias (from Latin, meaning "after the deed"), all stock prices are 30 days after companies filed their 10-Ks with the SEC. This one-month delay gives investors time to digest the most recent year's performance.

A small company located outside of New York City generates $600 million in annual revenues as a distributor of toothpaste, shampoo, and aspirin. It's a mundane business, to be sure. Still, this family controlled outfit has been profitable on an accrual basis every year for the past 5 years. What makes this company interesting is its letter to stockholders in the annual report. In it, management describes the successful year the company just had and promises strong growth to come.

Sound intriguing? Want to go out and buy the stock right now? It's time for a second and third opinion.

As we see in Figure 7.3, the company has had defensive and enterprising losses for each of the past 10 years.

Not surprisingly, when you plot these losses on the Earnings Power Chart (see Figure 7.4) the company lands in the lower-left box. Do you still want to buy? Of course not. Now for the unveiling. The company is Allou Health & Beauty Care, of Brentwood, New York.

Postscript: In a complaint filed by the U.S. District Court in August 2003, Victor Jacobs and his three sons were accused of creating phony sales and inventory transactions and issuing false and misleading financial statements to shareholders and lenders. A separate but related complaint charged four men, including a Jacobs, of conspiracy to bribe a New York City fire marshal by

Figure 7.3

Allou Health & Beauty Care, Quality of Profits, 1998–2002

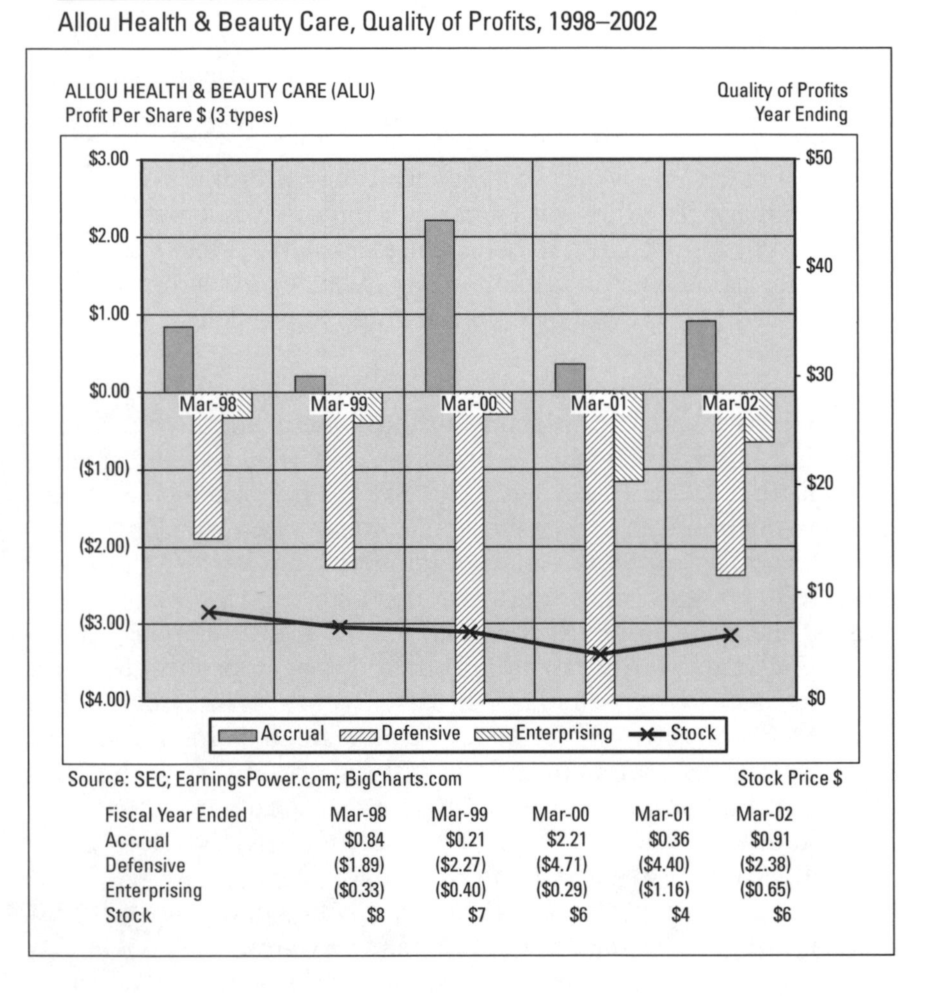

Fiscal Year Ended	Mar-98	Mar-99	Mar-00	Mar-01	Mar-02
Accrual	$0.84	$0.21	$2.21	$0.36	$0.91
Defensive	($1.89)	($2.27)	($4.71)	($4.40)	($2.38)
Enterprising	($0.33)	($0.40)	($0.29)	($1.16)	($0.65)
Stock	$8	$7	$6	$4	$6

promising him $100,000 in cash in exchange for issuing a false incident report. Allou's Brooklyn warehouse, which held the company's alleged inventory, burned down on September 25, 2002. Prosecutors said the defendants fabricated about $220 million in bogus sales and nearly $200 million in purchases of nonexistent inventory. The fraud complaint also alleged that the company kept two sets of financial books to deceive auditors and regulators.[2]

Figure 7.4

Allou Health & Beauty Care, Earnings Power Chart, 1998–2002

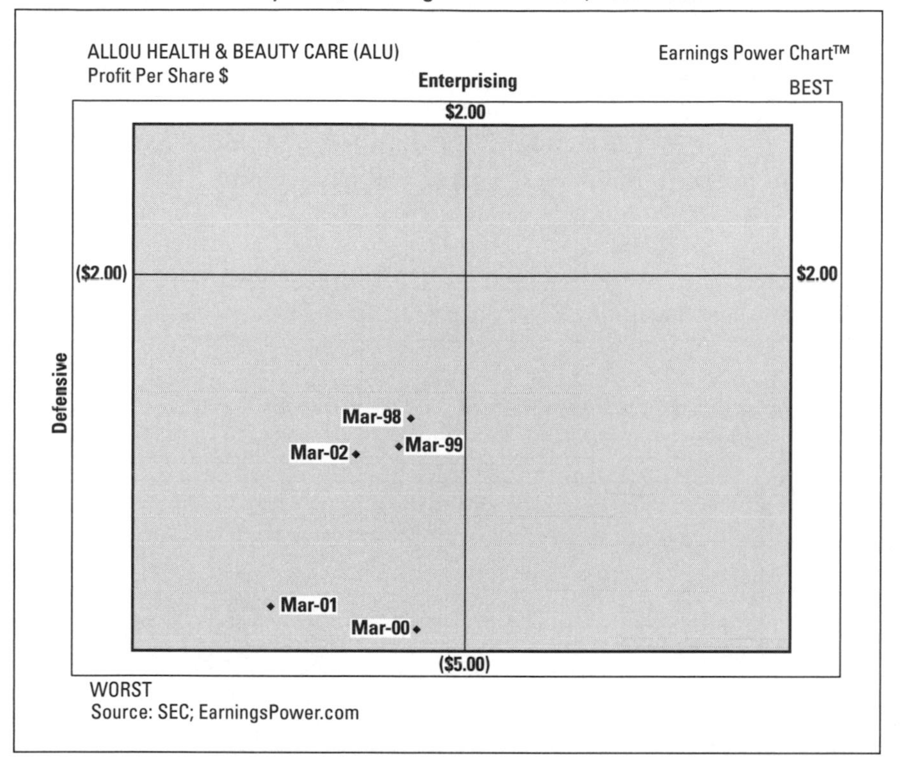

The stock, which traded as high as $8 in 2002, is now worthless.

I have followed Allou for years and been tempted to buy it several times because it always looked cheap, valuation-wise. In fact, Allou was the first company I ran through my Earnings Power Chart. That exercise not only dashed my initial optimism about the company but also kept me from making what would have turned out to be a bad investment.

Here's another scenario. A maker of precision measurement instruments posted four consecutive years of accrual profit growth. For the fiscal year ended March 1998 it made $0.11 a share; fiscal 1999, $0.12 a share; fiscal 2000, $0.64 a share; and fiscal 2001, $0.99 a share.

Due to its rapid earnings growth, the company was ranked #3 on the Forbes 200 Best Small Company list for 2001. Is that reason enough to buy the stock? We'll see.

Although the company did show growth in enterprising profits for three years running, its defensive losses grew steadily due to investment in working capital. The Quality of Profits Chart in Figure 7.5 shows a big disparity, or loose correlation, between accrual, defensive, and enterprising results.

Figure 7.5

Measurement Specialties, Quality of Profits, 1998–2001

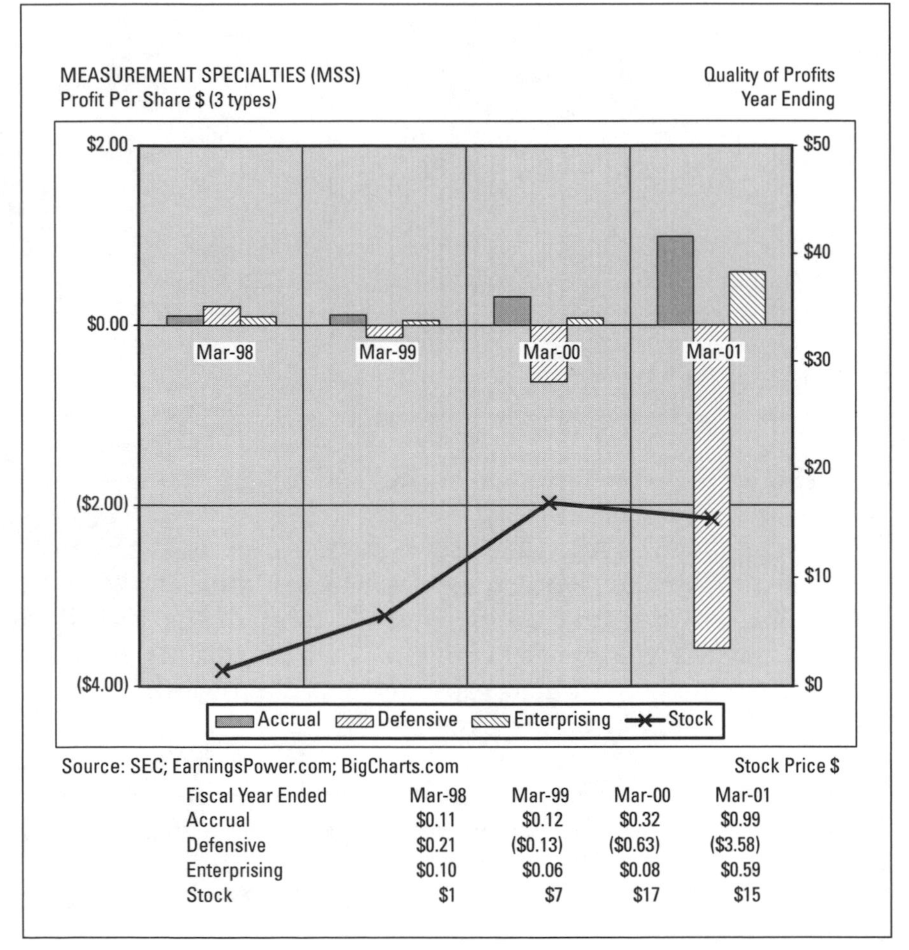

Fiscal Year Ended	Mar-98	Mar-99	Mar-00	Mar-01
Accrual	$0.11	$0.12	$0.32	$0.99
Defensive	$0.21	($0.13)	($0.63)	($3.58)
Enterprising	$0.10	$0.06	$0.08	$0.59
Stock	$1	$7	$17	$15

On the Earnings Power Chart (see Figure 7.6) the company lands in the lower-right box. Do you heed the caution or buy?

The company is Measurement Specialties Inc., which later violated its debt covenants with its banks, fired its CFO, and had its stock temporarily de-listed. By using the Earnings Power Chart you avoided an investment that could have cost you money. The stock, which traded for more than $25 in late 2000, eventually fell below $5 a share.

In 1997 a large U.S. industrial company, one that has earned a place in U.S. history, posted an accrual profit of $1.88 a share. What's more, the company also recorded a defensive profit—especially impressive since this, too, followed a loss from the

Figure 7.6

Measurement Specialties, Earnings Power Chart, 1998–2001

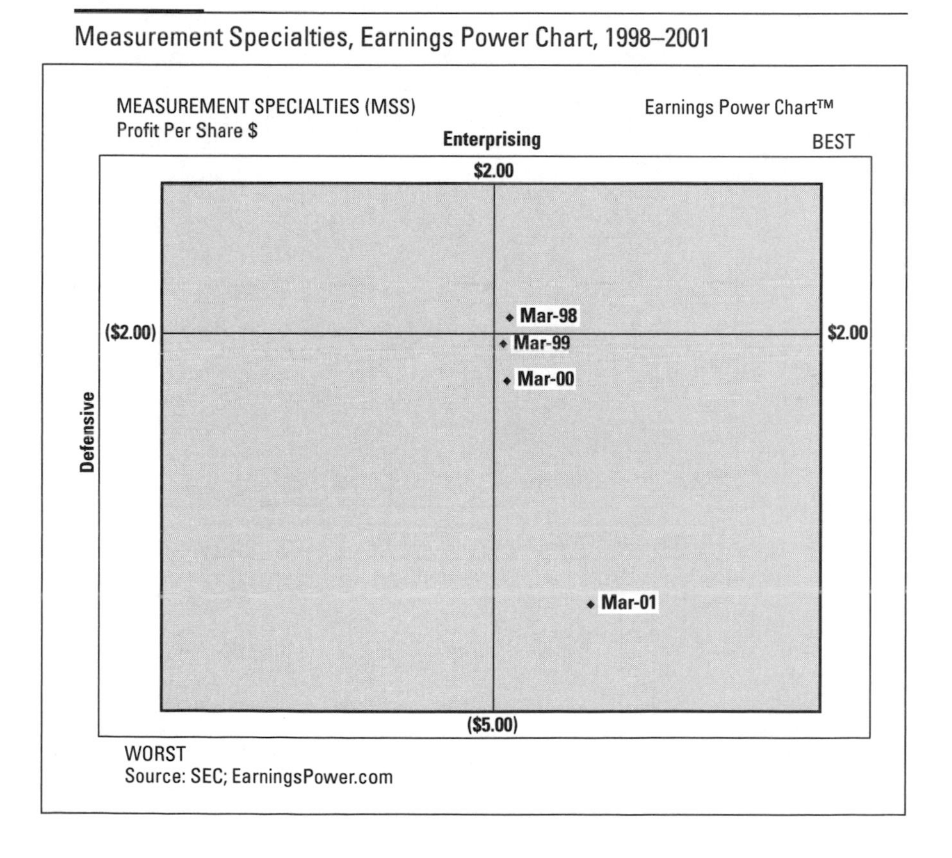

prior year. Naturally, this apparent turnaround story catches your attention. Still, is this reason enough to buy the stock?

Unfortunately, as we see in Figure 7.7, the company lost money on an enterprising basis in 1997.

In the Earnings Power Chart (see Figure 7.8) this stock lands in the upper-left box. You might be tempted to buy into this turnaround story since the company has posted accrual and

Figure 7.7

Bethlehem Steel, Quality of Profits, 1996–2000

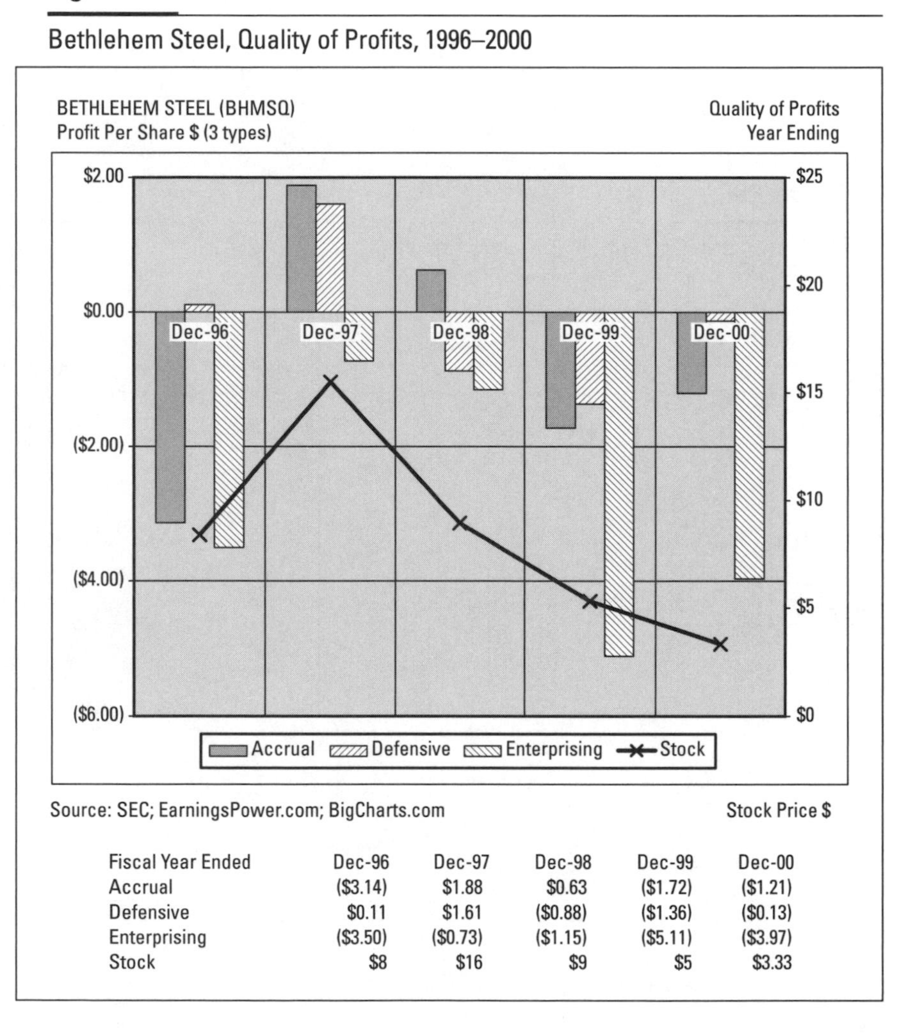

Fiscal Year Ended	Dec-96	Dec-97	Dec-98	Dec-99	Dec-00
Accrual	($3.14)	$1.88	$0.63	($1.72)	($1.21)
Defensive	$0.11	$1.61	($0.88)	($1.36)	($0.13)
Enterprising	($3.50)	($0.73)	($1.15)	($5.11)	($3.97)
Stock	$8	$16	$9	$5	$3.33

Figure 7.8

Bethlehem Steel, Earnings Power Chart, 1996–2000

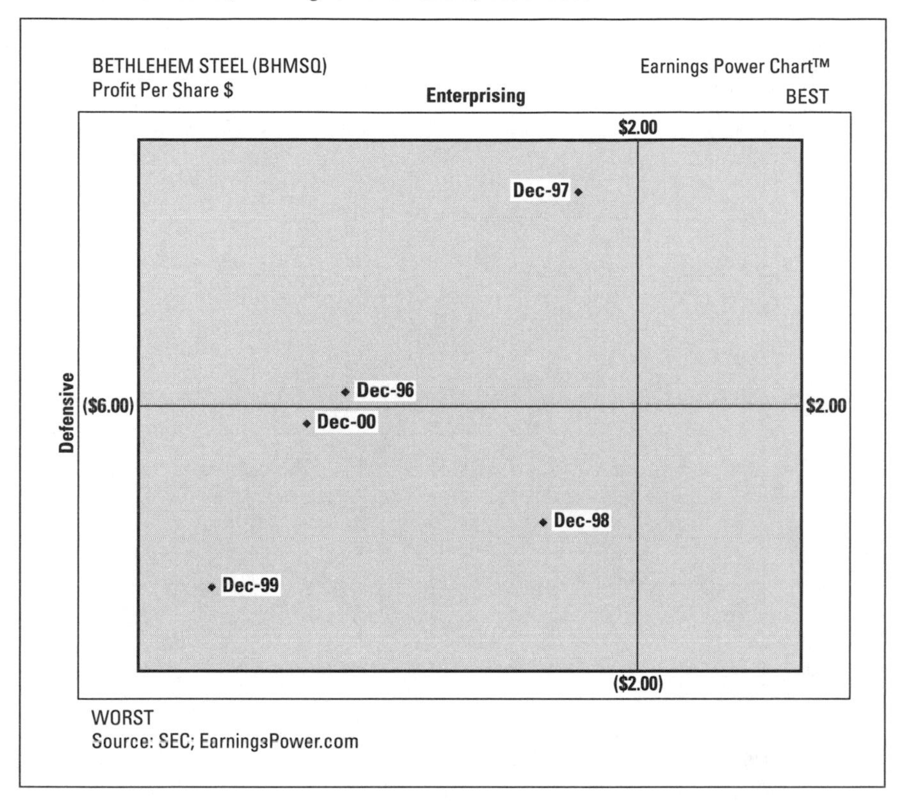

defensive profits and its enterprising loss narrowed. The stock, by the way, was trading about $50 a share in 1997.

The company is Bethlehem Steel. A few years after posting these results, the venerable steel company went bankrupt, completely wiping out its owners' equity position.

The lesson bears repeating. Even if a company shows revenue increases and is profitable on an accrual basis, its underlying results might not be as good, at least from a defensive and enterprising perspective, as they first appear.

As we see in Figure 7.9, Nortel Network's last good year was 1997. Incredibly, in mid-2000 it was a $75 stock. What's the story here?

Figure 7.9

Nortel Networks, Quality of Profits, 1997–2001

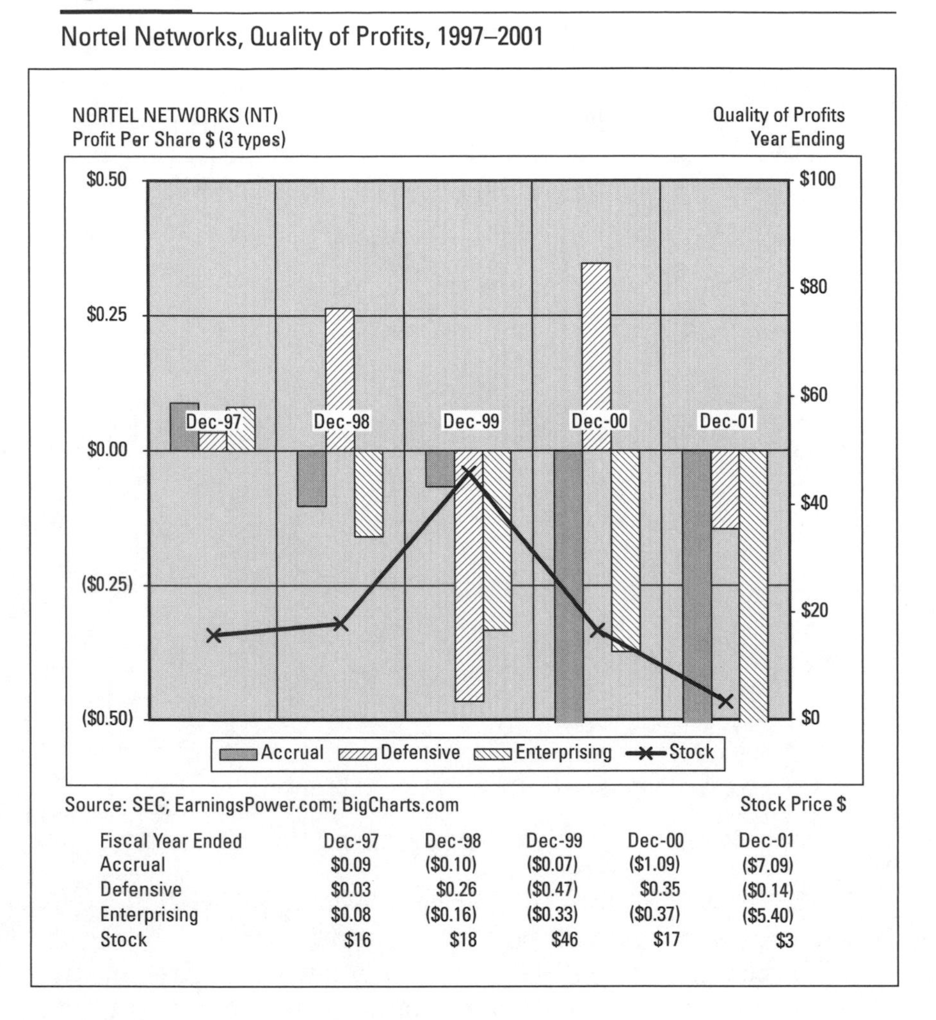

Fiscal Year Ended	Dec-97	Dec-98	Dec-99	Dec-00	Dec-01
Accrual	$0.09	($0.10)	($0.07)	($1.09)	($7.09)
Defensive	$0.03	$0.26	($0.47)	$0.35	($0.14)
Enterprising	$0.08	($0.16)	($0.33)	($0.37)	($5.40)
Stock	$16	$18	$46	$17	$3

Let's assume it is early 1998 and this company has caught your attention. Looking at its results for fiscal 1997 on the Quality of Profits Chart (see Figure 7.9), you note that it has accrual, defensive, and enterprising profits and that these figures are tightly correlated. But one year of results does not a trend make. To determine if it has authentic earnings growth, it's advisable to look at more than one year's results.

Jumping forward one year, Nortel's results are mixed. The good news is it had defensive profits, the bad news is it had accrual and enterprising losses. Nortel's Quality of Profits chart is deteriorating as time goes on.

Looking at Nortel on the Earnings Power Chart (see Figure 7.10) we see that in 1997 it had a toehold on the Earnings Power Box. From 1998 onward the company was in less favorable positions on the Earnings Power Chart.

As an investor with the benefit of the Earnings Power Chart methodology, what would you have done? If Nortel caught your eye in 1997, you might have considered making a starter

Figure 7.10

Nortel Networks, Earnings Power Chart, 1997–2001

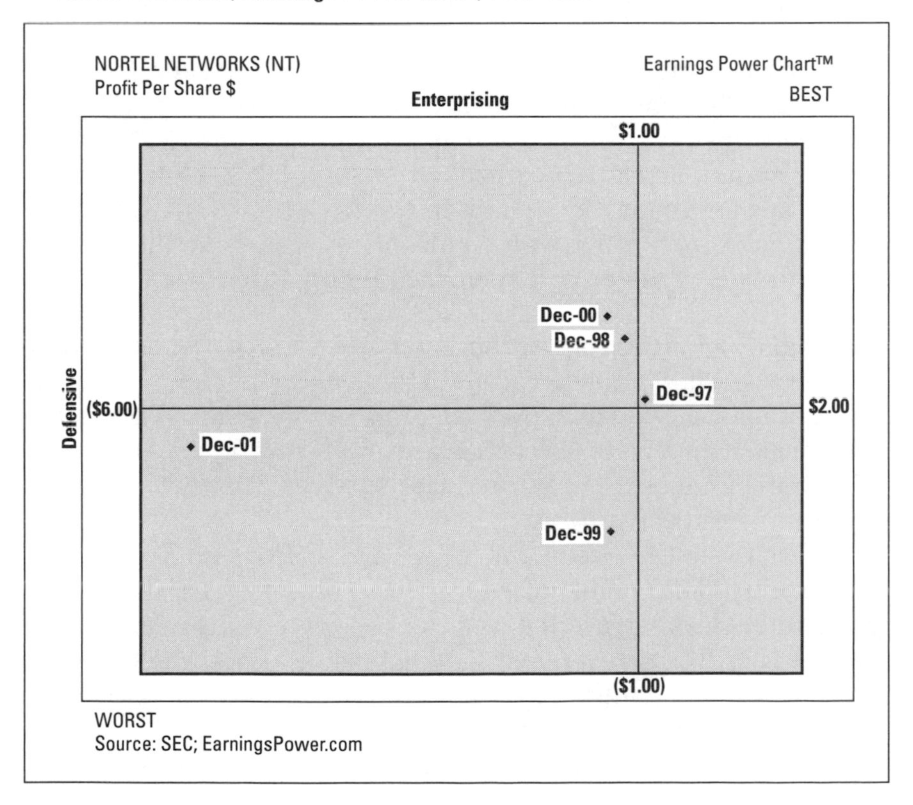

investment. But the accrual loss in 1998 should have been a warning signal that most likely would have prevented you from adding to your position and perhaps even prompted you to sell all your shares. With both defensive and enterprising losses in fiscal 1999, you most certainly would want to liquidate your holding. In April 2003, Nortel's stock sold for $3 a share.

It can be difficult to have the conviction to stay with a decision to sell a stock or not buy if the stock price is rising. There might be times that you second-guess the Earnings Power Chart because it forces you to leave money on the table. In the case of Xerox, however, to err on the side of caution was clearly the best move.

Xerox's shares were trading around $15 at the beginning of 1994 and rose to more than $60 in mid-1999. Looking at the Quality of Profits Chart in Figure 7.11, you can see that Xerox has a defensive loss even though it has accrual and enterprising profits.

The Earnings Power Chart confirms this opinion (see Figure 7.12). The results for 1996 are in the lower-right box, a position that this company continued to occupy for the next several years. Xerox's stock, which peaked at over $60 a share in mid-1999, sold for about $10 a share in the Spring of 2003. Using the Earnings Power Chart, you would have missed the stock's big rise, but you would have also missed its big fall.

Now, let's look at Tyco International Ltd., which, under Dennis Kozlowski, was an acquisition story. During the 1990s the Bermuda-based conglomerate acquired more than 700 companies in such disparate industries as fire alarms, medical devices, fiber-optic undersea cable, financial services, tubular steel, and environmental consulting.

What was the effect of all these acquisitions on Tyco's earnings quality? The Quality of Profits Chart (Figure 7.13) shows Tyco was profitable on an accrual basis for the three years ending fiscal 2001. Crucially, however, Tyco had defensive losses in all three of those years, and enterprising losses in two out of three years.

Viewed on the Earnings Power Chart (Figure 7.14) Tyco never occupied the Earnings Power Box during these years. No

Figure 7.11

Xerox, Quality of Profits, 1996–2000

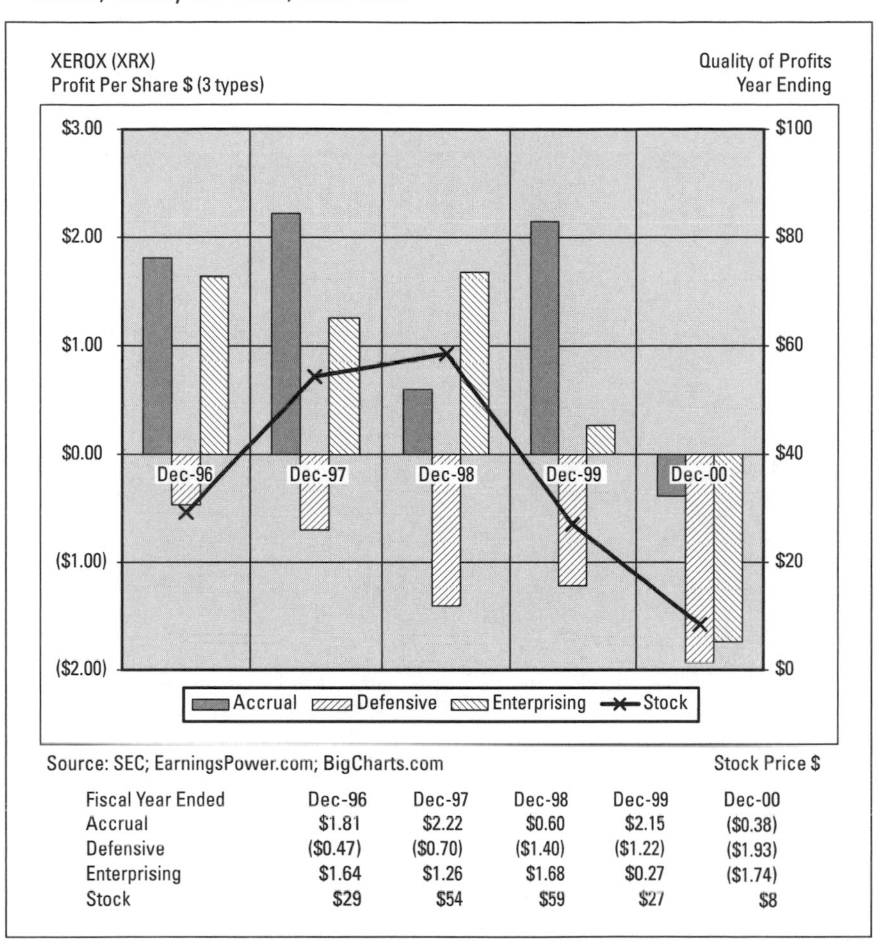

Fiscal Year Ended	Dec-96	Dec-97	Dec-98	Dec-99	Dec-00
Accrual	$1.81	$2.22	$0.60	$2.15	($0.38)
Defensive	($0.47)	($0.70)	($1.40)	($1.22)	($1.93)
Enterprising	$1.64	$1.26	$1.68	$0.27	($1.74)
Stock	$29	$54	$59	$27	$8

matter that Tyco was viewed as a growth company, it clearly did not earn that designation according to the Earnings Power Chart.

Tyco's financials would have steered the investor seeking authentic earnings power clear of this stock long before serious problems beset the company. According to news reports, Tyco was under SEC investigation from 1999 until 2000. In 2002 a new SEC investigation began. Kozlowski and other former com-

Figure 7.12

Xerox, Earnings Power Chart, 1996–2000

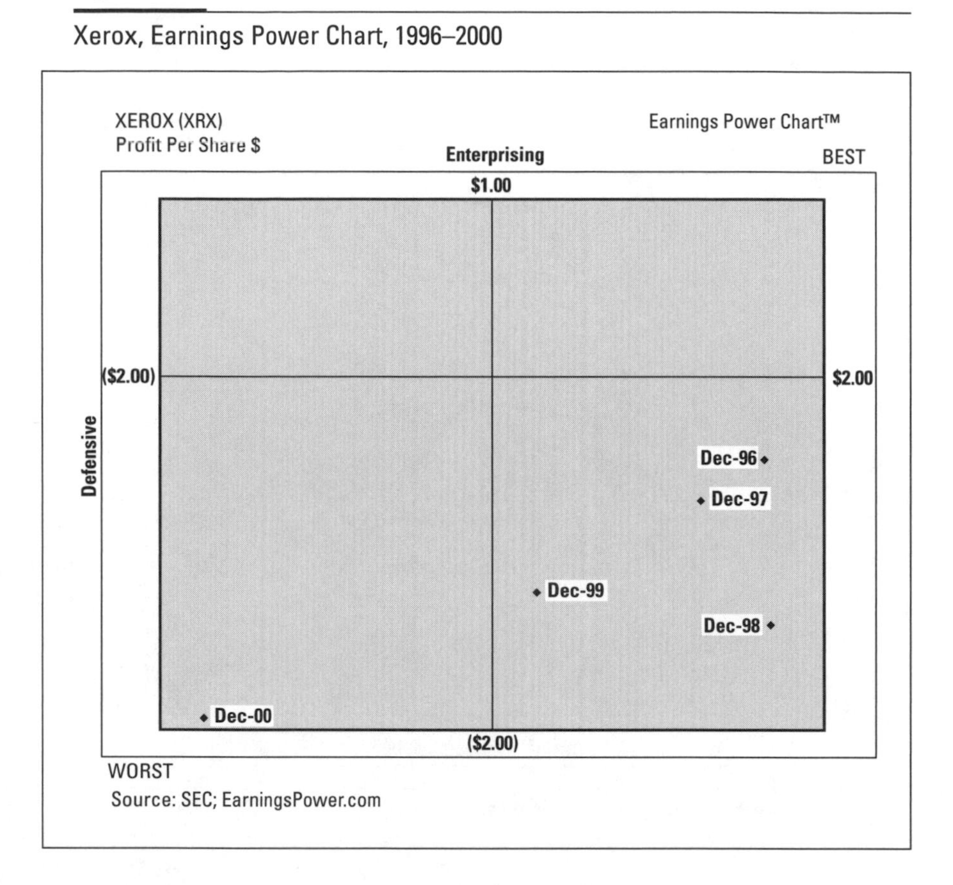

pany officials have also been under investigation for allegedly fraudulent activities. Tyco stock, which sold for $60 at the end of 2001, later fell to less than $10 per share before recovering to the mid-teens by early 2003.

Sometimes a good company with consistent earnings growth stalls. That's why you can never just make an investment after you've identified a good growth prospect, and then walk away. You have to pay attention and, year after year, run the company through the Earnings Power Chart.

The Gap showed good growth in accrual, defensive, and enterprising profits from fiscal 1996 through fiscal 1999 (see

Figure 7.13

Tyco, Quality of Profits, 1999–2001

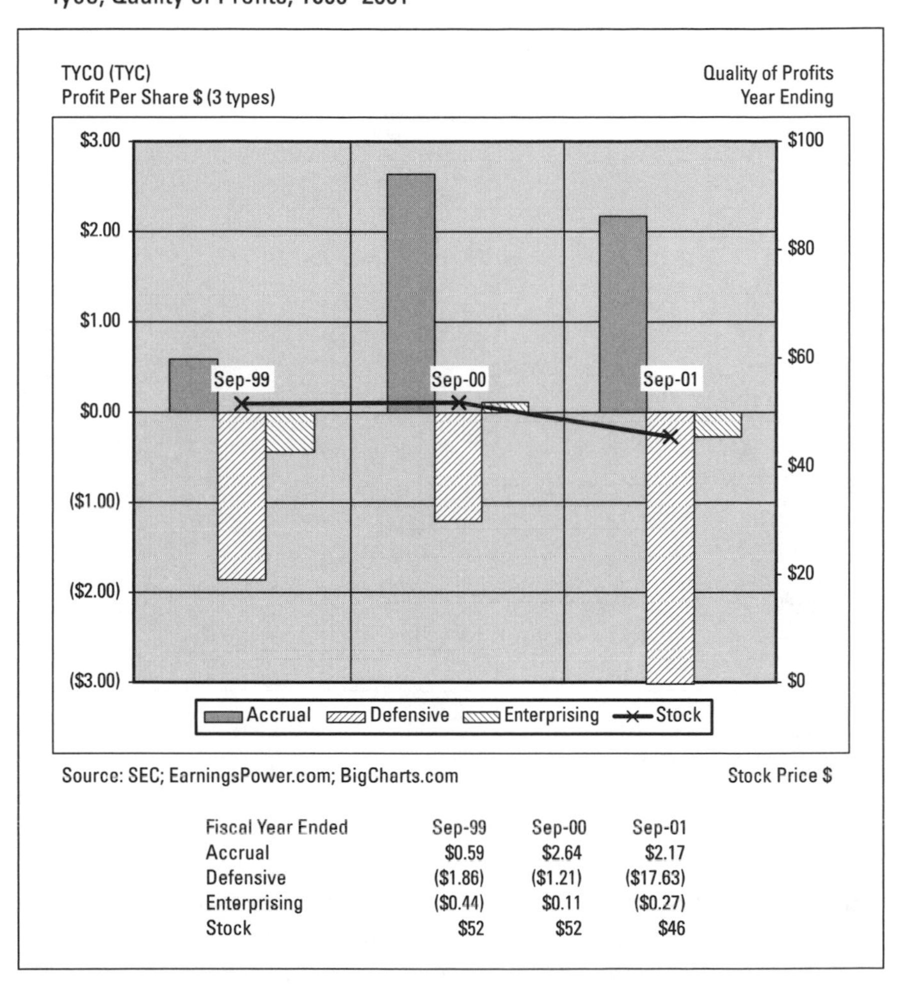

Fiscal Year Ended	Sep-99	Sep-00	Sep-01
Accrual	$0.59	$2.64	$2.17
Defensive	($1.86)	($1.21)	($17.63)
Enterprising	($0.44)	$0.11	($0.27)
Stock	$52	$52	$46

Figure 7.15). The stock for this retailer of casual clothing rose from about $10 to more than $50 by early 2000. If you had identified The Gap as a growth stock during this period, you were sitting on big capital gains.

But could you assume that the stock price would keep rising on continued strength in its financial results?

The Gap's results for fiscal 2000 show the beginning of a sharp disparity. Although the company posted stronger accrual

Figure 7.14

Tyco, Earnings Power Chart, 1999–2001

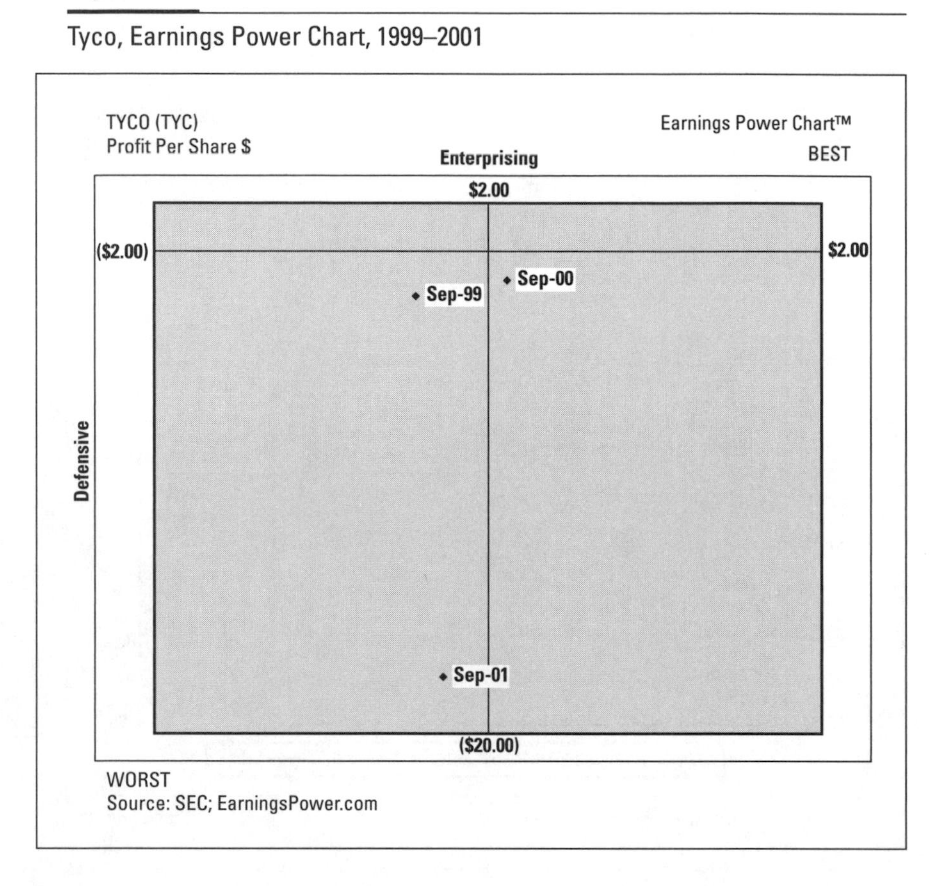

and enterprising profits, it had only a small defensive profit. In fiscal 2001 it had a defensive loss and lower enterprising profits.

As the Earnings Power Chart in Figure 7.16 shows, The Gap, which had occupied the Earnings Power Box between 1996-1999, almost slipped out in fiscal 2000. In fiscal 2001 it dropped into the lower-right box.

What was going on behind the scenes that the rise in accrual profits from fiscal 1998 to 1999 and 2000 masked? In fiscal 2000 The Gap had only a small defensive profit because its capital-spending program was accelerating. Higher capital spending means a higher investment in fixed capital, a use of

Figure 7.15

The Gap, Quality of Profits, 1996–2002

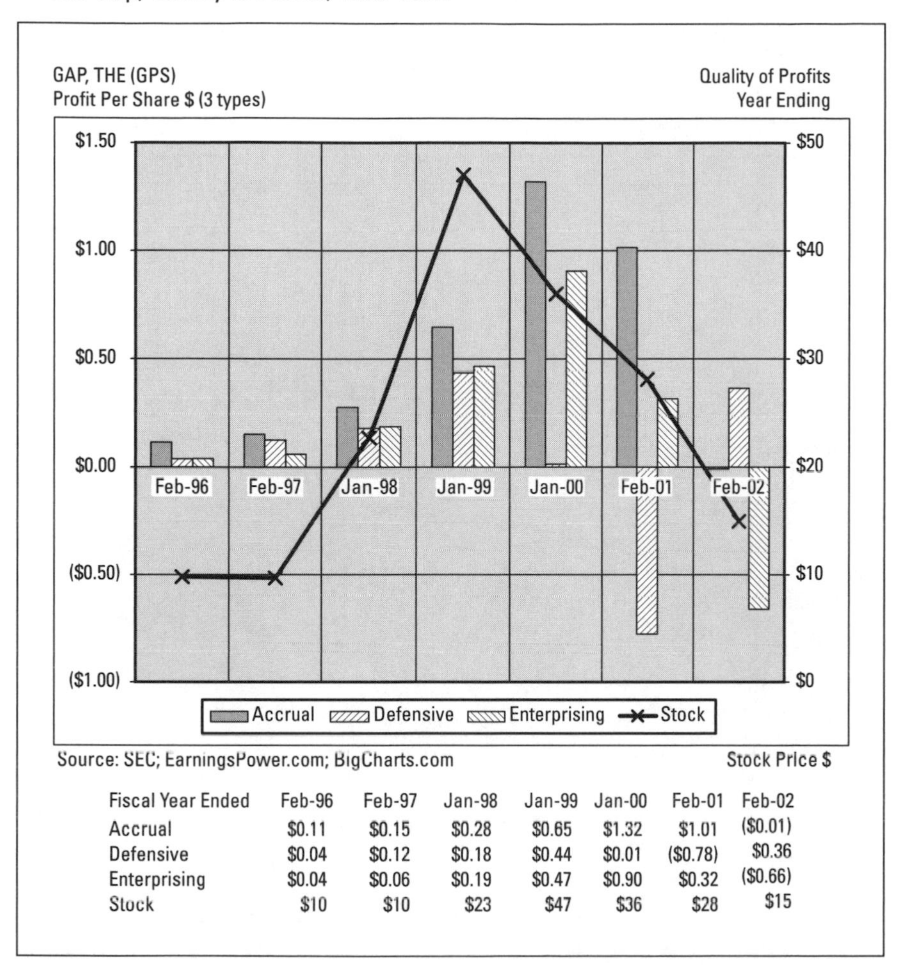

Fiscal Year Ended	Feb-96	Feb-97	Jan-98	Jan-99	Jan-00	Feb-01	Feb-02
Accrual	$0.11	$0.15	$0.28	$0.65	$1.32	$1.01	($0.01)
Defensive	$0.04	$0.12	$0.18	$0.44	$0.01	($0.78)	$0.36
Enterprising	$0.04	$0.06	$0.19	$0.47	$0.90	$0.32	($0.66)
Stock	$10	$10	$23	$47	$36	$28	$15

cash (expense) in the defensive income statement. In 2000 The Gap spent $1.3 billion—an amount roughly 50 percent higher from the previous year's results, and more than triple the amount from a few years earlier—to upgrade stores and install new merchandising displays. Investments in working capital, another direct charge in the defensive income statement, were also well above previous years' figures. If we examine The Gap's

Figure 7.16

The Gap, Earnings Power Chart, 1996-2002

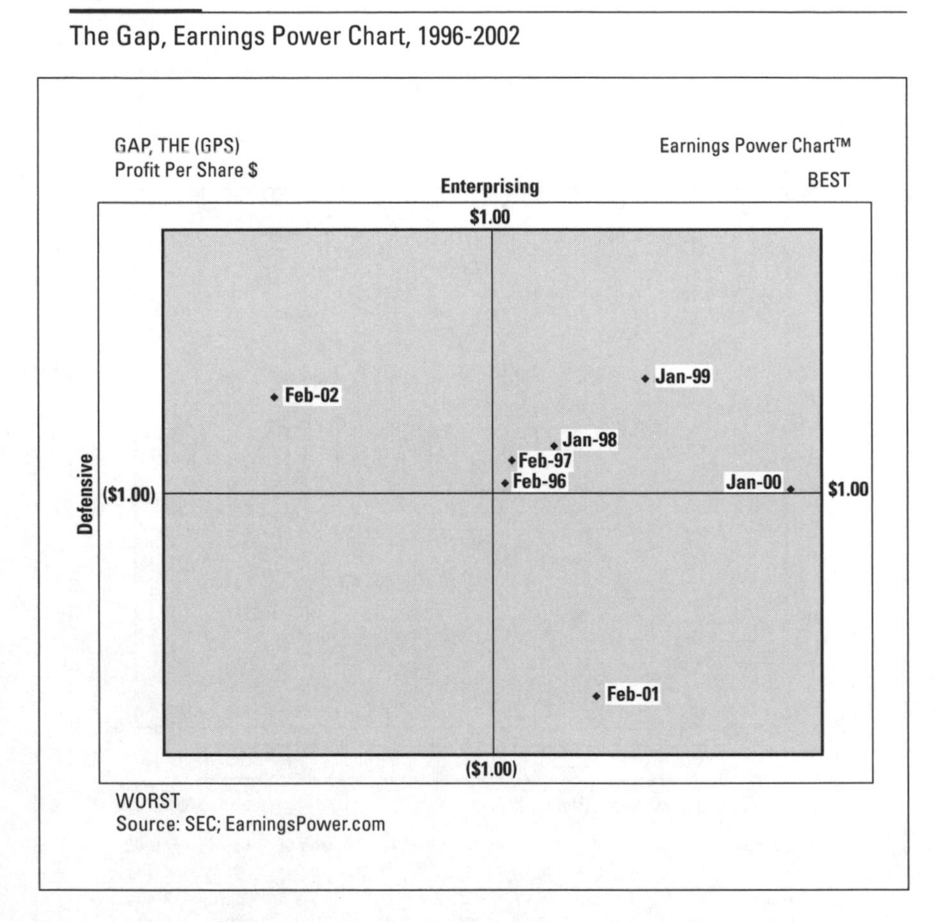

results, it's hard to say that fiscal 2000 signaled an outright sell. That would have been a tough call, even with the decline in defensive profits. But you can see why someone might have decided to book some stock profits by selling part of their position and also pay closer attention to future results. By the time fiscal 2001 results were released, this investor would not have been caught off-guard when The Gap's far-greater defensive loss presaged poor accrual results in fiscal 2002.

The Earnings Power Chart isn't suitable for banks because of their highly leveraged capital structure or natural resource companies because of their sensitivity to commodity prices. For all the other companies, however, this two-dimensional approach will guide you toward companies with authentic earnings power and away from those that have poor fundamentals—even if the accrual income statement looks impressive.

To do well in the stock market, you need an edge. Use the Earnings Power Chart to help give you that edge.

CHAPTER 8

Earnings Power Archetypes

All companies—whether publicly owned or private—are situated in one of the four boxes of the Earnings Power Chart. The best companies (but not necessarily the best stocks) are situated in the upper-right box, the Earnings Power Box; the worst, those that can't self-fund and are destroying value, in the lower-left box. Companies in the upper-left and lower-right boxes have room for improvement and warrant caution.

As Figure 8.1 reveals, Enron Corporation, WorldCom, Lucent Technologies, and Wrigley were all profitable in the accrual sense of the word for their respective years shown.

However, according to the Earnings Power Chart, only Wrigley is situated in the Earnings Power Box (Figure 8.2). As for the other companies, Lucent is in the lower-right box, Enron the lower-left box, and WorldCom the upper-left box. Four profitable companies the way accountants define profits, but only one had authentic earnings power. *In which boxes are the companies you own situated*?

While viewing a company's performance for one year is useful, you will also want to look at the last *several* years' worth of results. As Winston Churchill noted, "The farther back you can look, the farther forward you are likely to see." Heeding Churchill's

Figure 8.1

Archetypes, Quality of Profits

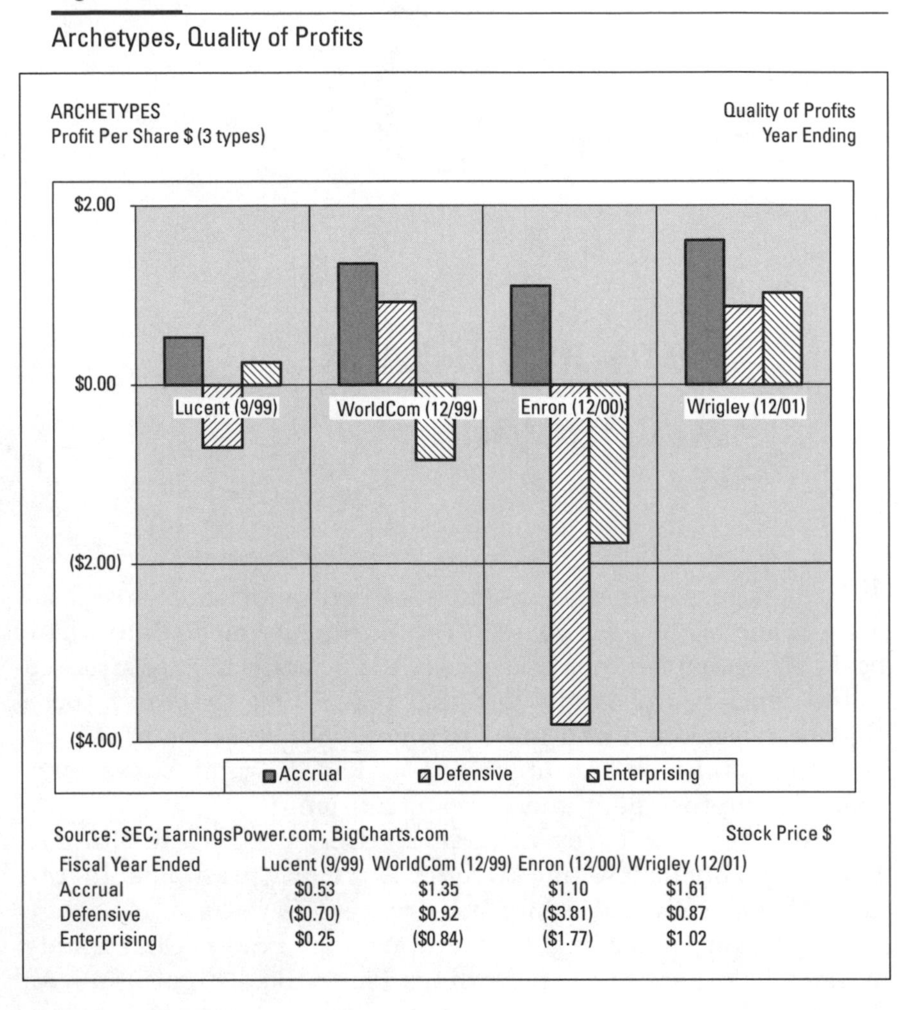

Fiscal Year Ended	Lucent (9/99)	WorldCom (12/99)	Enron (12/00)	Wrigley (12/01)
Accrual	$0.53	$1.35	$1.10	$1.61
Defensive	($0.70)	$0.92	($3.81)	$0.87
Enterprising	$0.25	($0.84)	($1.77)	$1.02

advice, in this chapter we look at several years worth of results for each of these four companies.

My goal here is not to write a complete account of what went right and/or wrong for each company. I'll save that for others. Instead, my purpose is rifle-specific: Did the Earnings Power Chart tell us *before* the accrual income statement that, in the case of Enron, WorldCom and Lucent, earnings quality was poor or declining? My other question is whether Wrigley, accord-

Exhibit 8.2

Archetypes, Earnings Power Chart

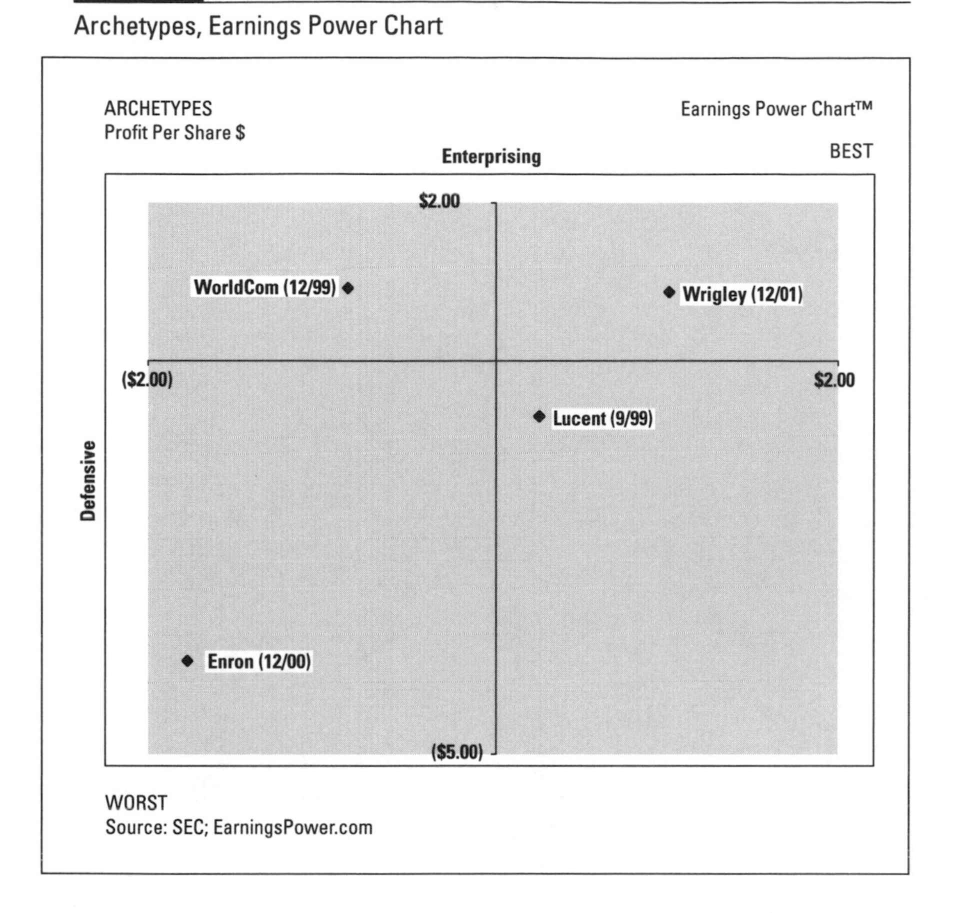

ing to Earnings Power Chart, has the makings of a great growth stock for the next decade?

I should also mention that all charts in this book, including this chapter, are based on data from annual reports or 10-K filings made by the companies *for the year indicated*. All too often companies restate prior year results. By using data from the original filings, I hope to keep any *ex post facto bias* to a minimum. Investors, after all, do not have the benefit of hindsight. Also, as stated previously, all stock prices in this book are 30 days after the company filed its 10-K with the SEC.

Now, let's go to the charts.

THE LOWER-LEFT BOX: ENRON CORPORATION

For the year ending December 31, 2000 Enron was profitable on an accrual basis but had defensive and enterprising losses (Figure 8.3).

Therefore, viewed through the Earnings Power Chart (Figure 8.4), Enron was situated in the lower-left box that year.

Figure 8.3

Enron, Quality of Profits, 1996–2000

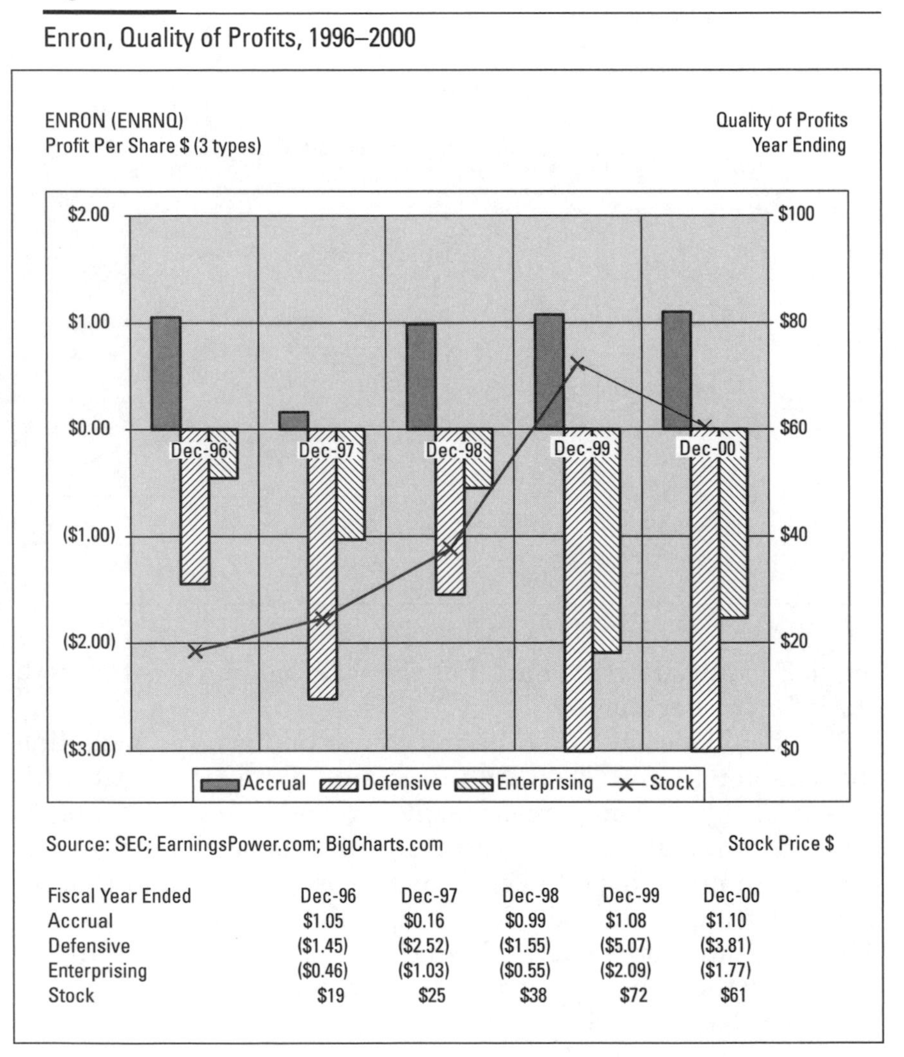

Fiscal Year Ended	Dec-96	Dec-97	Dec-98	Dec-99	Dec-00
Accrual	$1.05	$0.16	$0.99	$1.08	$1.10
Defensive	($1.45)	($2.52)	($1.55)	($5.07)	($3.81)
Enterprising	($0.46)	($1.03)	($0.55)	($2.09)	($1.77)
Stock	$19	$25	$38	$72	$61

Figure 8.4

Enron, Earnings Power Chart, 1996–2000

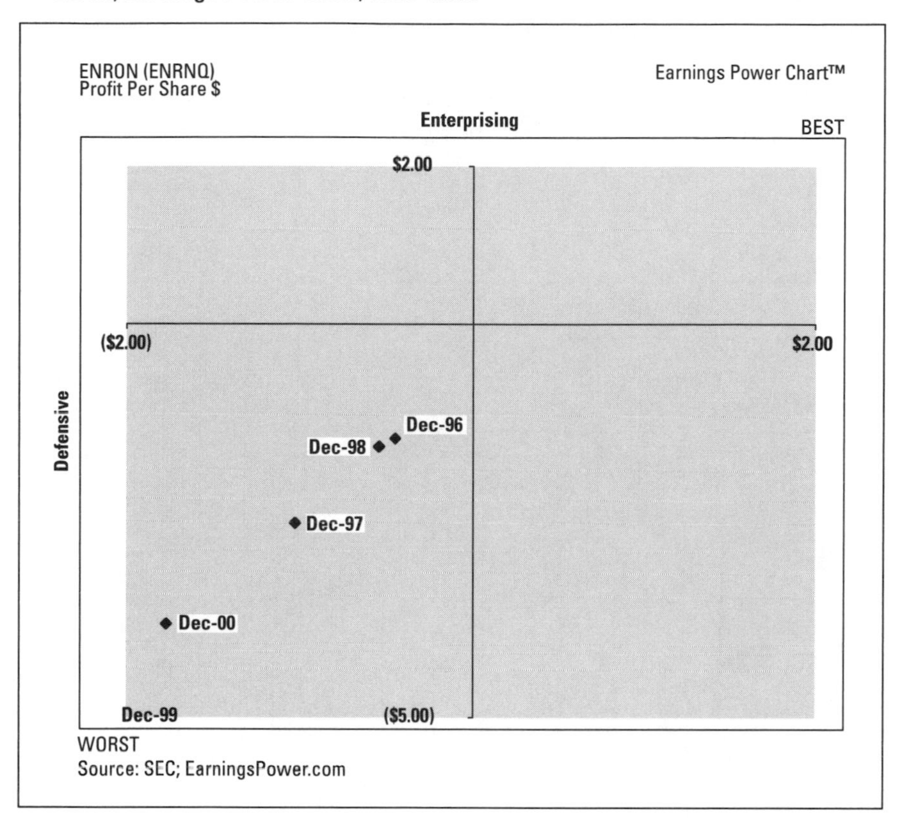

Companies in the lower-left box are unable to self-fund and create value. Incredibly, the Houston-based energy trader had been there since at least 1996. In terms of earnings quality, companies in the lower-left box are strictly bottom of the barrel.

It's puzzling why so many investors felt compelled to buy Enron. I suppose a rising stock price is partly to blame. But after topping out over $90 a share Enron's scrip began to nosedive as reports of alleged malfeasance surfaced. By the time the company filed for bankruptcy in December 2001 its shares were worthless. Crucially, if you viewed Enron through the Earnings Power Chart, you would have seen this company for what it really was years sooner.

The Upper-Left Box: WorldCom Inc.

For the year ending December 31, 1999 WorldCom was profitable on an accrual and defensive basis but had enterprising losses (Figure 8.5).

Therefore, viewed through the Earnings Power Chart (Figure 8.6), WorldCom was situated in the upper-left box that year.

Figure 8.5

WorldCom, Quality of Profits, 1997–2001

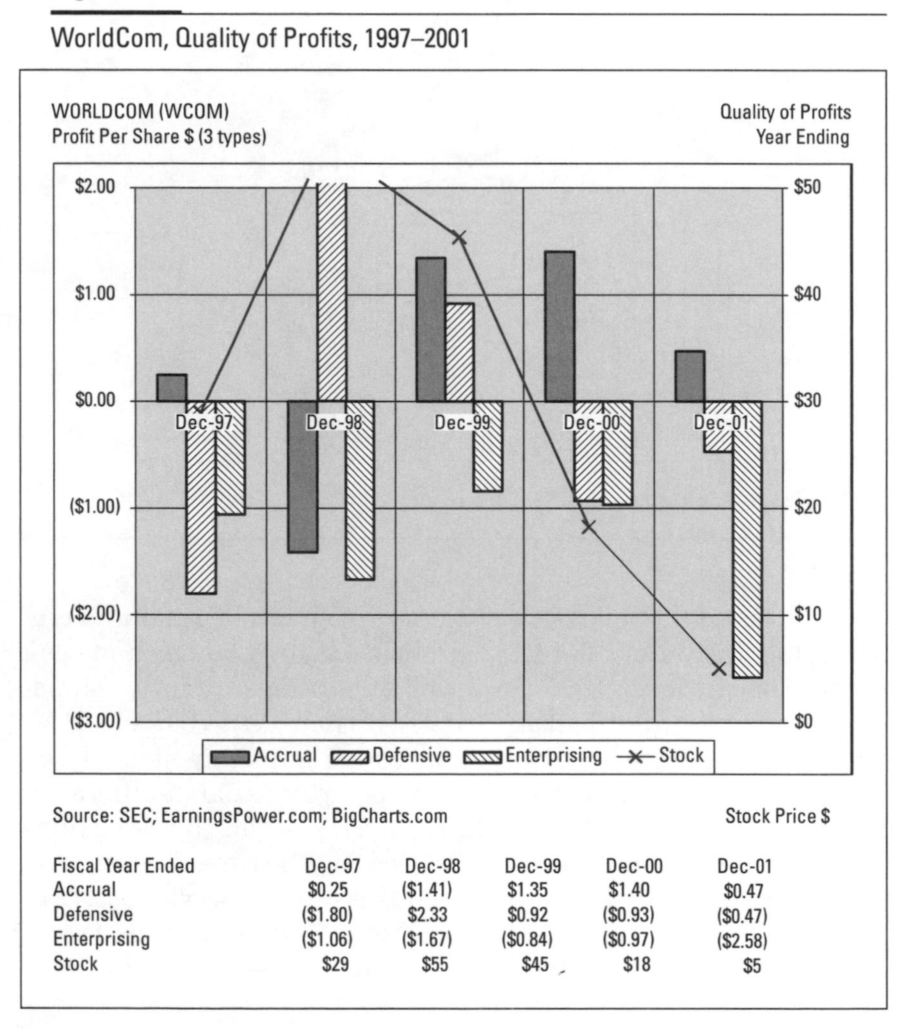

Fiscal Year Ended	Dec-97	Dec-98	Dec-99	Dec-00	Dec-01
Accrual	$0.25	($1.41)	$1.35	$1.40	$0.47
Defensive	($1.80)	$2.33	$0.92	($0.93)	($0.47)
Enterprising	($1.06)	($1.67)	($0.84)	($0.97)	($2.58)
Stock	$29	$55	$45	$18	$5

Exhibit 8.6

WorldCom, Earnings Power Chart, 1997–2001

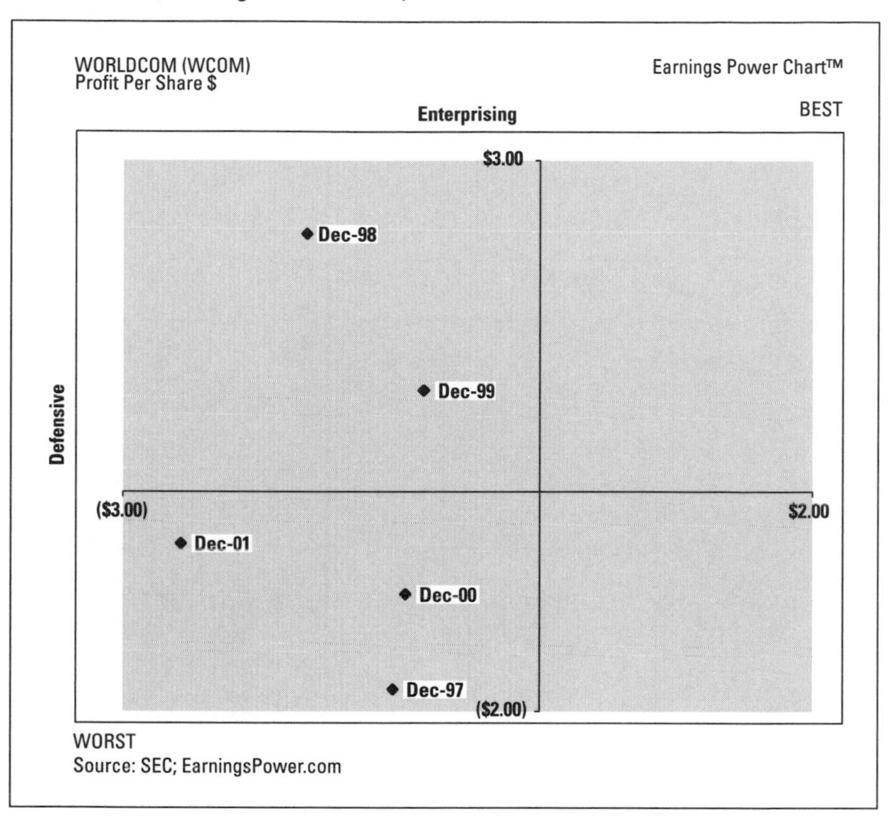

Companies in the upper-left box are able to self-fund but are destroying value.

Despite WorldCom's mixed earnings quality, the stock climbed from $10 in 1994 to over $60 by 1999. But then in 2002 the Clinton, Mississippi-based long-distance phone operator filed for bankruptcy and its stock fell to pennies a share. According to news reports, Bernie Ebbers, the company's one-time billionaire CEO and former physical education teacher, milkman, bar bouncer, car salesman, and motel chain owner, had his lieutenants use shady tactics to boost revenue and reduce expenses (including treating certain costs as capital spending).

The Lower-Right Box: Lucent Technologies

For the year ending September 30, 1999 Lucent Technologies was profitable on an accrual and enterprising basis but had defensive losses (Figure 8.7).

Therefore, viewed through the Earnings Power Chart (Figure 8.8), Lucent was situated in the lower-right box that year.

Figure 8.7

Lucent Technologies, 1997–2000

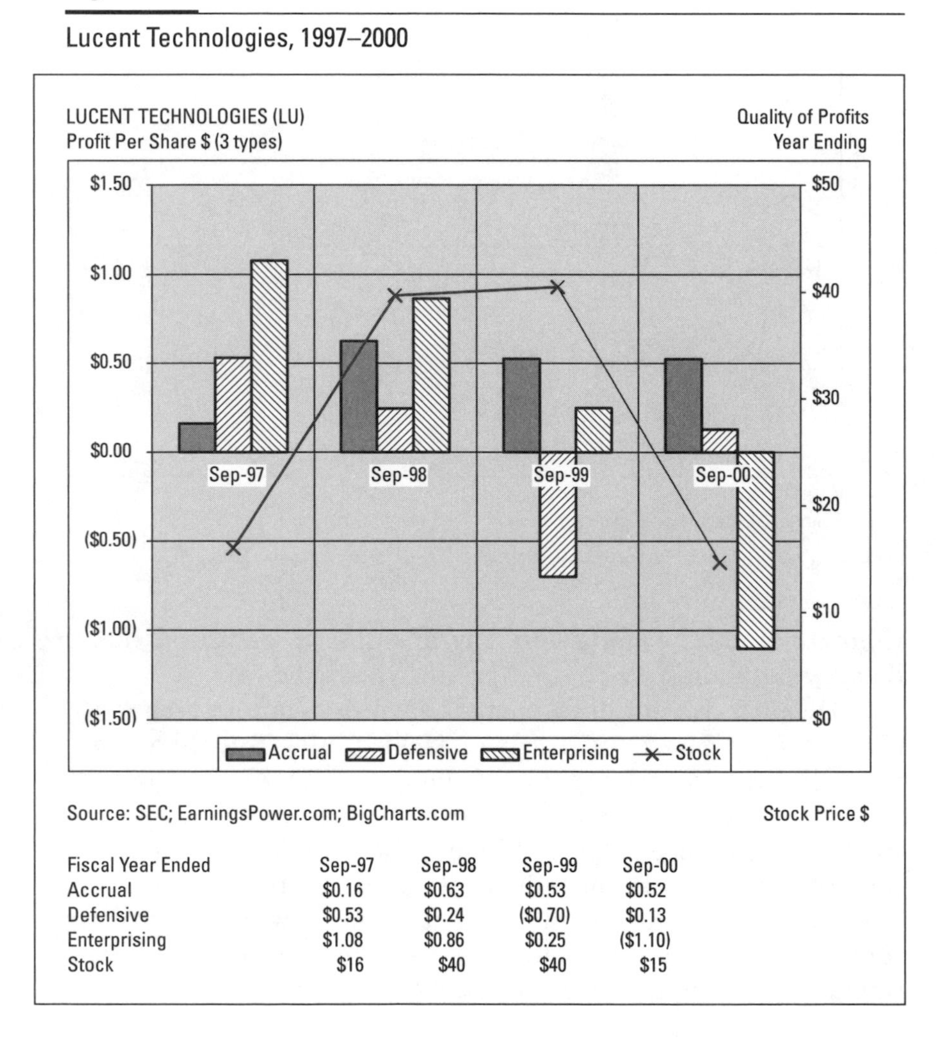

Fiscal Year Ended	Sep-97	Sep-98	Sep-99	Sep-00
Accrual	$0.16	$0.63	$0.53	$0.52
Defensive	$0.53	$0.24	($0.70)	$0.13
Enterprising	$1.08	$0.86	$0.25	($1.10)
Stock	$16	$40	$40	$15

Figure 8.8

Lucent Technologies, Earnings Power Chart, 1997–2000

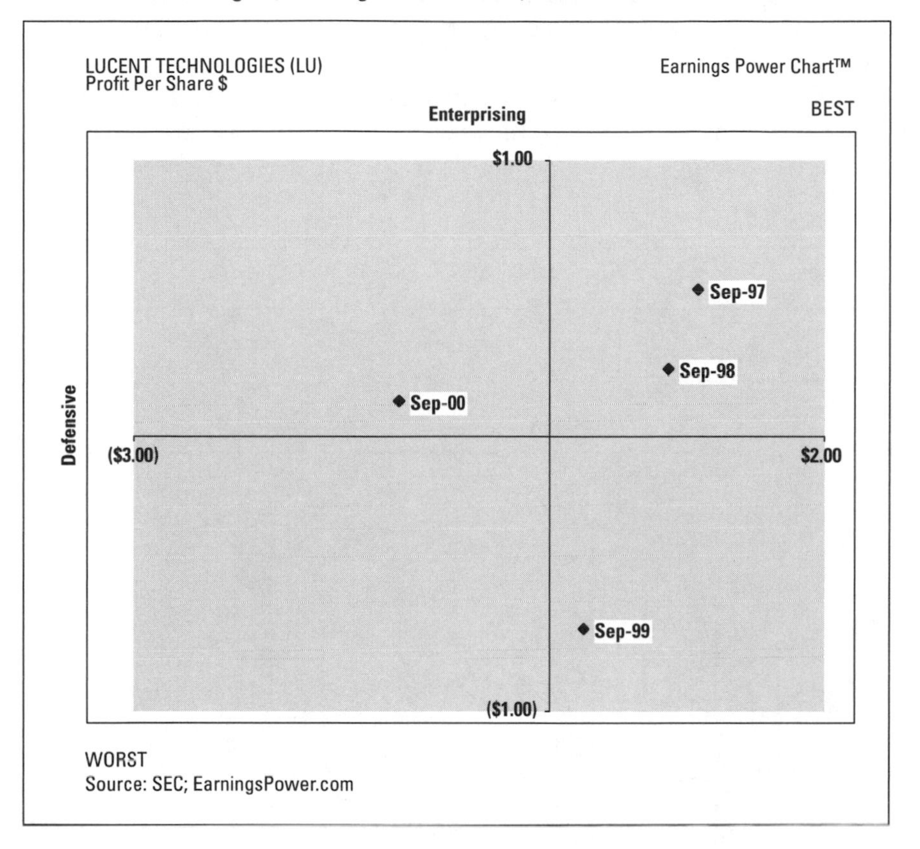

Companies in the lower-right box are creating value but not able to self-fund.

Spun off from AT&T in 1996, Lucent possessed authentic earnings power in fiscal 1997. The company was also able to self-fund and create value in fiscal 1998, but at a reduced rate. By the time fiscal 1999 rolled around the company had slid into the lower-right box, and in fiscal 2000 it side-stepped over to the upper-left box. Lucent's stock, which peaked at over $60 in late 1999, now trades for a couple of bucks.

UPPER-RIGHT BOX: WM. WRIGLEY JR. COMPANY

As we first learned in Chapter 7 and see once again in Figure 8.9, Wrigley was profitable on an accrual, defensive, and enterprising basis in 2002.

When a company like Wrigley has defensive and enterprising profits, it is situated in the upper-right box, or Earnings

Figure 8.9

Wrigley, Quality of Profits, 1998–2002

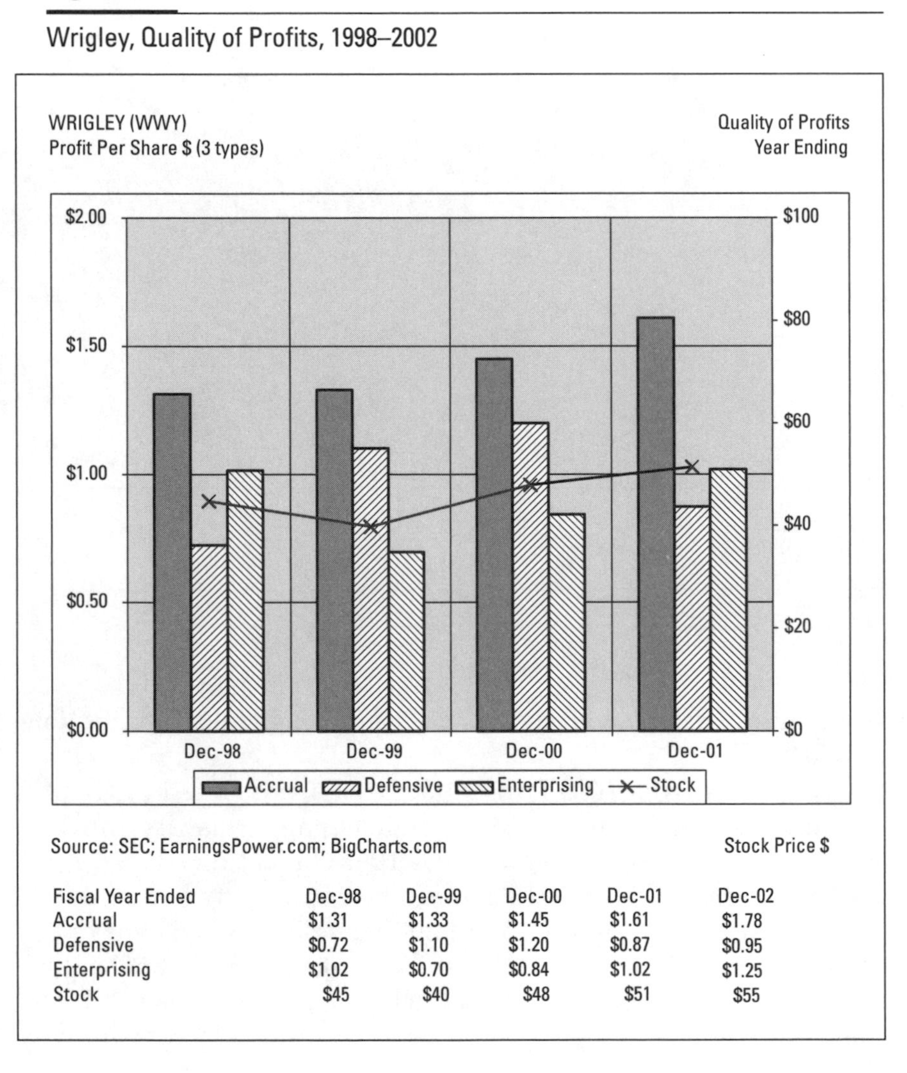

Fiscal Year Ended	Dec-98	Dec-99	Dec-00	Dec-01	Dec-02
Accrual	$1.31	$1.33	$1.45	$1.61	$1.78
Defensive	$0.72	$1.10	$1.20	$0.87	$0.95
Enterprising	$1.02	$0.70	$0.84	$1.02	$1.25
Stock	$45	$40	$48	$51	$55

Power Box, of the Earnings Power Chart (see Figure 8.10). If you believe that Phoebus Apollo's advice to his son of *Medius tutissimus ibis* ("You will go safest in the middle course") is sensible, then as a long-term cautiously greedy investor stick with companies in the Earnings Power Box. In terms of earnings quality, the middle course is the ability to self-fund and create value.

Now that we have looked at the charts our four archetype companies, let us return to the two questions posed at the beginning of this chapter.

Our first question is whether the Earnings Power Chart revealed the problems at Enron, WorldCom and Lucent before

Figure 8.10

Wrigley, Earnings Power Chart, 1998–2002

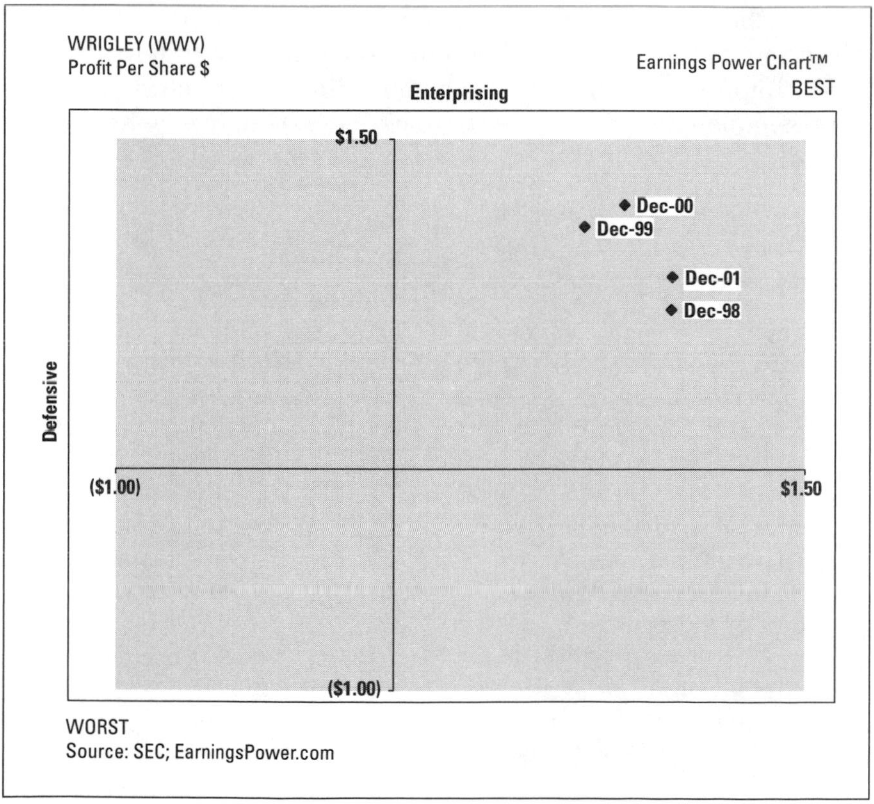

WRIGLEY (WWY)
Profit Per Share $
Earnings Power Chart™
BEST
Enterprising
$1.50
Dec-00
Dec-99
Dec-01
Dec-98
Defensive
($1.00)
$1.50
($1.00)
WORST
Source: SEC; EarningsPower.com

they appeared on the accrual income statement. In Enron's case the answer is an unequivocal yes. The company had been in the lower-left box since at least 1996. As for WorldCom, it was in the upper-left and lower-left boxes prior to its demise. Sadly, many investors perceived it to be a blue chip growth stock. Lucent has the most interesting chart. For the first two years it had authentic earnings power. Of course, the deterioration in fiscal 1998 results versus the prior year was an important "tell." If you owned the stock, you should have sold part of your position. You should have sold the rest of your position after fiscal 1999's results were announced. That's just common sense.

Our second question is whether Wrigley has the makings of a great growth stock? As a long-term cautiously greedy investor we want companies (1) situated in the Earnings Power Box and (2) moving in the upper-right direction. Although Wrigley passes the first test, it comes up short on the second test. As Figure 8.10 shows, there is no sign of dramatic movement in an upper-right direction. Wrigley is a terrific company, but as we'll learn in the next chapter it doesn't have the same impressive chart pattern that some of the great growth stocks in recent years have produced.

How To Read The Charts

Are these two alternate income statements infallible? No, of course not. Nothing works all the time. That said, it's important to know how to read the Quality of Profits and Earnings Power Charts so you can achieve the best possible results with the least amount of risk. Here are the types of scenarios that you will encounter, and what to do.

1. *Accrual profits increase, as do defensive and enterprising profits*. This is the ideal scenario. If you believe the firm's competitive advantages are still intact and you are comfortable with the current price-earnings ratio (see Chapter 13 to learn more), then buy more stock.

2. *Accrual profits increase but defensive and/or enterprising profits lag or fall from prior year levels*. Sell some of your stock in case the growth story is ending. Also, if you are able, figure out what is happening to the business, and why. If the defensive

income statement shows weakness, is it due to investment in fixed capital? Investment in working capital? If the problem is with the enterprising income statement, is management reducing its spending on R&D or advertising? Is the company over-paying for its acquisitions?

3. *Accrual profits stay flat with declines in defensive and/or enterprising profits.* Here again, prudence dictates that you reduce your holdings (especially if the price-earnings ratio gives you vertigo). The company may resume its growth curve, but why not wait for proof?

4. *Accrual profits decline, as do defensive and/or enterprising profits.* Sell everything unless you are sure the company's problems are transitory.

CHAPTER 9

The Best Chart: A Staircase

If a company is in the Earnings Power Box every year that's a good reflection of a company's past performance. But what about *future* performance? Does the company have the potential to be a great growth stock for the next decade?

To answer this question we look at three companies whose stocks have generated tremendous capital gains for their stockholders. These companies are Microsoft Corporation (1990-1999), Apollo Group (1995-2002), and Paychex (1990-2002). Each displays constant growth in defensive and enterprising profits over a long period, no mean feat. Plotting this X-Y relationship on the Earnings Power Chart, the progression resembles a staircase, hence the Earnings Power Staircase company designation. Earnings Power Staircase companies embody the consistent, profitable growth qualities that Charlie Munger, vice chairman of Berkshire Hathaway, once referred to when he said: "I'd personally rather buy a company whose business is good enough where we can buy it and then sit on our ass." That's the 'long-term' in long-term cautiously greedy.

Our first uber-company is Microsoft Corporation.

MICROSOFT CORPORATION, FISCAL 1990-1999

Microsoft's accrual, defensive, and enterprising profits all rose steadily during fiscal 1990-1999, as Figure 9.1 reveals.

Therefore, as the Earnings Power Chart (Figure 9.2) shows, Microsoft qualifies as an Earnings Power Staircase company. (This is the same chart that we saw in the introduction.) Not only does the software maker possess authentic earnings power,

Figure 9.1

Microsoft Corporation, Quality of Profits, 1990–1999

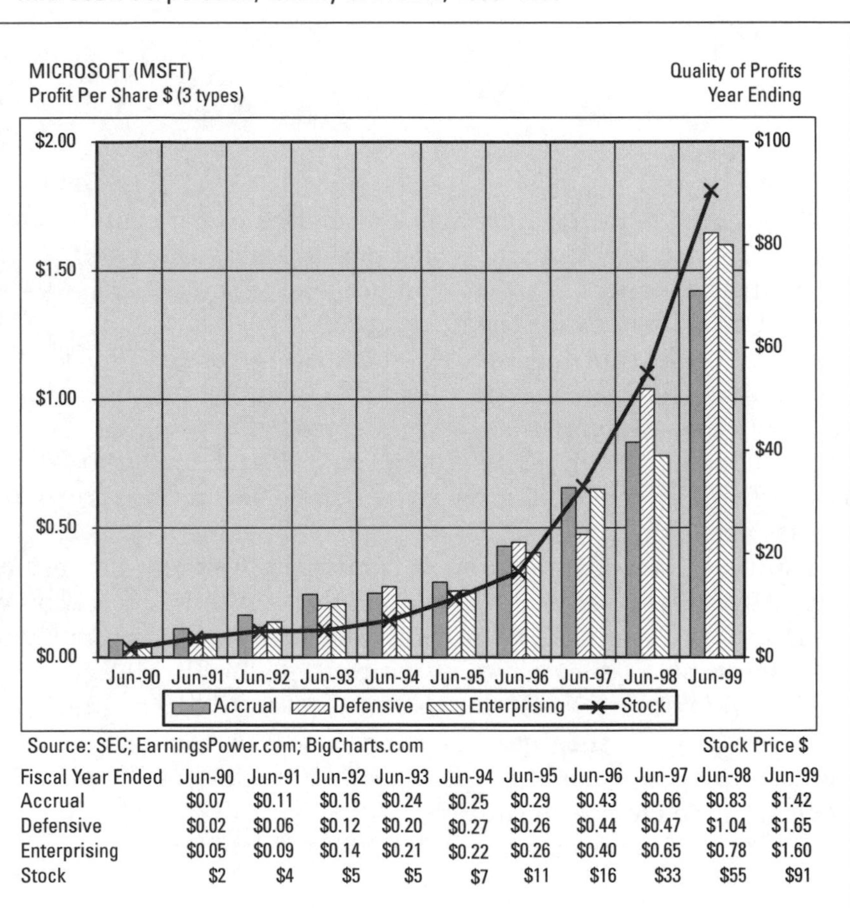

Fiscal Year Ended	Jun-90	Jun-91	Jun-92	Jun-93	Jun-94	Jun-95	Jun-96	Jun-97	Jun-98	Jun-99
Accrual	$0.07	$0.11	$0.16	$0.24	$0.25	$0.29	$0.43	$0.66	$0.83	$1.42
Defensive	$0.02	$0.06	$0.12	$0.20	$0.27	$0.26	$0.44	$0.47	$1.04	$1.65
Enterprising	$0.05	$0.09	$0.14	$0.21	$0.22	$0.26	$0.40	$0.65	$0.78	$1.60
Stock	$2	$4	$5	$5	$7	$11	$16	$33	$55	$91

Figure 9.2

Microsoft Corporation, Earnings Power Chart, 1990–1999

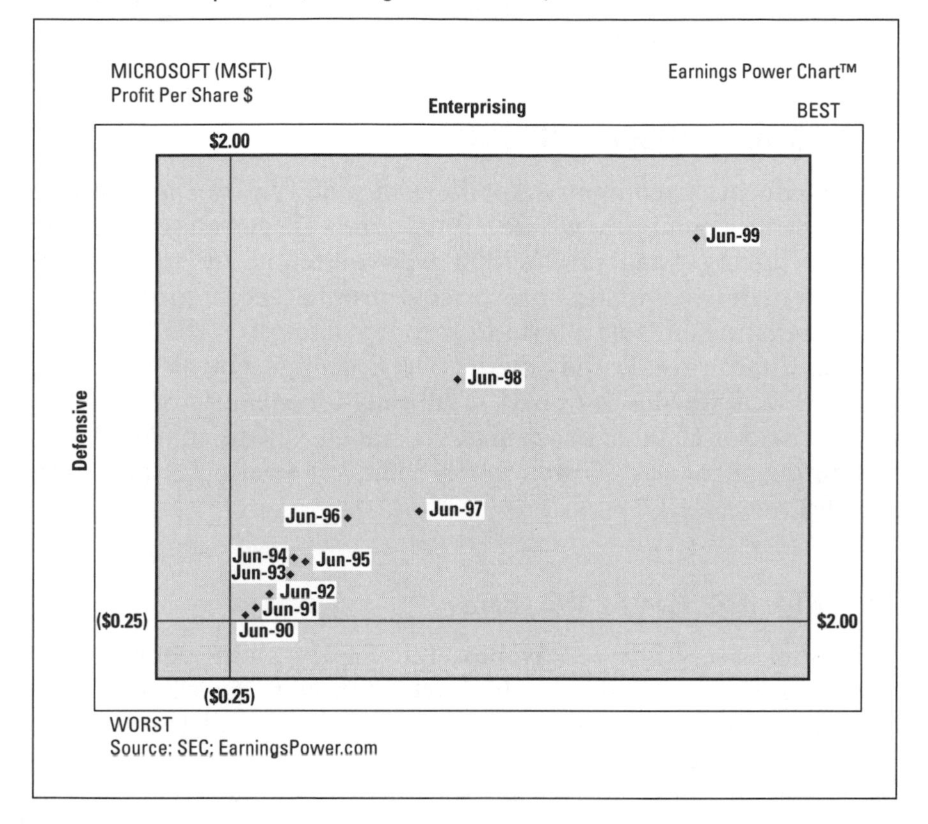

but it has profitable growth, that is, it generates year-over-year gains in both defensive and enterprising profits. This is the chart of a company that you want to buy and hold on to for a long time. As mentioned in Chapter 1, if you bought $10,000 worth of Microsoft Corporation at the beginning of 1990 those shares would be worth $966,000 at the end of 1999.

Postscript: By the early 2000s Microsoft was moving from a technology high-flier to a mature industrial giant. In 2003, for instance, the company stopped issuing stock options in favor of restricted stock, the latter which reward employees even when the stock falls. Microsoft also declared its first dividend, in part because it has nearly $50 billion in cash and short-term investments. As of August 2003 the stock is down 56 percent from its pre-crash high due to a variety of causes, including fears of slower earnings growth.

APOLLO GROUP, FISCAL 1995-2002

Adult education company Apollo Group of Phoenix is another example of a company whose robust gains in per-share accrual profits during fiscal 1995-2002 was matched by impressive growth in defensive and enterprising profits (see Figure 9.3).

Recasting our two alternate earnings figures on the Earnings Power Chart reveals that distinctive Earnings Power Staircase pattern that warms the heart of all long-term cautiously greedy investors. A $10,000 investment in Apollo Group made at the beginning of fiscal 1995 was worth $320,000 as of February 2003 (see Figure 9.4).

PAYCHEX, INC., FISCAL 1990-2002

Our final case study is Paychex, Inc. for the fiscal years 1990-2002. As Figure 9.5 shows, the Rochester, New York-based payroll services provider generated rapid gains in all three of its income statements.

Plotting these results on the Earnings Power Chart (see Figure 9.6) shows Paychex to be an Earnings Power Staircase company. Not only was the firm situated in the Earnings Power Box throughout the decade, it kept moving in an upper-right direction. A $10,000 investment in Paychex made at the beginning of 1990 was worth $370,000 at the end of 2002.

Companies that are situated in the Earnings Power Box and keep moving in an upper-right direction every year have profitable growth; not only do they get bigger, but as evidenced by the expansion in defensive and enterprising profits, they also get better. As we have seen, these Earnings Power Staircase companies can generate tremendous capital gains if you give them time to blossom.

Figure 9.3

Apollo Group, Quality of Profits, 1995–2002

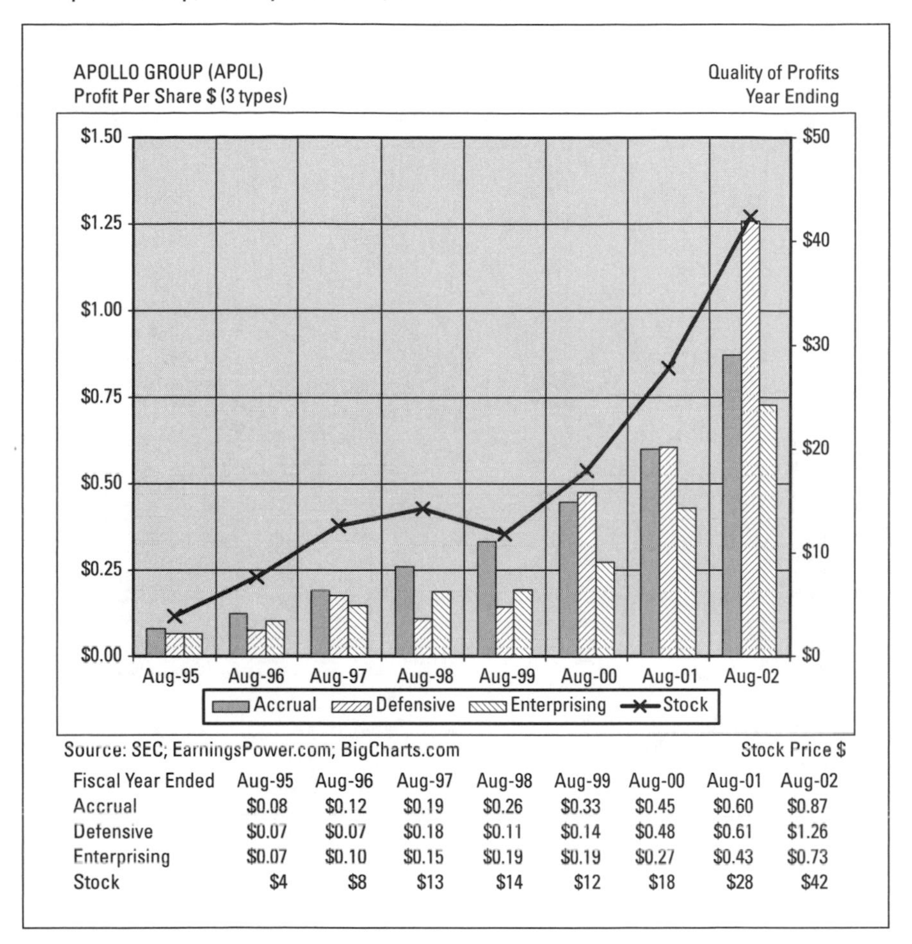

Fiscal Year Ended	Aug-95	Aug-96	Aug-97	Aug-98	Aug-99	Aug-00	Aug-01	Aug-02
Accrual	$0.08	$0.12	$0.19	$0.26	$0.33	$0.45	$0.60	$0.87
Defensive	$0.07	$0.07	$0.18	$0.11	$0.14	$0.48	$0.61	$1.26
Enterprising	$0.07	$0.10	$0.15	$0.19	$0.19	$0.27	$0.43	$0.73
Stock	$4	$8	$13	$14	$12	$18	$28	$42

This observation raises an interesting point:

How many "steps" (years) do you need to see before a company qualifies as an Earnings Power Staircase? I think two years of operating history is sufficient. Your goal is to buy one of these companies in their youth; if you wait five years the price-earnings ratio will get bid up by other investors who appreciate the firm's sterling qualities.

Figure 9.4

Apollo Group, Earnings Power Chart, 1990–1999

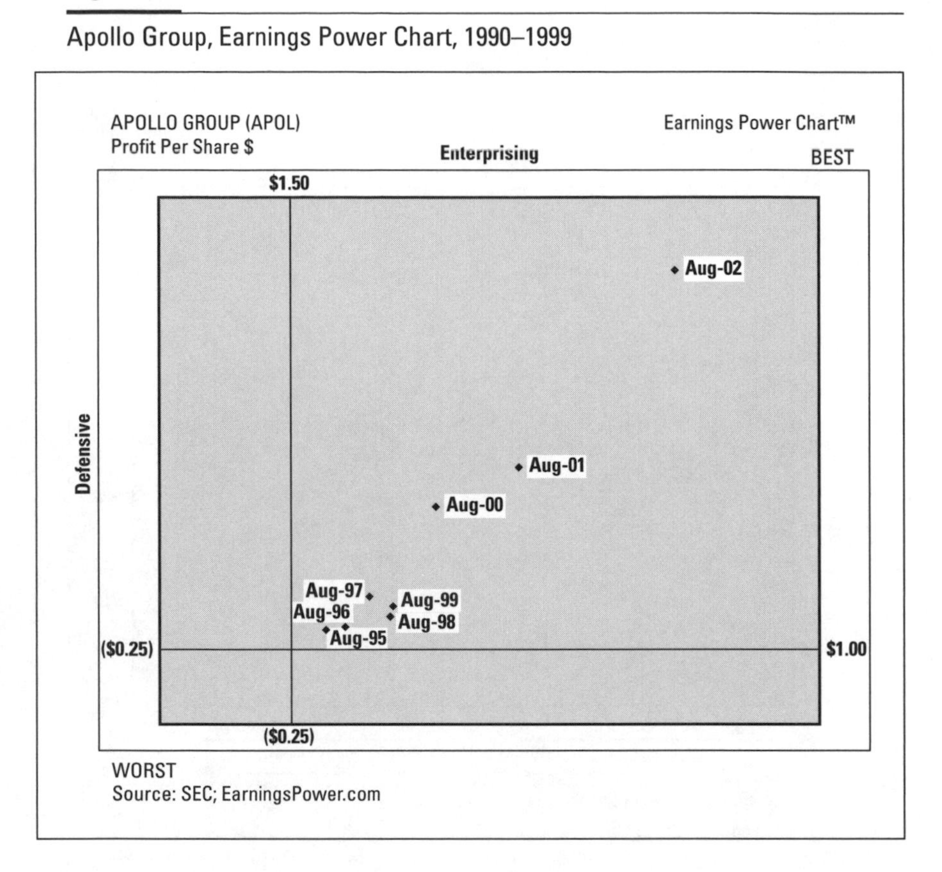

Figure 9.5

Paychex, Quality of Profits, 1990–2002

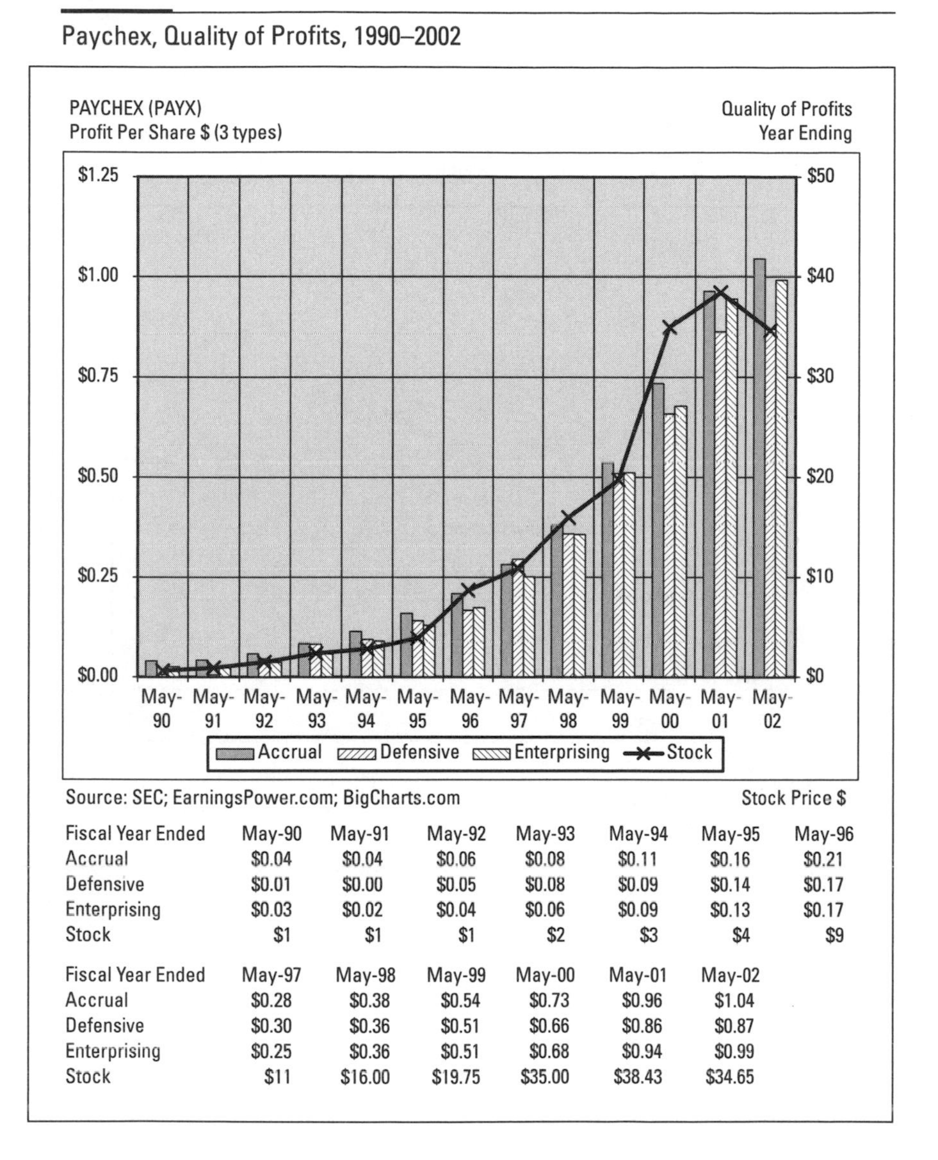

Fiscal Year Ended	May-90	May-91	May-92	May-93	May-94	May-95	May-96
Accrual	$0.04	$0.04	$0.06	$0.08	$0.11	$0.16	$0.21
Defensive	$0.01	$0.00	$0.05	$0.08	$0.09	$0.14	$0.17
Enterprising	$0.03	$0.02	$0.04	$0.06	$0.09	$0.13	$0.17
Stock	$1	$1	$1	$2	$3	$4	$9

Fiscal Year Ended	May-97	May-98	May-99	May-00	May-01	May-02
Accrual	$0.28	$0.38	$0.54	$0.73	$0.96	$1.04
Defensive	$0.30	$0.36	$0.51	$0.66	$0.86	$0.87
Enterprising	$0.25	$0.36	$0.51	$0.68	$0.94	$0.99
Stock	$11	$16.00	$19.75	$35.00	$38.43	$34.65

Figure 9.6

Paychex, Earnings Power Chart, 1990–2002

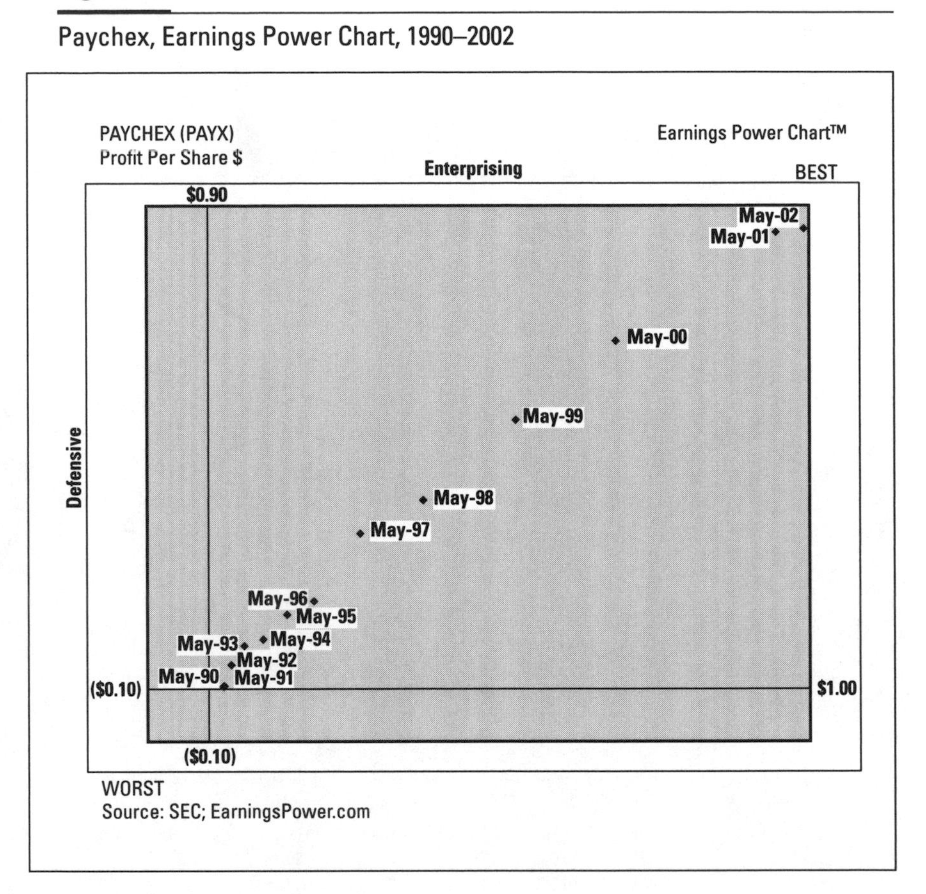

CHAPTER 10

There Are No "One Decision" Stocks

Many years ago, my great-grandfather John C. Stevens bought shares in a company called American Electric Power. When he died, my grandmother inherited the shares, which she held onto for the rest of her life. It never occurred to her to sell or even take a second look at what she owned; after all, her father had purchased the stock. When my grandmother passed away, the shares were bequeathed to me—a thoughtful and generous gesture.

When the stock certificates arrived, my curiosity was piqued. What had this stock done in the last 40 or 50 years? Then I looked at American Electric Power's price chart between 1965 and 2000: The stock had gone nowhere.[1] Talk about opportunity cost! For whatever reason, whether benign neglect or sentiment, no one had bothered to check on the status of the electric utility.

The lesson here is that when it comes to individuals stocks, the philosophy of buy-and-hold makes sense *provided you buy and hold the right stocks*. If you buy-and-hold the wrong stocks, you risk losing money or wasting your time. American Electric Power may have been a great stock when great-grandfather Stevens bought it, but in the last 35 years it's been a real snoozer. We should have sold the shares long ago and put the money elsewhere.

The rigor of the earnings power methodology doesn't end when you instruct your broker to acquire a round lot (one hundred shares). As Heraclitus observed: "Everything flows and nothing abides; everything gives way and nothing stays fixed." The great growth stock of the last decade might become today's sad tale, the struggling turnaround of a year ago might be on its way to a stellar performance. The only way you will know is by updating a firm's performance every year using the Earnings Power Chart.

When it comes to stocks that have enjoyed both glory days and suffered reversals of fortunes, Cisco Systems and Dell Computer stand out. In fact, you'd be hard-pressed to name two other companies that generated more fevered attention in recent years than this pair. Interestingly, both were founded in 1984.

CISCO SYSTEMS

Founded by a group of computer scientists from Stanford University, Cisco Systems boasts a history of innovation. Its engineers, according to the San Jose, California–based company, have been prominent in developing Internet Protocol (IP), the basic language for communicating over the Internet and in private networks.

We divide the Cisco drama into two acts: fiscal 1990-1995 and fiscal 1996-2002.

Fiscal 1990–1995 (ending July)

Figure 10.1 shows that during fiscal 1990-1995 Cisco's rapid gains in accrual profits were matched stride-for-stride by increases in both defensive and enterprising profits.

Transferring these results to the Earnings Power Chart (see Figure 10.2), we find Cisco was situated in the Earnings Power Box, meaning it possessed authentic earnings power. Moreover, Cisco's steady progression in an upper-right direction meant it was an Earnings Power Staircase company. As we learned in Chapter 9, when a company forges a Staircase, *that's* the hallmark of a great growth company. In Cisco's case, not only was it getting bigger, it was getting better. An impressive accomplishment, to be

Figure 10.1

Cisco Systems, Quality of Profits, 1990–1995

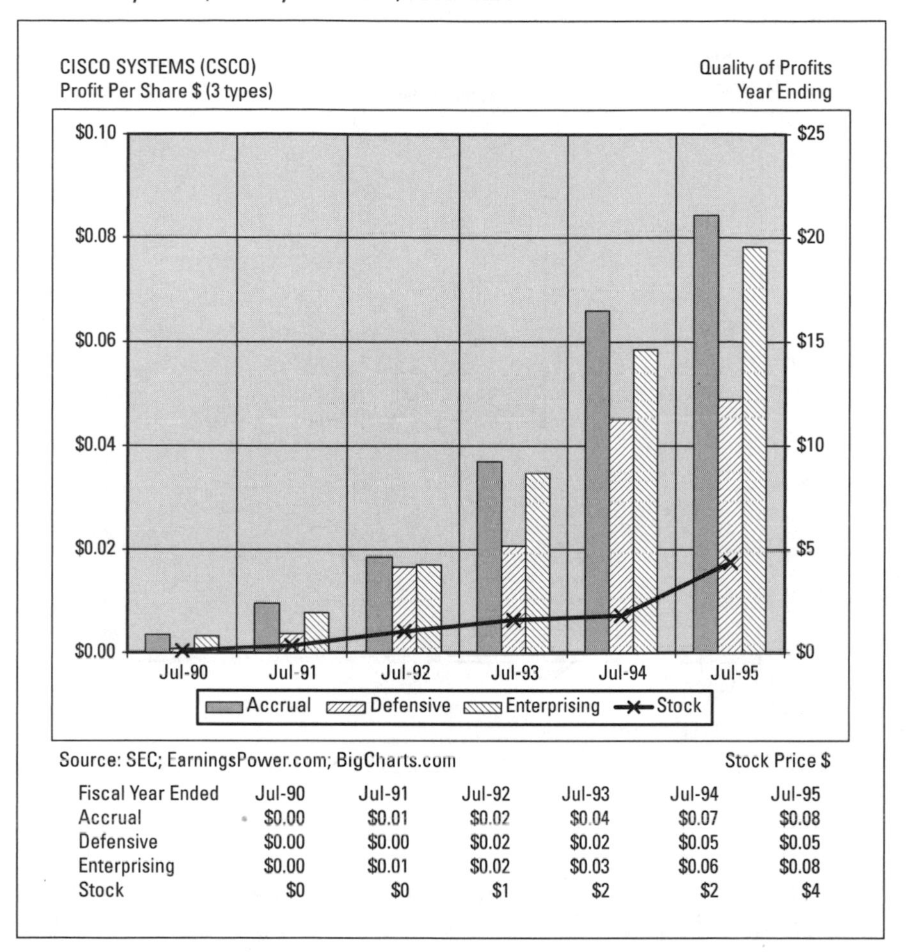

Fiscal Year Ended	Jul-90	Jul-91	Jul-92	Jul-93	Jul-94	Jul-95
Accrual	$0.00	$0.01	$0.02	$0.04	$0.07	$0.08
Defensive	$0.00	$0.00	$0.02	$0.02	$0.05	$0.05
Enterprising	$0.00	$0.01	$0.02	$0.03	$0.06	$0.08
Stock	$0	$0	$1	$2	$2	$4

sure. During this period a $10,000 investment in Cisco's stock grew to $490,000.

Fiscal 1996–2002

Cisco continued to post strong growth in per-share accrual profits through fiscal 2000, albeit at a lower rate than before (see Figure 10.3).

Figure 10.2

Cisco Systems, Earnings Power Chart, 1990–1995

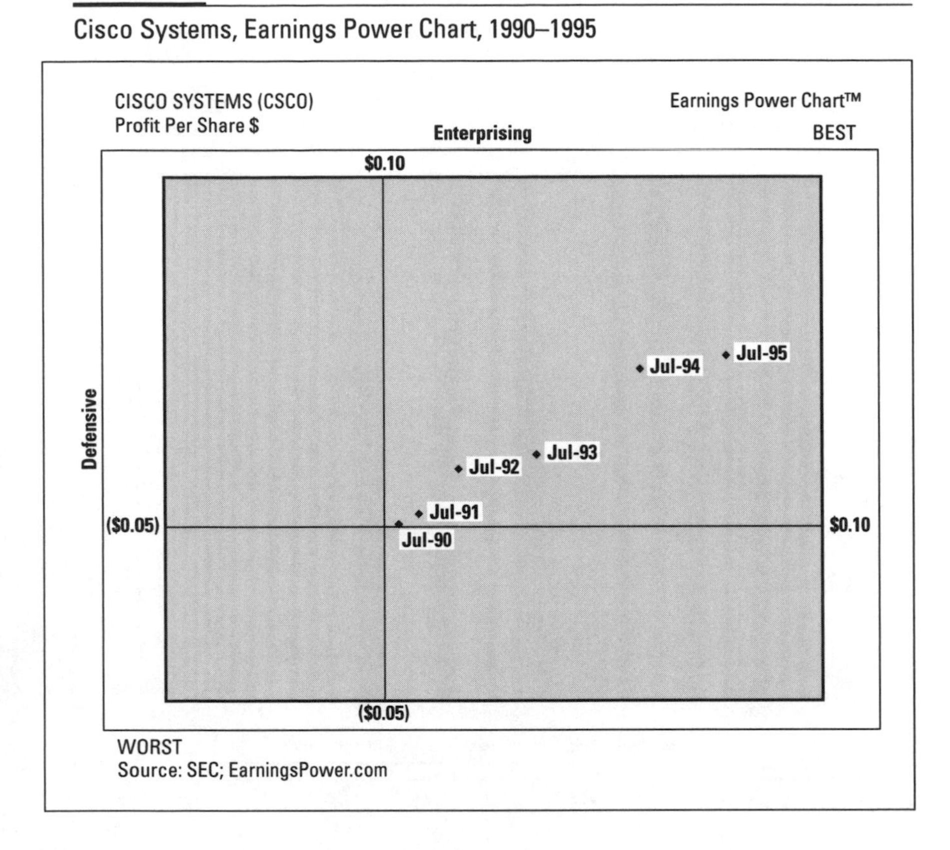

In fiscal 2001, though, Cisco stunned Wall Street by reporting a loss of $0.14 a share (accrual profits). With the Internet economy collapsing, Cisco got stuck with too many servers and routers, and had to write-down $2.5 billion of inventory. The stock, which had traded as high as $80 a share, fell almost 90 percent before bottoming out at under $10 a share. No matter that Cisco made $0.25 a share (accrual profits) in 2002, the consensus was this company's greatest days were behind it. As of this writing Cisco's stock trades at prices last seen at the end of 1998 (see Figure 10.4)

Figure 10.3

Cisco Systems, Quality of Profits, 1996–2002

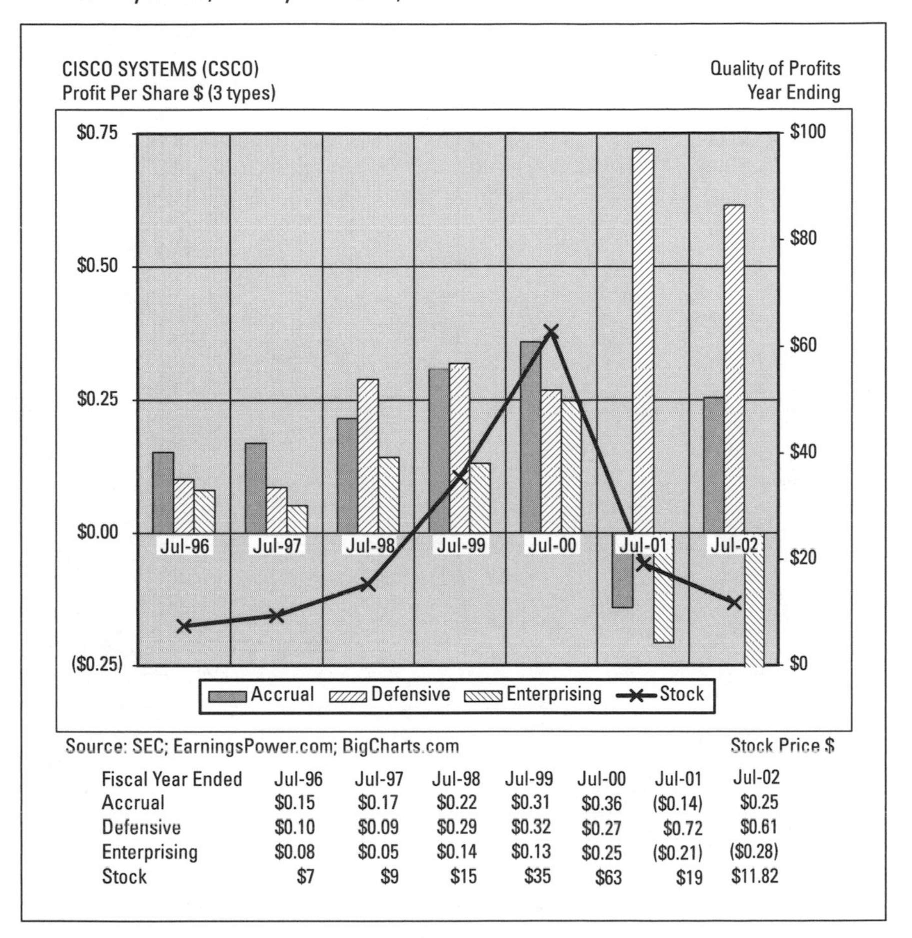

Fiscal Year Ended	Jul-96	Jul-97	Jul-98	Jul-99	Jul-00	Jul-01	Jul-02
Accrual	$0.15	$0.17	$0.22	$0.31	$0.36	($0.14)	$0.25
Defensive	$0.10	$0.09	$0.29	$0.32	$0.27	$0.72	$0.61
Enterprising	$0.08	$0.05	$0.14	$0.13	$0.25	($0.21)	($0.28)
Stock	$7	$9	$15	$35	$63	$19	$11.82

DELL COMPUTER

Dell Computer Corporation was founded by Michael Dell in his college dorm room with $1000 and a novel idea: namely, to sell computer systems directly to customers. The chairman and CEO of the company that bears his name is today, according to the company, the longest tenured CEO in the computer industry. (Just before this book went to press the stockholders approved a name change

Figure 10.4

Cisco Systems, Earnings Power Chart, 1996–2002

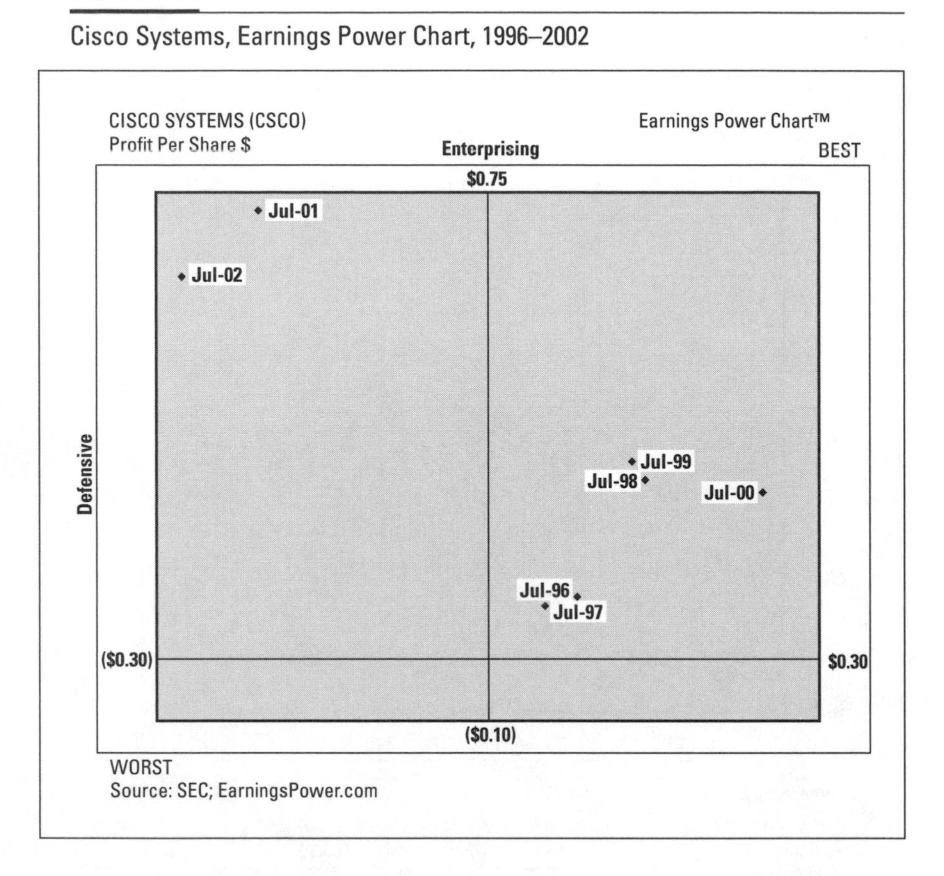

to Dell Inc. to better reflect its "broader range of technology products and services.") We divide the Dell story into three acts: fiscal 1990-1994, fiscal 1995-1999, and fiscal 2000-2002.

Fiscal 1990–1994 (Ending February)

Dell enjoyed steady gains in per-share accrual profits during fiscal 1990-1993, as Figure 10.5 shows. In 1992 and 1993, however, the company reported defensive losses. It appears the defensive income statement anticipated the problems that caused Dell to lose money on an accrual basis in 1994.

Figure 10.5

Dell Computer, Quality of Profits, 1990–1994

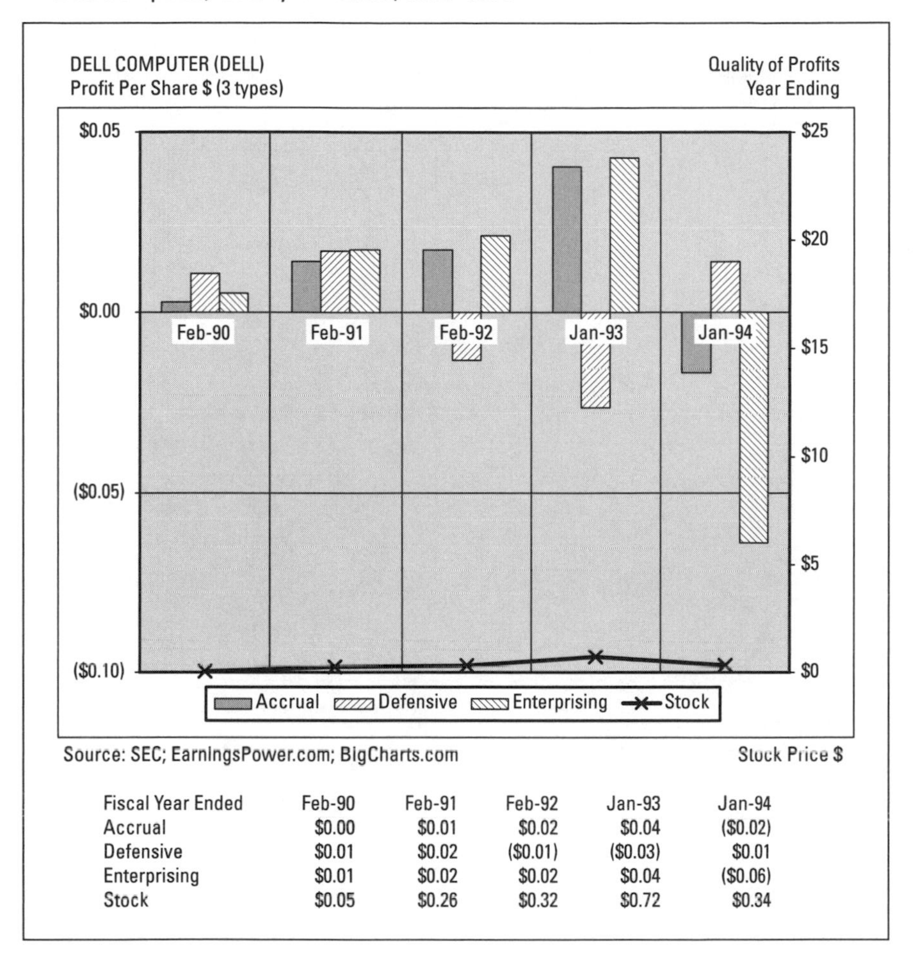

Fiscal Year Ended	Feb-90	Feb-91	Feb-92	Jan-93	Jan-94
Accrual	$0.00	$0.01	$0.02	$0.04	($0.02)
Defensive	$0.01	$0.02	($0.01)	($0.03)	$0.01
Enterprising	$0.01	$0.02	$0.02	$0.04	($0.06)
Stock	$0.05	$0.26	$0.32	$0.72	$0.34

Figure 10.6 shows Dell was an Earnings Power Staircase company in fiscal 1990 and 1991, but then the company slipped into the lower-right box in 1992. Dell remained in the lower-right box in 1993, and then moved to the upper-left box in 1994.

Figure 10.6

Dell Computer, Earnings Power Chart, 1990–1994

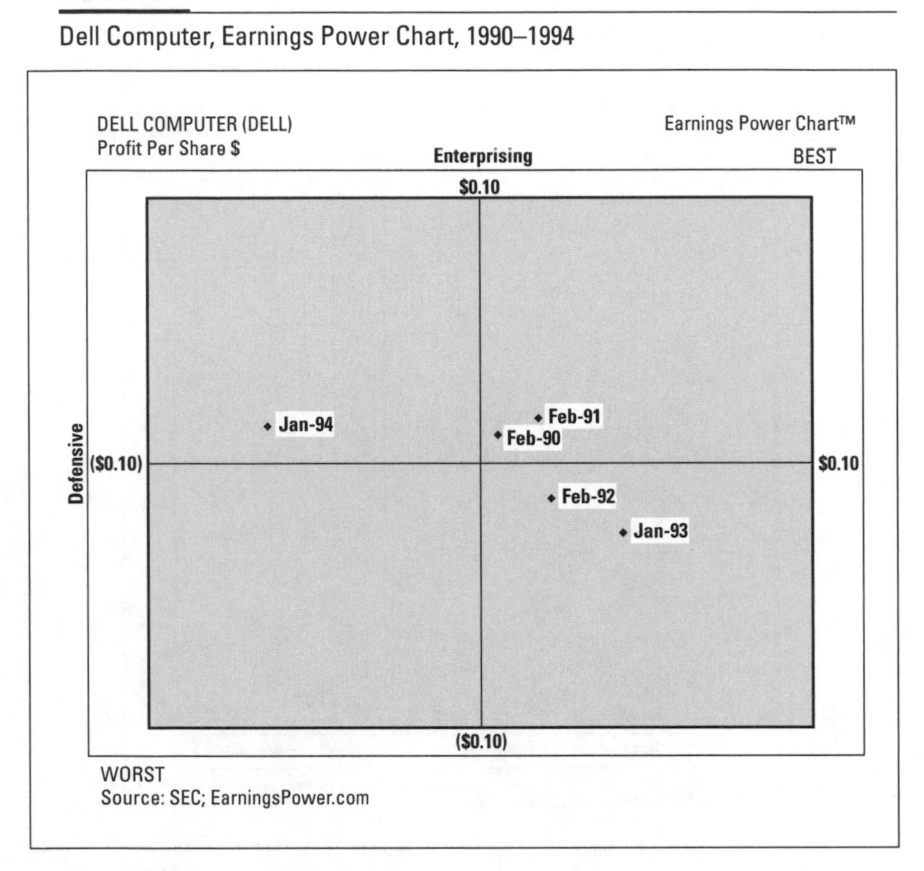

Fiscal 1995–1999

By the mid-1990s Dell fixed its earlier problems, as Figure 10.7 shows, and produced rapid gains in accrual, defensive, and enterprising profits.

Dell moved back into the Earnings Power Box in 1995 (see Figure 10.8). What's more, it began forging another staircase pattern, the hallmark of a great growth company. Wall Street liked what it saw, and the stock rose from a split-adjusted $0.72 to $50. A $10,000 investment in Dell made at the beginning of fiscal 1994 was worth $692,000 at the end of fiscal 1999.

Figure 10.7

Dell Computer, Quality of Profits, 1994–1999

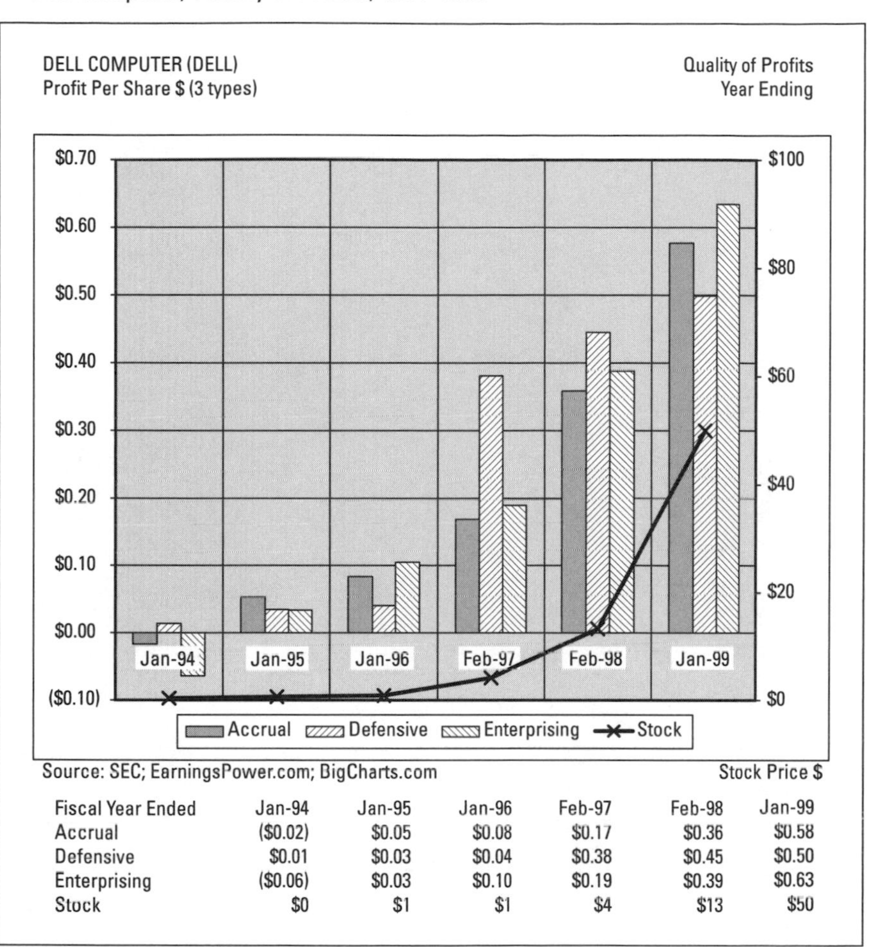

Fiscal Year Ended	Jan-94	Jan-95	Jan-96	Feb-97	Feb-98	Jan-99
Accrual	($0.02)	$0.05	$0.08	$0.17	$0.36	$0.58
Defensive	$0.01	$0.03	$0.04	$0.38	$0.45	$0.50
Enterprising	($0.06)	$0.03	$0.10	$0.19	$0.39	$0.63
Stock	$0	$1	$1	$4	$13	$50

Fiscal 2000–2002

As Figure 10.9 shows, Dell's per-share accrual profits continued growing at a steady clip through fiscal 2001, but fell in 2002 (see Figure 10.9).

Dell is still producing that desirable staircase pattern, but as Figure 10.10 shows the results of late appear wobbly.

Figure 10.8

Dell Computer, Earnings Power Chart, 1994–1999

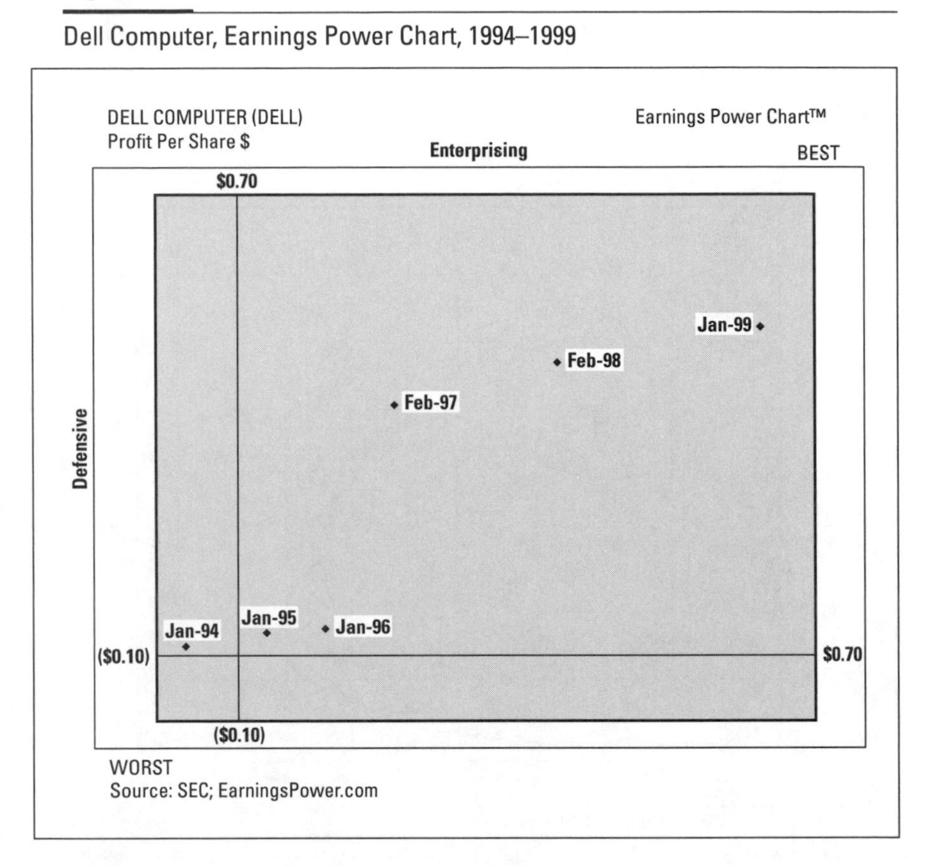

LESSONS LEARNED FROM CISCO AND DELL

Here are two lessons to be learned from Cisco Systems and Dell Computer that apply to all companies.

First, earnings quality for most companies will change from one year to the next. This is due to a variety of factors, including entrance of new competitors, a saturated market, changing consumer preferences, and the loss of a key executive. In Dell's case we saw its strong performance of 1990-1991 dissipate in 1992-1994 and then return in 1995. *Keep watching your companies.*

Second, while Earnings Power Staircase companies can generate substantial capital gains, pay attention to valuation. In

Figure 10.9

Dell Computer, Quality of Profits, 1998–2002

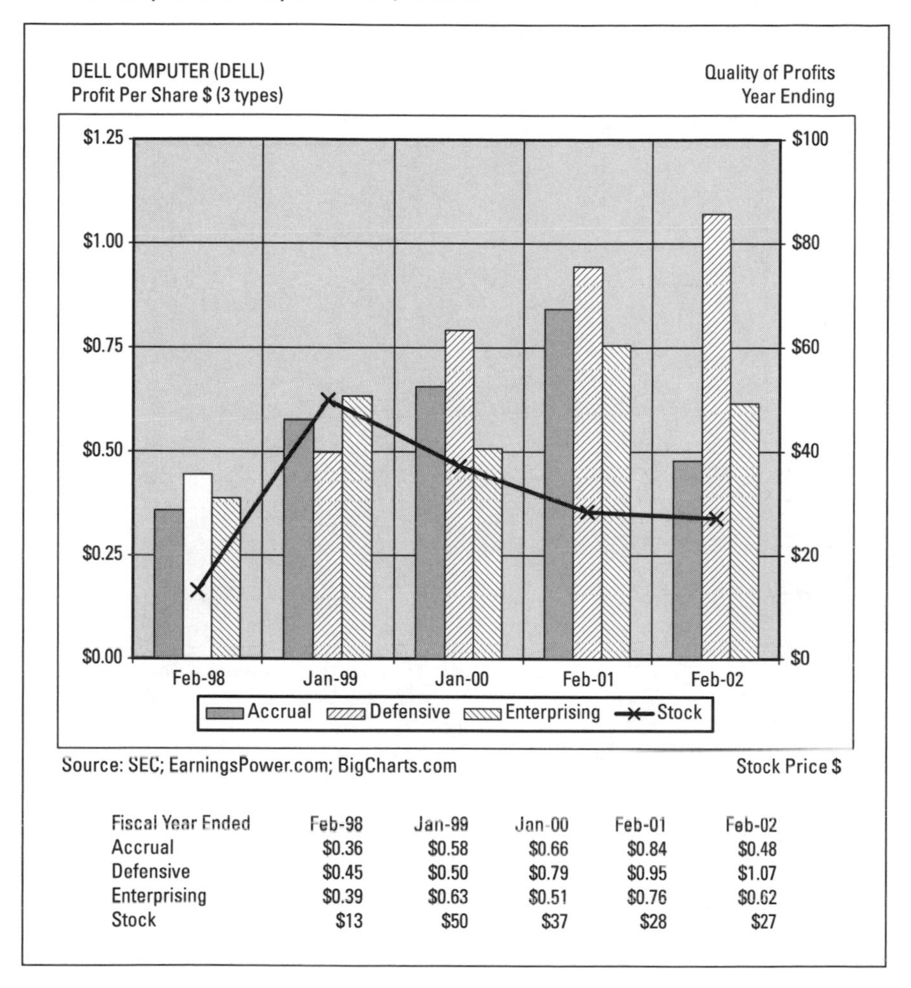

Fiscal Year Ended	Feb-98	Jan-99	Jan-00	Feb-01	Feb-02
Accrual	$0.36	$0.58	$0.66	$0.84	$0.48
Defensive	$0.45	$0.50	$0.79	$0.95	$1.07
Enterprising	$0.39	$0.63	$0.51	$0.76	$0.62
Stock	$13	$50	$37	$28	$27

mid-1999 Cisco System's price-earnings ratio was 184x, according to Morningstar. But then business conditions changed for the worse, and the stock fell from $80 a share to under $10. Cisco's $400 billion loss in market value makes Enron's $66 billion loss look like child's play. (Of course, Cisco is still in business.) *Even great companies can be lousy stocks if you pay a rich multiple of earnings.* See Chapter 13 for additional remarks on valuation.

Figure 10.10

Dell Computer, Earnings Power Chart, 1998–2002

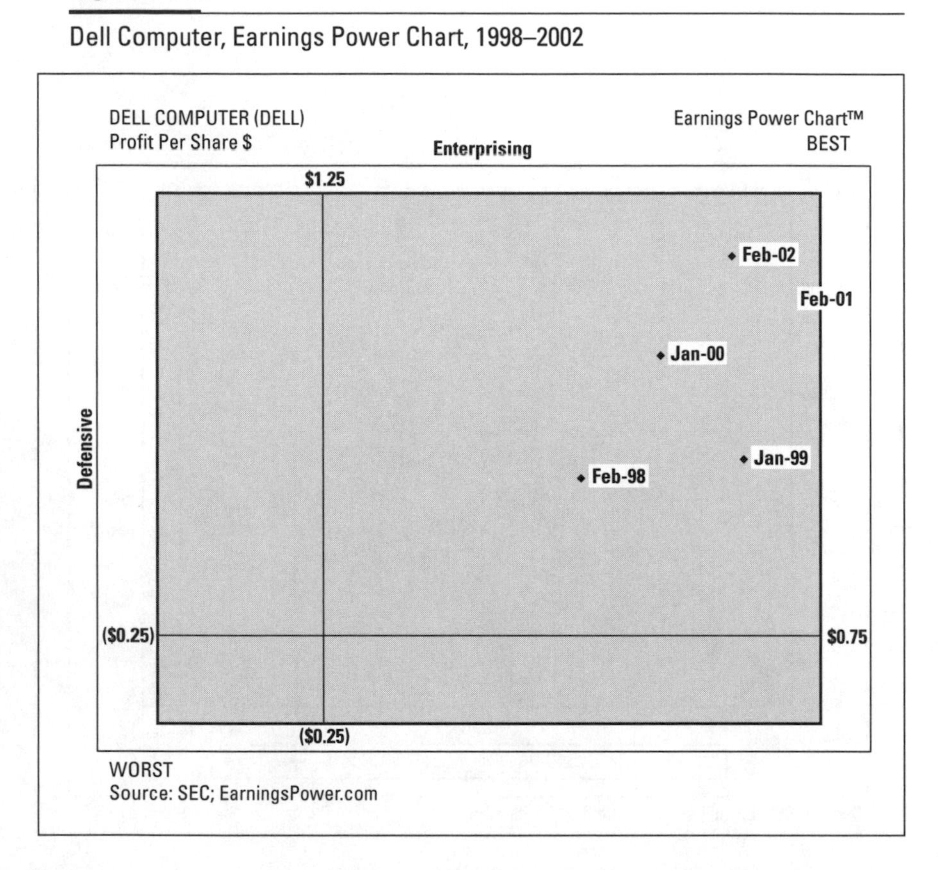

CHAPTER 11

Earnings Power Ratios

Charles F. Montgomery, antique expert and longtime director of the Winterthur Museum in Delaware, developed a methodical, almost scientific, way to evaluate antiques because he wanted to demystify the process by which collectors make decisions about quality and authenticity. His checklist became known as Montgomery's Fourteen Points of Connoisseurship: form, ornament, color, materials, craft, technique, trade practices, function, style, finish, attribution, provenance, condition, and evaluation.

You should be as systematic as Montgomery when you evaluate promising investments, checking off the merits and demerits of each company as you go. That way you can find the best possible merchandise and avoid the investment dreck.

To this end, I introduce two additional yardsticks by which to size up your investments. The debt repayment period is based on the defensive income statement, the return on greenest dollar on the enterprising income statement. These are advanced concepts that build upon the earnings power methodology.

DEBT REPAYMENT PERIOD

There are advantages to borrowing money. For one thing, debt is a deductible expense. Also, lenders are willing to accept a lower expected return, so this lowers a company's weighted average cost of capital, or WACC. But too much debt can pop a company's rivets, resulting in bankruptcy.

How can you tell whether a company has overleveraged itself? One way to ascertain credit quality is to calculate the debt-to-equity ratio. This measures the amount of debt a company employs in relation to its corporate net worth. Many investors shun companies with debt-to-equity ratios over 75 percent because of the high degree of financial risk.

The debt-to-equity ratio has its place in every investor's quiver, to be sure. Still, companies don't repay borrowed money by selling assets, unless they are overextended and in trouble. Also, banks loan money to businesses based on their ability to service the debt, and stockholders' equity is just an extra cushion of safety. Last, the fixed capital for many companies is of little use to other businesses, even though the assets may be carried on the balance sheet at considerable value.

A better gauge of creditworthiness is the debt repayment period. This ratio tells you how long, in years, a firm needs in order to repay debt and equivalents based on its most recent year's worth of defensive profits. The rule: The lower the debt repayment period, the better. As a rule, I avoid companies with debt repayment periods over five years. They're not worth the risk.

Debt includes working capital lines of credit, the current portion of long-term debt, long-term debt, and capital leases. You will find these amounts on the balance sheet, under the section for liabilities. Debt equivalents, for our purposes, are capitalized operating leases (see Table 11.1).

Since Wrigley has no debt, let's examine WorldCom's balance sheet. On December 31, 1999, it had short-term debt of $5 billion, long-term debt of $13.1 billion, and capitalized operating leases of $7.3 billion.

Short-term debt	\$5.0 billion
Long-term debt	\$13.1 billion
Operating leases	\$7.3 billion (See Table 11.1)
Total debt & equivalents	\$25.4 billion

As shown, WorldCom had \$25.4 billion of debt and equivalents at the end of 1999. Meanwhile, defensive profits for the long-distance phone company totaled \$2.7 billion. WorldCom's debt repayment period, therefore, is estimated at 9.4 years:

$$\text{Debt repayment period} = \frac{\text{Debt \& equivalents}}{\text{Defensive profits}}$$

$$= \frac{\$25.4 \text{ billion}}{\$2.7 \text{ billion}}$$

$$= 9.4 \text{ years}$$

At 9.4 years, WorldCom's debt repayment period was nearly twice our prescribed five-year threshold. Do yourself a favor and let others own Wall Street's highly leveraged companies. If a company has authentic earnings power, it won't need to borrow much money. In 2002 WorldCom filed for bankruptcy protection, listing some \$107 billion in assets and \$41 billion in debt.

Because many companies' defensive profits go up one year and down the next (especially for the cyclicals), you may also want

Table 11.1

How To Calculate WorldCom's Capitalized Operating Leases (figures in millions)

	Future Value	Discount Rate @8%	Present Value
Year 1	\$2,193	0.9259	\$2,031
Year 2	\$1,929	0.8573	\$1,654
Year 3	\$1,895	0.7938	\$1,504
Year 4	\$1,631	0.7350	\$1,199
Year 5	\$1,313	0.6806	\$894
Capitalized operating leases			\$7,281

to calculate the debt repayment period using *normalized* defensive profits. This is the sum of the last four four years' worth of defensive profits divided by 4. Four years is usually sufficient to smooth out the effects of the typical business cycle, which usually takes four years to run its course.

The reason we use defensive profits as the denominator for the debt repayment period formula is because the defensive income statement expenses investment in fixed and working capital in the year incurred. In the enterprising income statement, these uses of cash are not deducted dollar-for-dollar. As a result, a firm's true cash-generating ability may be overstated.

RETURN ON GREENEST DOLLAR

At any given moment a company will have a myriad of investment opportunities from which to choose. The company might, for example, decide to sell a product or service today but wait several weeks to get paid, an investment in working capital. It might build a new research lab, an investment in fixed capital. It might launch a new marketing campaign, an investment in intangibles. The firm might also invest in goodwill if the purchase price of an acquisition exceeds the seller's corporate net worth. Each option has a certain risk-reward profile. Stockholder value can be enhanced, but it can also be destroyed, so making the right choices is critical.

How, then, to determine whether management is getting the biggest bang on your buck? One approach is to estimate what I call the return on greenest dollar. The more money a firm earns on its latest investment in enterprising capital (that is, debt, stockholders' equity, capital equivalents), the better. The 'green' in return on greenest dollar refers to last year's investment in the business, rather than total capital. This is a subtle but important distinction.

The return on greenest dollar ratio is calculated by dividing the year-to-year change in enterprising net operating profit after taxes (eNOPAT), by the year-to-year change in enterprising capital. eNOPAT is the sum of enterprising profits and enterprising interest, that is, what the firm earns before taking into account the cost of financing the business. The prefix 'e' for enterprising, denotes that we have, among other things, capitalized intangibles.

By way of example, in 2002 Wrigley's enterprising profits were \$281.5 million, and its enterprising interest \$152.6 million. (Because I'm using data from the last six years' worth of financial statements, eNOPAT is slightly different from the amount calculated in Chapter 6.) eNOPAT, as shown below, totaled \$434.1 million in 2002:

$$\begin{aligned}\text{eNOPAT} &= \text{Enterprising profits} + \text{enterprising interest}\\ &= \$281.5 \text{ million} + \$152.6 \text{ million}\\ &= \$434.1 \text{ million}\end{aligned}$$

In 2001, Wrigley's eNOPAT was \$364.1 million. Also, its enterprising capital for December 31, 2001, and December 31, 2002, was \$1102.4 million and \$1484.7 million, respectively:

$$\begin{aligned}\text{Return on greenest dollar}\\ &= \frac{\text{Change in eNOPAT}}{\text{Change in enterprising capital}}\\ &= \frac{\$434.1 \text{ million} - \$364.1 \text{ million}}{\$1484.7 \text{ million} - \$1102.4 \text{ million}}\\ &= \frac{\$70.1 \text{ million}}{\$382.3 \text{ million}}\\ &= 18\%\end{aligned}$$

As calculated, Wrigley's return on greenest dollar in 2002 was 18 percent. This means the \$382.3 million investment in enterprising capital made in 2002 produced an additional \$70 million of eNOPAT. That's a fine return on investment, especially when you consider the yield of a U.S. Treasury obligation. In late-August 2003 the yield on a 10-year Treasury was 4.46 percent, well-below the return Wrigley earned on its latest investment in the business

Companies with authentic earnings power tend to produce high returns on greenest dollar every year. A high return on greenest dollar tells you management is allocating capital intelligently. (For more on this topic, please see the section on acquisitions in Chapter 12.) Many erstwhile blue chip companies get into trouble by investing in low-yielding projects in order to maintain the illusion of earnings growth. It's much harder to fool the return on greenest dollar equation, however. Successive disappointing returns on greenest dollar will eventually pull down a firm's total return on capital, which in turn will hurt enterprising profits.

Using the debt repayment period and return on greenest dollar, let's take one more look at our four archetypes from Chapter 8. Our interest here is to see if we can develop any rules of thumb to distinguish between good companies like Wrigley from bad companies like Enron, WorldCom, and Lucent Technologies. (Table 11.2)

As Table 11.3 shows, Enron's debt repayment period was "n/a" for 'not applicable' between 1997-2000 due to defensive losses. Meanwhile, its return on greenest dollar was erratic and never topped 14 percent.

Table 11.2

Earnings Power Ratios

Income Statement	Ratio	Answers the question . . .
Defensive	Debt repayment period	Is this company able to cover its debt in a reasonable period?
Enterprising	Return on greenest dollar	What is the percentage return management is earning on its most recent investment in the business?

Table 11.3

Enron Corporation

Fiscal year	1997	1998	1999	2000
DRP (year)	n/a	n/a	n/a	n/a
RGD (%)	0%	14%	Negative	8%

Source: SEC, EarningsPower.com

WorldCom's debt repayment period, as we see in Table 11.4, was six years in 1998 and 9 years in 1999. Due to defensive losses, results for 2000 and 2001 were not applicable. Meanwhile, its return on greenest dollar peaked at 66 percent in 1999 and then was negative in 2000 and 2001.

Lucent Technologies had low debt repayment periods in fiscal 1997 and 1998. In 1999 the company had a defensive loss, so the ratio is not applicable. The next year, in 2000, the debt repayment period was 11 years. As for Lucent's return on greenest dollar, the numbers went from negative returns in 1997 and 1998 to 2 percent in 1999 and then 15 percent in 2000 (see Table 11.5).

Wrigley had a net cash position during 1999-2002, meaning it had more cash and marketable securities than debt and equivalents. Meanwhile, its return on greenest dollar, which was negative in 1999, was in double-digits between 2000-2002. It is interesting to note that the percentage return has declined every year since 2000. If you own shares of Wrigley, this is a number to keep your eye on. (see Table 11.6).

Table 11.4

WorldCom

Fiscal year	1998	1999	2000	2001
DRP (year)	6	9	n/a	n/a
RGD (%)	2%	66%	Negative	Negative

Source: SEC, EarningsPower.com

Table 11.5

Lucent Technologies

Fiscal year	1997	1998	1999	2000
DRP (year)	2	5	n/a	11
RGD (%)	Negative	Negative	2%	15%

Source: SEC, EarningsPower.com

Table 11.6

William Wrigley Jr. Company

Fiscal year	1999	2000	2001	2002
DRP (year)	Net cash	Net cash	Net cash	Net cash
RGD (%)	Negative	54%	28%	18%

Source: SEC, EarningsPower.com

Table 11.7

Microsoft Corporation

Fiscal year	1995	1996	1997	1998
DRP (year)	Net cash	Net cash	Net cash	Net cash
RGD (%)	52%	219%	82%	47%

Source: SEC, EarningsPower.com

Now let's look at our Earnings Power Staircase companies. How do they fare with these two measures? Like Wrigley, Microsoft had net cash during fiscal 1995-1998. Moreover, its return on greenest dollar was over 40 percent every year (see Table 11.7). This is an impressive performance on both counts.

Apollo Group was also in a net cash position during fiscal 1998–2001. As for the return on greenest dollar, the numbers speak for themselves (see Table 11.8).

Our final case study is Paychex. During fiscal 1998-2001 it had either net cash or a debt repayment period of zero years. Meanwhile, the return on greenest dollar numbers are all triple-digit. No wonder Paychex is one of the great growth stocks of the last decade (see Table 11.9).

If you already built a defensive and enterprising income statement for a company, it takes just a few more minutes of work to estimate its debt repayment period and return on greenest dollar ratios.

With respect to the debt repayment period, look for companies that generate defensive profits every year in sufficient

Table 11.8

Apollo Group

Fiscal year	1998	1999	2000	2001
DRP (year)	0	2	1	Net cash
RGD (%)	13%	18%	82%	47%

Source: SEC, EarningsPower.com

Table 11.9

Paychex

Fiscal year	1998	1999	2000	2001
DRP (year)	Net cash	Net cash	0	0
RGD (%)	234%	276%	175%	229%

Source: SEC, EarningsPower.com

quantity to repay all debt and equivalents in five years or less. As an additional safety measure, calculate the debt repayment period using normalized defensive profits. This emphasis on credit quality is consistent with the goal of the defensive investor who wants to avoid committing serious mistakes or sustaining losses. Meanwhile, the enterprising investor who wants to own companies that are both sound and more attractive than the average will pay close attention to the return on greenest dollar. As we just learned, Microsoft, Apollo Group, and Paychex all generated high returns on the incremental investment in their business.

You will improve your stock market results by buying companies with low debt repayment periods and high returns on greenest dollar.

CHAPTER 12

Measuring Management

If you intend to own a stock for a year or two, the quality of a firm's management is inconsequential. But if your timeframe is several years (a must if you are a growth investor), it's vital that you determine whether management is working for you. Strong management bodes well for your stock. Management that's weak or unscrupulous can spell trouble.

What are some clues that management is representing your best interests? It's difficult for an outsider to get a complete picture of management conduct, but here are some hints that, taken as a whole, can give you a good idea.

EXECUTIVE STOCK OWNERSHIP

Stock ownership is a sign that management's interests are aligned with stockholders. Managers who own company stock tend to be more responsive than those who have been granted large options packages and have little of their own wealth on the line. You can find information on how much stock executives and directors own by looking in the proxy.

CANDOR

You also want to read the annual letter to stockholders for the last four or five years. This is the chief executive's opportunity to write a frank account of the company's recent performance, warts and all. If you read actively and take notes, you'll see a story unfold. Pay special attention to the *tone* of the letter. Does the chief executive address you as if you were a majority owner? Or do you feel as if you are just a cog in the wheel?

Consider, for example, this brassy sentence from Enron's 2000 annual report:

> *Enron's performance in 2000 was a success by any measure. The company's net income reached a record in 2000. Enron is laser-focused on earnings per share, and we expect to continue strong earnings performance.*[1]

Of course, we know otherwise: 2000 was a bad year for Enron, just like 1996, 1997, 1998, and 1999. We know that because Enron was situated in the Earnings Power Chart's lower-left box. Use the Earnings Power Chart to check whether management is being straight with its owners.

Here are other questions to get answers to:

- What went right during the year? What went wrong?
- Does the CEO take credit for the good things that happen but blame debacles on forces beyond his or her control (for example, the economy, a coup in a foreign land, El Niño, tennis elbow)?
- Does the CEO discuss how much money the company made during the year? If management trumpets pro forma earnings or EBITDA, that's a bad sign.
- Do past predictions match the company's actual performance?
- Does the CEO seem overly promotional? (A company that goes to great lengths to sell its stock may be ignoring its business.)
- Is there a lot of industry mumbo-jumbo?
- Do initiatives that are announced with great fanfare in

prior years seem to disappear without explanation?
- Are the company's financials easy to grasp?

You will also want to listen to quarterly conference calls. This is when management discusses the highs and lows of the last 90 days. Does management evade tough questions? If so, that's a concern. Perhaps they are trying to hide something. Many companies even post the calls on their Web sites, which means you can listen at your convenience.

THE CEO'S RESUME

If you were to go into business with strangers, you'd make an effort to get to know them first. Where did they grow up? What colleges did they attend? Do they have stable job histories? Are their family lives happy? That sort of thing.

When you buy a company's stock it pays to do the same kind of research. Start with the chief executive officer (CEO). Read the annual report, 10-K, and proxy to answer the following questions:

- How long has the CEO been with the company?
- How long has the CEO been in the same job?
- How long was the CEO employed by previous employers?
- Where was the CEO educated?
- What contributions did the CEO make at previous employers? (If a past employer was a public company, you may want to run that firm's numbers through the Earnings Power Chart.)
- Does the CEO's compensation seem reasonable?
- Does the CEO receive overly generous perks?

Also check whether the CEO is also chairman of the board of directors. This is a conflict of interest because the board's job, among other things, is to hire the CEO and monitor that person's progress. When the CEO and the board chair are the same person (which, unfortunately, happens all too often), other directors may be reluctant to speak their minds. This, in turn, can result in a CEO staying at the helm too long.

EXECUTIVE COMPENSATION

The fiscal year ending January 2, 1999, marked the third consecutive year of accrual losses for the Warnaco Group (see Figure 12.1). Still, the maker of women's underwear (Olga, Valentino, Scaagi, Ungaro, Bob Mackie, Fruit of the Loom) awarded its chairman, president, and CEO, Linda Wachner, a salary of $2.7 million, a bonus of $6 million, a restricted stock grant worth $6.5 million, and a package of options that was valued at $58.2 million, for a grand total of $73.4 million. Imagine how much money Wachner would have deserved if Warnaco had been situated in the Earnings Power Box that year instead of the lower-left box (see Figure 12.2). The stock, which reached its apogee of $45 in mid-1998, fell to pennies a share by the time the company filed for bankruptcy in 2001. (In 2003 Warnaco emerged from bankruptcy with a debt-free balance sheet and without Linda Wachner at the helm.)

If a company that interests you is situated in the Earnings Power Box, you're happy to pay the CEO any reasonable sum. What you don't want to do, however, is pay a king's ransom to executives whose companies are situated in the other three boxes, especially if the companies have been there for more than one year. Such was the case with Warnaco.

Executive compensation is an important issue for investors. So check the proxy to see if the company indicates how increasing stockholder value is tied to specific performance targets for executive officers. Do executives get large bonuses even if the company reported a loss? That's a negative. Are remuneration plans designed to enhance stockholder value? That's a positive.

BOARD OF DIRECTORS

The responsibility of the board of directors is to enhance the long-term value of the company for its stockholders. In executing its responsibilities a board has specific functions in addition to the general oversight of management and the company's business

Figure 12.1

Warnaco, Quality of Profits, 1995–1999

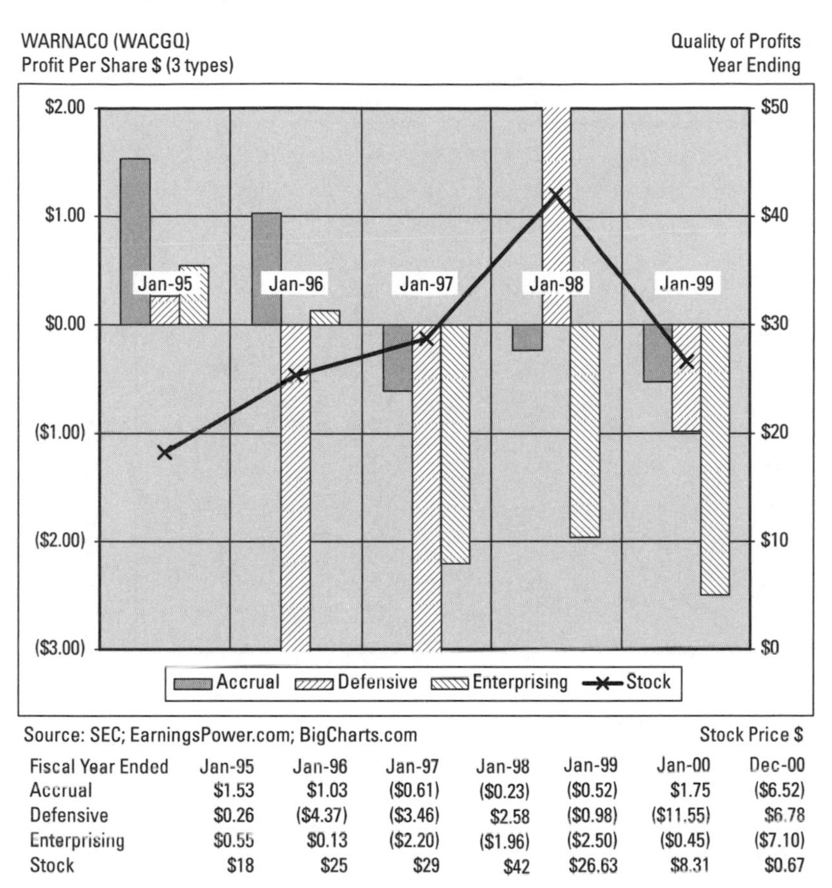

Source: SEC; EarningsPower.com; BigCharts.com

Stock Price $

Fiscal Year Ended	Jan-95	Jan-96	Jan-97	Jan-98	Jan-99	Jan-00	Dec-00
Accrual	$1.53	$1.03	($0.61)	($0.23)	($0.52)	$1.75	($6.52)
Defensive	$0.26	($4.37)	($3.46)	$2.58	($0.98)	($11.55)	$6.78
Enterprising	$0.55	$0.13	($2.20)	($1.96)	($2.50)	($0.45)	($7.10)
Stock	$18	$25	$29	$42	$26.63	$8.31	$0.67

performance. These tasks might include evaluating strategic initiatives, reviewing financial and business goals, approving the terms of a large acquisition, checking the integrity of the financial statements, hiring outside counsel, and socializing with younger executives who moving up the chain of command.

Here again, the proxy is a trove of information. Questions to get answers to include:

- How many directors are there?
- How many of the directors are company employees or officers? The lower the percentage, the better. That's

Figure 12.2

Warnaco, Earnings Power Chart, 1995–1999

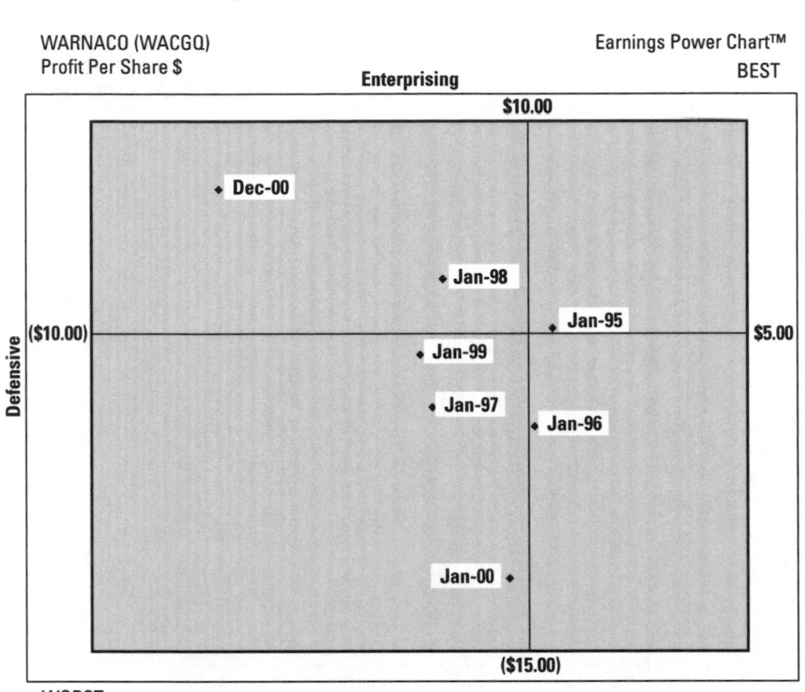

Source: SEC; EarningsPower.com

because employees who sit on the board might be reluctant to question the CEO's ideas for fear it may cost them their jobs.

- Who nominates new directors? That's best left to non-employees to avoid conflicts of interest.
- How many directors are related? If there are three or more board members with the same last name, I invoke my "Rigas rule," which means head for the hills. The Rigas rule is named for the Rigas family who controlled the board of scandal-ridden Adelphia Communications. The cable television company, it will be recalled, allegedly failed to disclose $2.3 billion in company-guaranteed loans to the family of founder John Rigas. Alas, four of the nine directors of the company were Rigas's.

(Now-bankrupt Allou Health & Beauty Care, who we met in Chapter 7, had 3 family members on its board.)

- Do any directors do business with the company? If so, this is a conflict of interest.
- How long are directors' terms? One-year terms are best, because with longer tenures some directors may get complacent.
- Are all directors up for re-election every year? Staggered elections are a bad sign because it can insulate the board from angry blocs of investors who might want to toss out all the directors at once.
- Do all directors attend at least 75 percent of their board and committee meetings?
- Does the company disclose how it evaluates directors?
- What percentage of the audit committee is independent? The more independence, the better.
- Do all directors own shares in the company?
- Did they buy the stock themselves, or was it given to them?

One thing that can potentially weaken the effectiveness of a board is interlocking director relationships. Often, executives of one company serve on the board of another and vice versa. For example, if you learn that the chairman of Company A is on the board of Company B, find out if the chairman of Company B is on the board of Company A. If so, this may mean the board is not as independent as it seems, even if the majority of its other members are non-employees. When a board is not sufficiently independent, directors may go easy on management and be reluctant to ask tough questions about, for example, compensation or investments.

RELATED-PARTY TRANSACTIONS

Watch for "related-party transactions," which are potential conflicts of interest. Things to look for include employees or directors who own stock in companies that are suppliers or customers; friends or relatives who do business with the company; and family members who are consultants.

General Electric is a company that has a clear policy on this issue. The company states on its Web site that directors "will be considered 'independent' if the sales to, and from, GE are less than one percent of the revenues of the companies they serve as executive officers, and if loans provided by GE to a company they serve as executive officers, and loans received by GE from such companies, constitute less than one percent of total assets. Moreover, if a GE director serves as an officer or director of a charitable organization, the GE director will be considered 'independent,' if GE donates less than one percent of that organization's annual charitable receipts."[2]

Walt Disney Company, on the other hand, has room for improvement. In its 2003 proxy, we learn that children, spouses, in-laws and even directors do business with Disney in one way or another. For example, a daughter of one director was paid $95,000 as a marketing manager, the son of another director made $176,000 in salary and bonus, and a director's wife was paid $386,000 by a company in which Disney has a 50 percent equity interest. Through an aviation company he owns, director and vice chairman Roy Disney (Walt's nephew) was paid $624,000 as reimbursement for business travel. The father-in-law of Robert Iger, Disney's president and chief operating officer, was paid $70,000 during the year for unspecified services. Also, Disney director and former United States Senator George Mitchell, through his law firm, received $443,000 in fees for legal and regulatory services. The architect Robert A. M. Stern, who was also on the board, was paid $105,000 in fees and expenses for blueprints. (Even the head of a school attended by the children of Michael Eisner, the chairman and chief executive, was a director at one time.) It should make you nervous to see so many board members with such close financial ties to the company. The incestuous nature of Disney's board may help explain why the stock has fared poorly over the last several years.

INDEPENDENT AUDITOR

As part-owner of a company you want to have confidence that the financial statements are credible. So check if the independent auditor earns substantial sums by also providing consulting services to the firm. To keep the consulting revenue flowing the outside accountant may be afraid to challenge unscrupulous management over its accounting. According to *BusinessWeek*, in 2000 Enron paid Arthur Andersen $25 million in audit fees and another $27 million for other services, including tax preparation and internal auditing.[3] The proxy will tell you all the fees paid to the independent auditor.

Also check the proxy to see if there is a periodic evaluation of auditor independence. If the same auditor has worked with the same management team for many years, the auditor may be reluctant to speak up for fear of rocking the boat.

ACQUISITIONS

A hallmark of top-notch management is wise investment of capital. It's human to make mistakes, but in business if management keeps pouring capital into wasteful projects, the company is destined for the lower-left box of the Earnings Power Chart.

What are some of the ways in which management can invest its capital? A partial list includes:

- Put the money in the bank to build up the checking account balance
- Invest in working capital assets such as receivables or inventory
- Invest in fixed capital assets like plant, property, and equipment
- Acquire other companies
- Pay down accounts payable and accrued liabilities
- Pay down debt
- Increase the dividend payout
- Repurchase stock

Acquisitions are the riskiest bets. That's because most deals don't work out as planned. In fact, various studies peg the failure rate as high as 80 percent.[4]

There are many reasons why the failure rate is so high: difficulties integrating billing and payroll procedures; cultures that don't mesh; key employees who get fed up and leave; overpayment, which transfers the bulk of future gains from the merger to the stockholders in the seller company; buyers who don't fully understand the businesses they just bought; failure of expected synergies to materialize; integration efforts that frustrate customers and employees; overestimates of expected cost savings; and an emphasis on cost cutting that leads to poor customer service.

Because acquisitions are so vexing, find out how many acquisitions the company has made over the last several years. The more acquisitions a firm makes, the more cautious you should be. Tyco International (see Chapter 7) is a case in point. During the 1990s it bought more than 700 companies. We now know the miserable results from that strategy.

As mentioned in Chapter 4, you can also check a company's balance sheet to see if it has a high percentage of goodwill to total assets. The higher the ratio, the greater the likelihood that at least some of the goodwill will become impaired.

If a company you own announces an acquisition, check the deal terms. Hostile deals paid with cash seem to work best, while friendly deals paid with stock are the worst.

DEBT

A company with lots of debt might as well be wearing handcuffs and have their feet encased in cement. This is because high interest charges payable to banks or bondholders mean less money for investment in growth. That puts the company at a competitive disadvantage relative to its peers.

Savvy managers use debt sparingly. The debt repayment period (Chapter 11) will tell whether a company can repay its debt and equivalents in a reasonable period.

STOCKHOLDER DILUTION RATE

Companies like to issue stock options to employees because the pieces of paper are not treated as an expense. But a company that issues options profligately creates a burden for its non-employee stockholders. That's because the higher the dilution the rate, the smaller your claim on a firm's net assets and earnings power.

You can check whether a firm is granting too many options by tracking the number of diluted shares outstanding over the last several years. The following data from Morningstar.com shows Yahoo!'s diluted share count for the four years ending 2002 (in millions):

1999	516.0
2000	550.7
2001	569.7
2002	593.8

In Yahoo!'s case we see a 15 percent growth (dilution) in share count since 1999. Although some of this growth might be for a good reason, it's an item to put on your watch list if you're a Yahoo! stockholder.

DIVIDENDS

During most of the 1990s, investors shunned dividend-paying stocks. For one thing, dividends are taxable income, and who wants to pay taxes? Also, many of Wall Street's best-performing stocks did not even pay a dividend. Of course, with the sharp declines in the S&P 500 and Nasdaq in the last few years dividends are back in vogue. Many investors now reason that if a firm can pay a dividend, its earnings quality must be sound. You can cash a dividend check at the bank, after all, but you can't cash net income.

Dividends are fine as long as they are paid out of a *growing* stream of defensive profits. If, however, a firm is paying a dividend while its investment in fixed or working capital is turning an accrual profit into a defensive loss, that's troubling. You should ask yourself (and management) what purpose is served by depleting the company's cash reserves? Avoid these kinds of companies.

You can check whether a company can afford its dividend by dividing the annual payout by defensive profits. The dividend payout is reported in the financing section of the statement of cash flows. The lower the payout rate the more affordable the dividend. In contrast, a high dividend payout rate may unduly tax the firm's cash-generating ability. Anytime you see a payout rate over 50 percent of defensive profits, that's a sign of possible over-spending.

MORALE

Although it isn't an obvious or direct measure of management's competence, morale does reflect management's approach to one of the company's key assets. Happy employees give a firm a competitive edge. Dispirited employees, on the other hand, are a hidden cost that you should factor into your investment decisions.

You can scope out morale by searching the Internet for bulletin boards that let employees speak their mind. If the company is a retailer, go to the stores and chat up the employees.

Also, find out whether the company has been through several rounds of layoffs. Seeing their colleagues lose their jobs dampens employee enthusiasm, as the survivors spend valuable time trying to figure out who's next rather than paying attention to customers. Companywide reorganizations, especially if they happen repeatedly, are poison.

Many old-line industrial companies have employees that are party to collective bargaining agreements, so check if there is a history of strikes. With so many other companies to choose from, no need to get mixed up in a situation where there's a possibility of labor unrest.

Other clues of low morale include workplace safety violations and citations for unfair labor practices.

Liberty Hyde Bailey was once asked by a lady what to do about all the dandelions in her lawn. The famous botanist's pithy advice? "Learn to love them."

As an investor, you don't have to learn to love the dandelions in your portfolio; you can pull them out. In addition to using quantitative tools like the Earnings Power Chart, debt repayment period, and return on greenest dollar, look at the *qualitative* aspects of the business, including management. The longer you intend to own the stock, the bigger their role in determining whether your investment is a success.

CHAPTER 13

Graham's Classroom

As we learned in Chapter 1, if you are a growth investor you must successfully navigate three obstacles to achieve satisfactory results. These obstacles are valuation, competitive advantage, and earnings quality. Misjudge a company on any one of these items and you could sere a hole in your purse that takes years to mend.

This book is primarily concerned with the last of these three obstacles, earnings quality. I believe the quickest and easiest way for you to become a better investor is to know whether a profitable company has authentic earnings power. If you become proficient with the defensive and enterprising income statements, then you won't own the next Enron, Lucent, and WorldCom. *There will be more debacles—but you don't need to be the victim.* Having made sure a company is able to self-fund and create value, we return to the other two obstacles: competitive advantage and valuation. These topics are books unto themselves, but here are some things to think about.

COMPETITIVE ADVANTAGE

Companies like Wrigley that are situated in the Earnings Power Box have a competitive advantage that is hard to duplicate and that sets them apart from ordinary, run-of-the-mill businesses. But before you buy such a company's stock, determine (1) what the competitive advantage is, and (2) how long it will last.

Here are ways a firm can differentiate itself from competitors:

- World-class brands (for example, Coca-Cola, Nike, Wrigley)
- Stockholder-oriented management (see Chapter 12)
- Nurturing culture for employees
- Great customer service
- Creativity and innovation
- Valuable patents or trademarks
- Investment in R&D or advertising that contributes to top-line revenue growth
- High costs for customers to switch to competing products
- Dominant market share
- Efficient distribution routes
- Well-sited store locations
- Licensing agreements
- Lowest-cost production
- Pricing power
- Anti-trust laws that make it difficult for a rival to emerge

If you have trouble ascertaining a firm's competitive advantage(s), listen to what its leadership has to say. You can do this by reading the chairperson's letter to stockholders in the annual report, and by checking the company's press releases online. Companies are only too happy to crow about what makes them special. If the firm is in the retail business, go to a store and talk to the employees. The more competitive advantages a firm has, the better.

Now that you've identified the source or sources of the firm's competitive advantage, assess its durability. The longer you believe a firm's competitive advantage will last, the better. Of all the skills needed to do well as an investor, being able to answer the "how long will it last" question is the toughest—just ask anyone who owned technology stocks in the late 1990s.

Here are a few questions to ask yourself:

- What are this company's strengths? Weaknesses?
- What are its competitors' strengths? Weaknesses? (Keep in mind that these days a firm's competitors also include suppliers and customers.)
- Does the company offer products that satisfy basic human or business needs or wants?
- Is the company the lowest-cost producer? Lowest-cost producers can sustain their position in tough times and leverage their dominance when the economy comes roaring back.
- Does the company have financial muscle? A Fort Knox balance sheet can help keep a pesky competitor at bay.
- Does the company have a dominant or growing market share? A company that dominates its industry or is gaining market share is doing something right.
- Does the company compete in an industry that will support additional growth?

In trying to determine how long a firm will be able to maintain its dominance, think about the business model. Specifically, how does the company generate a dollar of revenue? Consider two businesses, one that sells luxury cars and another that sells chewing gum. All else being equal, given the choice between owning a company that makes expensive products or services that are bought occasionally and the company that makes cheap (in price, not quality) products or services that are bought frequently, opt for the latter. The cheap products/repeat purchase model is safer because with each sale customers are reminded once again why they like the company's product. Also, top-line revenue is more predictable when the product or service is bought often. Last, in a recession people will be inclined to hold onto their luxury automobiles for another year but go ahead and buy another pack of gum. Wrigley fits the cheap product/repeat purchase model, which augurs well for its continued prosperity.

Be careful with companies that sell "superior technology." In the short-run, superior technology may mean rapid growth in defensive and enterprising profits. But being situated in the Earning Power Box is also a magnet that attracts competitors, and competitors, as we have learned, like to introduce new products and services that are newer, faster, cheaper, and more efficient. If you're a consumer, innovation is wonderful; if you're a business owner, however, innovation can be your enemy, possibly rendering your products or services obsolete overnight. (To remind me of this point, I have on my desk a cartoon from *The New Yorker* entitled "French Army Knife." The knife pictured has 12 corkscrews. If the 12 corkscrews is a firm's superior technology, you can bet competitors are working day-and-night on a *13-corkscrew* knife!)

Perhaps the most important competitive advantage is management. Does management have the ability to continue its outstanding performance? Does management allocate capital well? Are management's interests properly aligned with stockholders'? (See Chapter 12 for more on this topic.)

In addition to its pristine balance sheet, Wrigley's competitive advantage is enhanced by world-class brands and international operations in several countries. In the United States, Wrigley sells nearly half of all chewing gum. In 18 European markets it has an 80 percent or greater market share.

So Wrigley gets the green light in our analysis, not only for its earnings quality but also on the basis of competitive advantage.

When assessing a firm's competitive advantage, use the Earnings Power Chart to check how its competitors are doing. To illustrate, let's compare Wrigley to Hershey Foods Corporation, which makes chocolate products such as Hershey's Kisses and Reese's peanut butter cups as well as gum and mints such as Ice Breakers, Breath Savers, and Bubble Yum; Tootsie Roll Industries, maker of Tootsie Roll and Tootsie Roll Pop candies; Lance Inc., which sells retail snack foods like Cape Cod potato chips and "Toast-Chee" crackers to convenience stores, supermarkets, gas stations, and vending machines; and Topps Company, maker of Bazooka bubble gum and sports cards.

The Quality of Profits chart (Figure 13.1) shows all five companies have accrual profits. It's also apparent that Hershey not only has the tallest earnings profits, but it is the only company to have defensive and enterprising profits that exceed its accrual results. Wrigley displays a good correlation among its three results and Tootsie Roll also has profits in all three categories, although its correlation is looser. Topps has a defensive

Figure 13.1

Wrigley Peer Survey, Quality of Profits, 2002

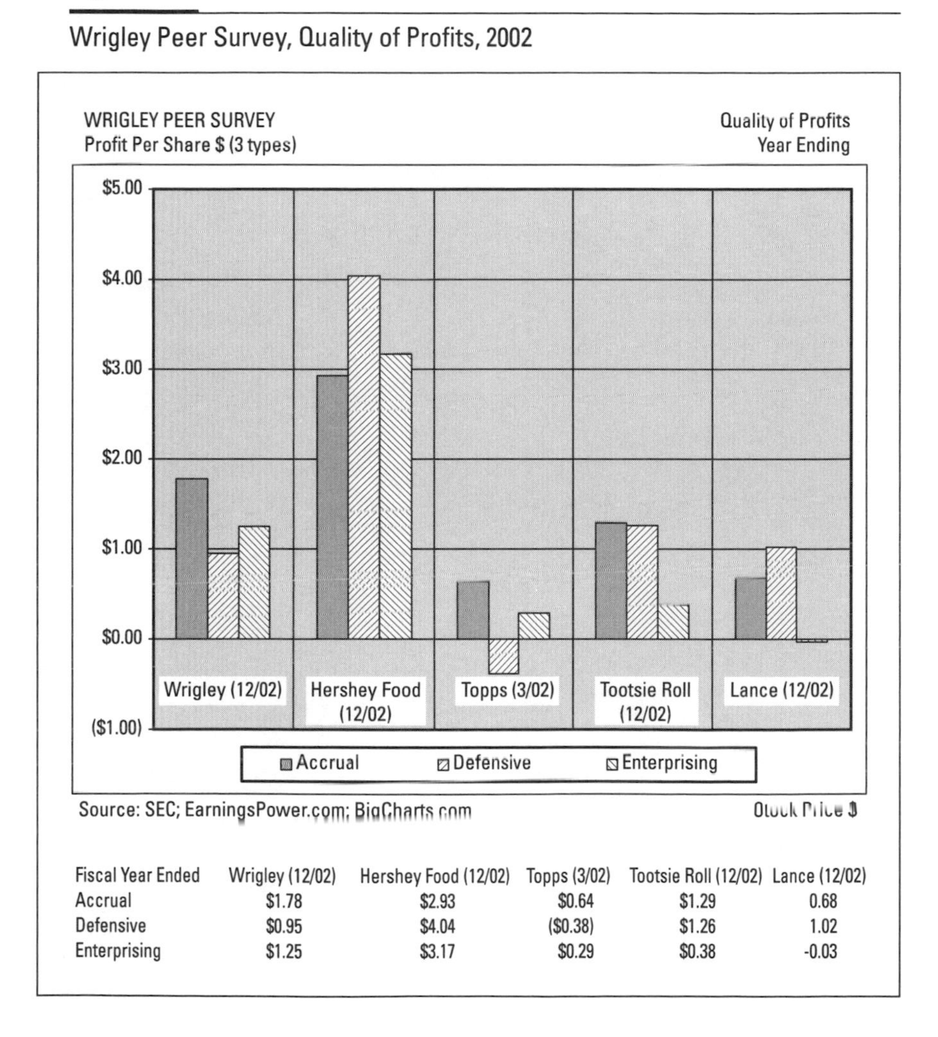

Fiscal Year Ended	Wrigley (12/02)	Hershey Food (12/02)	Topps (3/02)	Tootsie Roll (12/02)	Lance (12/02)
Accrual	$1.78	$2.93	$0.64	$1.29	0.68
Defensive	$0.95	$4.04	($0.38)	$1.26	1.02
Enterprising	$1.25	$3.17	$0.29	$0.38	-0.03

loss but an enterprising profit, Lance the opposite—a defensive profit but an enterprising loss.

Viewing these companies' results via the Earnings Power Chart (Figure 13.2) provides an interesting comparison of their earnings quality. But a one-year comparison is merely a snapshot. It's best if you can repeat this examination going back four or five years.

If one of your companies does lots of business with a handful of publicly traded customers, use the Earnings Power Chart to monitor *their* performance. If a few important customers get into trouble, then your stock is sure to feel the pain. Call Investor Relations to find out if there is a customer concentra-

Figure 13.2

Wrigley Peer Survey, Earnings Power Chart, 2002

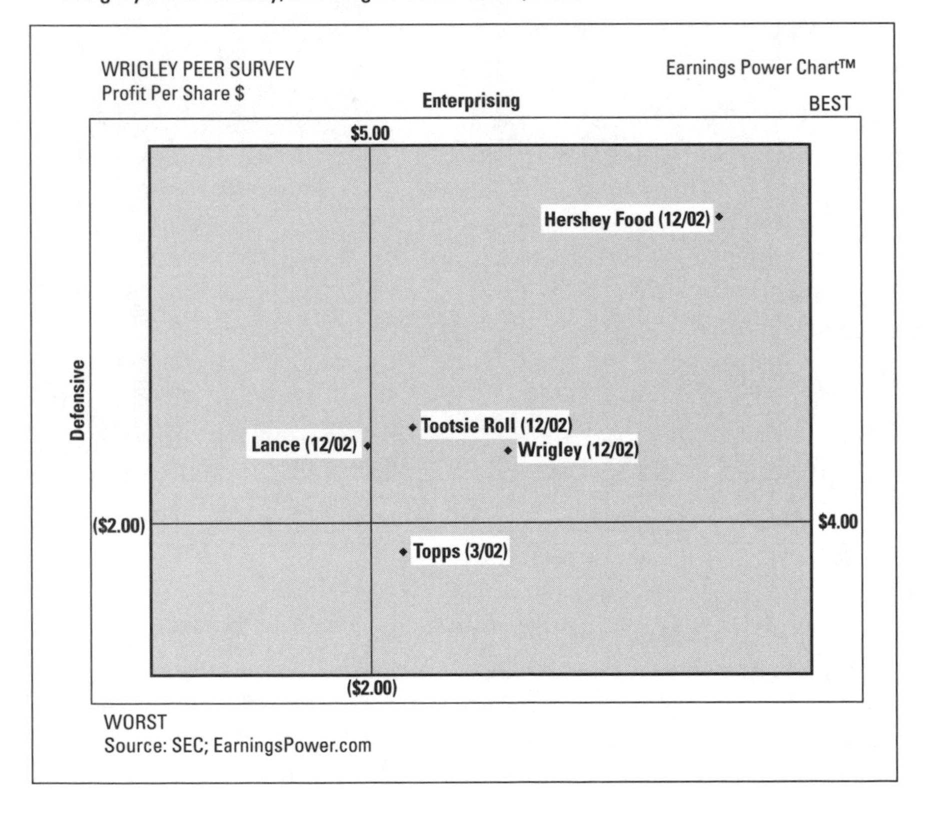

tion risk. In Wrigley's case, no mention is made in its annual report of customer concentration.

VALUATION

Our third and final test is valuation. The price you pay for any stock determines your return, and even Earnings Power Staircase companies can make for lousy stocks if you overpay. So what is the right price to pay for an earnings power company?

If a company has authentic earnings power, I turn to the Croesus test, after King Croesus of Lydia, who was known for his wealth and the prosperity of his kingdom. (If the company is not situated in the Earnings Power Box, then you should have less confidence in the quality of a firm's accrual profits.) The first assumption under the Croesus test is that you are rich enough not just to buy a few shares of stock but to acquire the entire company! That puts valuation in a much broader context. Now, consider these five steps:

1. *Decide the total return that you want.* For illustration purposes, let's assume that after assessing Wrigley's earnings quality and competitive advantage, you want to earn a 15 percent total return every year for the next 10 years. That's your minimum required rate of return. (Of course, just because you *want* to earn 15 percent doesn't mean it will happen.) A firm's total return is the sum of the dividend yield plus any capital appreciation, that is, a higher stock price. Thus,

Total return = Dividend yield + Capital appreciation

In Wrigley's case, right now it has a dividend yield of 1.5 percent. That means if we want a total return of 15 percent, the other 13.5 percent must come from capital appreciation. Expressed another way:

$$\begin{aligned} \text{Capital appreciation} &= \text{Total return} - \text{Dividend yield} \\ &= 15\% - 1.5\% \\ &= 13.5\% \end{aligned}$$

2. *Calculate Wrigley's market value.* With 225.576 million shares outstanding and a closing price of $57 on April 30, 2003,

Wrigley has a market value of $12.9 billion. Thus, to buy the entire company (remember, you're as rich as Croesus), it will cost you $12.9 billion (in millions except stock price).

If a company employs lots of debt, add that amount to the market value figure. This adjustment increases your cost of ownership. If, on the other hand, the business is flush with cash or marketable securities, then subtract the amount from market value. This adjustment lowers your purchase price. In Wrigley's case its debt and cash balances are insignificant in relation to its market value, so we don't make any adjustments.

$$\begin{aligned}\text{Market value} &= \text{Shares outstanding} \times \text{Stock price}\\ &= 225.576 \times \$57\\ &= \$12{,}858\end{aligned}$$

3. *Calculate Wrigley's market value 10 years out.* Since growth investing means making a long-term commitment let's assume you you plan to own Wrigley for ten years and then will sell the company to another Croesus. If Wrigley's stock goes up 13.5 percent as required, at the end of year 1 its market value must be $14.6 billion. This process repeats itself the next year, so by the end of year 2 the firm's market value must be $16.6 billion. By the end of year 10, Wrigley's market value must be $45.6 billion for you to achieve your 13.5 percent capital appreciation per year, as shown in Table 13.1. (Remember, we assume the other 1.5 percent annual gain is from dividends.)

4. *Estimate the P/E ratio at the end of 10 years (a guess, to be sure).* Now, let's assume you sell Wrigley at the end of year 10. What will the company sell for? Let's say Wrigley's terminal P/E ratio is 17x (a realistic assumption if the gum maker is still situated in the Earnings Power Box). That means earnings in year 10 must be $2.7 billion. (Divide the $45.6 billion market value by 17.)

5. *Finally, the sanity test.* In 2002, Wrigley's accrual profits totaled $402 million. So to reach $2.7 billion in year 10, the company's earnings must go up 6.7 times, which is the equivalent of a 21 percent compound annual growth rate.

Table 13.1

Wrigley Company's Forecasted 10-Year Growth in Market Value (in millions, except growth rate)

Year	Beginning Market Value	Growth Rate	Ending Market Value
1	$12,858	13.5%	$14,594
2	$14,594	13.5%	$16,564
3	$16,564	13.5%	$18,800
4	$18,800	13.5%	$21,338
5	$21,338	13.5%	$24,218
6	$24,218	13.5%	$27,488
7	$27,488	13.5%	$31,199
8	$31,199	13.5%	$35,411
9	$35,411	13.5%	$40,191
10	$40,191	13.5%	$45,617

Can Wrigley attain this earnings growth rate? We won't know the answer for sure until 2012. Still, Wrigley's past earnings growth rate offers a clue to what the future may hold. According to Morningstar, Wrigley's earnings grew an average of 10.8 percent a year for the 10 years ending 2002. In light of past performance, a 21 percent earnings growth rate for the next 10 years seems, well, ambitious. Don't you agree? If you want to obtain a 15 percent total return every year for the next decade, you would not want to buy Wrigley at its current stock price.

Alas, it's our third obstacle—valuation—that prevents us from buying Wrigley's stock. Wrigley has authentic earnings power, as well as several competitive advantages. So far, so good. But when we combine 2002 accrual profits (the most recent year available) with its recent stock price, the Croesus Test tells us the earnings growth rate needed to support our minimum required rate of return is well above its historic growth rate. It's not even close.

What to do? We will put Wrigley on our watch list and reassess the situation if the stock price drops sharply.

The Valuation Conundrum

The best companies (but not necessarily the best stocks) are Earnings Power Staircase companies. Not only are the companies getting bigger, they are getting better. You can be assured that Earnings Power Staircase companies have one or more competitive advantages; you just have to figure out what they are and how long they will last.

Of course, other investors will also want to own these corporate masterpieces. As a result, many Earnings Power Staircase companies have high price-earnings ratios.

To mitigate the risk that you overpay for growth that never materializes, here are four suggestions:

1. *Profitable growth.* Is may sound obvious, but make sure the company is forging that all-important staircase pattern. It would be unfortunate to pay a high price-earnings ratio for low-quality earnings. Unfortunately, investors do it all the time. Don't you be one of these people.
2. *Consider the smaller companies.* Try to buy an Earnings Power Staircase in its youth when most of its profitable growth lies ahead.
3. *Dollar-cost average.* There is no need to buy a full position today. Instead, dollar-cost average. Here's how. Let's assume you earmarked $10,000 to invest in a company. Instead of investing the entire sum all at once, buy $2,500 worth of stock today. If the fundamentals remain intact, then buy another $2,500 of stock a year later. If the stock price of your second installment is below your starter position, then you're happy because you get more shares for your money. If, on the other hand, the second installment costs more than your starter position (that is, you can't buy as many shares), then you're happy because of the capital gains. Either way you'll be satisfied with the outcome.

Repeat in years three and four, at which point you will have a full $10,000 position.

4. *Buy the best companies in unpopular industries.* Robert L. Rodriguez, Chief Executive Officer, First Pacific Advisors and two-time recipient of Morningstar Mutual Fund's Manager of the Year, doesn't believe an investor can forecast the future with any degree of accuracy or consistency. "That is why we tend to focus on market leadership companies in industries or sectors that are out of favor." By doing this, Rodriguez explains, "one is hopefully deploying capital into areas where the expectations are low."[1]

When Benjamin Graham taught at Columbia University one of his favorite instructional methods was to take two companies and line them up side by side. "Ben's class became popular," Irving Kahn remembers, "because he didn't teach out of a book. What he talked about in class that afternoon was what you would see in the papers that night or the next morning. This motivated the guys not only to become analysts but to learn how people were making money in the market under today's conditions."[1]

So, in the spirit of Graham, it's not enough for you to just "look over my shoulder" as I do the calculations and go through the analysis. Now, it's up to you.

If Graham, in our imaginary classroom, already has Wrigley on the chalkboard, what other company should he evaluate? The choice is yours. Find a company that looks promising. Determine its defensive and enterprising results. Run a Quality of Profits analysis. Then, place the company on the Earnings Power Chart. Into which box does it fall? If the company is situated in the Earnings Power Box, is it forging a staircase? With respect to competitive advantage, what is it and how long will it last? And, last, is the firm's current market value low enough so you get your minimum required rate of return?

Moving forward, the following sidebar gives a checklist for finding a company to compare to Wrigley:

The Earnings Power Decision Gates

1. *Identify a promising investment opportunity.* (For more ideas of where to look, see Chapter 14.)
2. *Get the company's latest 10-K.* (Call the company's Investor Relations department or get it from the company's or from various other Web sites.)
3. *The initial screen.* (Use the earnings power five-minute test, as described in Chapter 4, to eliminate companies that aren't worth your time.)
4. *Obtain the financials.* (To do the in-depth financial study, you'll need the company's 10-Ks for the past five years as well as the latest proxy. Sources: www.sec.gov and www.freeedgar.com)
5. *In which box is the firm situated?* (Build defensive and enterprising income statements. Determine the company's position on the Earnings Power Chart. Does it occupy the upper-right box, the Earnings Power Box? See Chapter 5, 6 and 7.)
6. *Is the company an Earnings Power Staircase?* (If the company is in the Earnings Power Box, does it exhibit consistent, year-to-year growth in defensive and enterprising profits that conforms to the staircase pattern described in Chapter 9?)
7. *Ratio analysis.* (Calculate the debt repayment period to see if the company can repay its debts and equivalents in less than five years. Use the return on greenest dollar ratio to see if management is generating a return of at least 15 percent on last year's investment. See Chapter 11.)
8. *Management.* (Assess the company's management. Are their interests aligned with yours? See Chapter 12.)
9. *Competitive advantage.* (Do you know what makes this company special? Do you know how long it will remain unique? Unique companies are the best stocks to own over long periods. See Chapter 13.)
10. *Valuation.* (Use the Croesus test to see if you have a shot at making your minimum required rate of return.

If the stock price is too high right now, buy a few shares as a "starter" position. A year from now, you can add to your position—provided, of course, the firm's earnings quality remains intact. See Chapter 13.)

11. *When to sell?* (Watch the company's defensive and enterprising results for sudden changes, such as a decline in profits or an unexpected loss. Based on my research, the defensive and/or enterprising income statements are almost always better leading indicators of earnings trouble than the accrual ledger. See Chapter 14 for other red flags.)

In *Dramatic Art*, Voltaire observes: *Le mieux est l'ennemi du bien*—"The best is the enemy of the good." How true. We put off doing a task today because we think we'll have the time to do a better job tomorrow. But what happens is predictable: We end up doing nothing! Don't make this mistake. Start as soon as you can. The more companies you study the easier this gets.

In Chapter 14 we'll examine several ways to identify promising investment opportunities to get the ball rolling as well as companies to avoid.

CHAPTER 14

Get Started Today

Even if you're just a casual investor, it's hard to go through the day without becoming aware of companies that may be great stocks for the next several years.

There are many places to consider to expand your search for the next possible Earnings Power Staircase company (when you find it, hold on tight, reinvest any dividends, and buy more shares on your birthday or another important anniversary).

Your household is a good place to start your search. Do you see a product or service that you use every day? Many companies that have produced great wealth for their stockholders over the last quarter-century make goods or provide services that people use daily.

What about companies that you pass by often? Imagine if you lived in Rochester, New York, the headquarters of Paychex, for the last 10 or 15 years and had driven past its headquarters regularly, but without really paying attention. There you were, consumed with worries about the cost of a new roof, medical bills, your kids' college tuition, and all the while the answer to your financial worries was right outside your car window. Are you driving past the next Paychex everyday?

A fellow I know, more competitive than most people, pores over financial statements of companies for which his friends and family work. He doesn't want to get left behind if *they* hit the mother lode. Perhaps this technique will work for you.

Become an expert in an industry in which you have great personal interest, perhaps in your line of work or one related to a hobby. When you focus on investment opportunities in which you have specialized knowledge, then you have a leg up over other investors. If you don't know anything about a company, its industry, or its products, you will be at a disadvantage.

Every year business magazines such as *BusinessWeek*, *Forbes*, and *Fortune* publish lists of America's fastest-growing companies. These are good places to look. Winnow your research from there.

If you are a strategic thinker, try figuring out which companies will benefit from the broad demographic changes taking place around you. An obvious theme is the effects of an aging population on the health care industry. But don't overlook the restaurant, travel, gambling, and entertainment industries that should benefit from the largest, most affluent, and best-educated population of Americans over age 60 ever. Also consider which industries stand to *lose* from these trends.

Perhaps following insider buying will unearth a promising stock. Company officers and board members know their businesses better than everyone else. Insiders, after all, have first-hand knowledge of price increases, planned cost efficiencies, or the pending demise of a competitor that underbids every job. Also, because the SEC requires that officers and directors hold for at least six months shares that have gone up in price, they're mostly long-term investors. You can obtain data on insider purchases on many free Web sites including Yahoo! and CBS MarketWatch.

Perhaps you subscribe to Thomas Carlyle's "Great Man" theory. Carlyle (1795–1881) believed that the Hero, not the Establishment or the State, is the catalyst for change, and that the history of the world is the biography of great men. If you agree with Carlyle, then follow companies that are run by executives who have a long history of making money for their stockholders.

Sandy Weill's visage won't be chiseled onto Mount Rushmore, but the banker does have an impressive track record of making money for his stockholders. Starting with a small brokerage firm that he helped found in 1960, Weill began buying other companies. In 1986 he took over Commercial Credit, a sickly finance company that made high-interest loans to blue-collar workers. Then, Weill's Commercial Credit bought Primerica (owner of Smith Barney), Shearson, and Travelers in 1993. After his company took the Travelers name, Weill added Aetna's property and casualty business in 1996 and Salomon Brothers in 1997. In 1999, Weill merged Travellers with Citicorp. Do you know a Sandy Weill? (In mid-2003, Weill announced that he planned to relinquish his job as Citigroup's chief executive by the end of the year.)

Investigate companies that "master" investors are buying. Although topnotch fund advisors are loath to reveal the companies they are buying (to prevent others from taking a position in front of a big order), anyone who manages $100 million or more must file a 13-F report with the SEC within 45 days of the end of each quarter. So identify a manager whose investment style you find congenial and check their filings via Edgar online (see www.sec.gov) to see what they are buying and selling.

Use an Internet-based screening tool. With Microsoft's MSN Stock Screener, for instance, you can look for companies with, say, a market value in excess of $100 million, revenue that is growing at least 10 percent per year, return on equity of at least 15 percent, shares trading below two times revenue, and a debt-to-equity ratio of less than 75 percent. Use this list as the basis for further spadework.

By all means examine the companies you already own. Do they self-fund and create value? If not, sell. Call it addition by subtraction.

Here are companies to *avoid*:

- *Initial public offerings.* You may think you're buying the next Microsoft when it debuts, but the odds are stacked against you. Individual investors rarely get the choicest deals, and many IPOs run up so much on the first day of trading that they're overpriced by the time you can get to them. Also, IPOs are expensive. As Warren Buffett has pointed out, if you're selling part of your company to strangers, would you do so at any time other than when you believe you can get highest price? That's usually a time of great market enthusiasm and a warning to investors.

- *Fads.* This list includes Hula-Hoop makers, microbrewery stocks, celebrity restaurants, scooters, pet rocks, mood rings and their ilk. They may rise quickly, but they usually fall faster.
- *Companies whose clients are in trouble.* Problems, like salmon migrating to spawn, go *upstream.*
- *Cocktail party stocks.* You know what I'm talking about. This is the stock on everyone's lips. There's truth in the old saw that if you see a bandwagon, it's probably too late to jump on it.
- *Small customer base.* Check the footnotes to make sure the company's revenue isn't concentrated among a handful of customers. This is especially important for smaller companies. Several years ago ADDvantage Media Group (which later changed its name to ADDvantage Technologies Group) saw its stock zoom from pennies a share to $9 after it inked a deal with Wal-Mart to install solar-powered calculators on shopping carts. But when Wal-Mart pulled out it sent ADDvantage's stock plummeting, to $0.50. Companies must disclose in their financial statements whether a customer accounts for more than 10 percent of total revenue.
- *Leveraged balance sheets.* Staircase companies don't need to borrow lots of money.
- *Insider selling.* There's no reason to buy when executives are heavy sellers, although occasional or planned sales (to comply with SEC rules and avoid impropriety) are fine. Executives need to buy houses, send children to college, and pay divorce settlements too.
- *Serial acquirers.* Companies that embark on pell-mell acquisition sprees might generate impressive sales and

earnings gains in the short-run, but, like Icarus, they tend to crash. Also, when a company keeps buying other companies it's harder to determine its organic growth (that is, the internal growth from the existing business). All else being equal, firms with high organic growth rates are more desirable than firms with low organic growth rates.

- *Recurring "one-time" charges.* Companies with more than two years of unusual and/or extraordinary losses in the last 10 years are probably overstating their accrual profits or mismanaging their stockholders' capital. Companies that restate their earnings should also be avoided.
- *Management instability.* In the late 1990s Global Crossing's plush executive headquarters had a revolving door on the corner office, which several different CEOs had occupied in the years leading up to its bankruptcy. Other clues of potential turmoil are changes in auditor or outside legal counsel.
- *Change of business strategy.* In the late 1970s Philadelphia Savings Fund Society, the first savings institution of its kind in the country, was severely hurt by inflation as well as by Wall Street's offering of high-rate certificates of deposit and money market accounts. Uncertain what to do, PSFS eventually renamed itself Meritor Savings Bank, went public, and then got mixed up in new ventures such as credit cards and equipment leasing. But Meritor had no prior experience in these areas and it eventually lost hundreds of millions of dollars. When the federal regulators padlocked the doors in 1992 the stock was trading at 25 cents, well off its $10 high from just a few years earlier.
- *Old and famous companies that have passed their prime.* These are the brand-name growth stocks that have double-digit price-earnings ratios and single-digit revenue growth.
- *Companies with lots of goodwill as a percentage of total assets.* If goodwill is a big percentage of the firm's

assets, it might mean the company is a serial acquirer and is overpaying for its deals. If management later decides that the goodwill is "impaired," or no longer of any use to the company, that asset will have to be written off. This charge reduces the stockholders' equity account, which can lead to adverse debt ratios and violate loan covenants with banks and other lenders. Why take the risk?

- *Stock option dilution.* Companies that award employees fistfulls of stock options punish their stockholders. As Zeke Ashton, managing partner of Centaur Capital Partners and a Motley Fool contributor has observed, this largesse acts like a reverse dividend—the longer you hold the stock, the more your ownership gets re-distributed from you to company insiders.[1] Don't tolerate it. Avoid companies with dilution rates over 5 percent a year.
- *Ex-investment bankers.* Investment bankers know how to buy and sell companies and write fairness opinions (value a business), but few have the experience to use R&D to develop new products and services, devise low-cost manufacturing processes, and create distribution channels. Before Jean-Marie Messier racked up a huge debt following a $100 billion spending spree in an attempt to turn the French utilities company Vivendi into a global media conglomerate, he was investment bank at Lazard Freres & Co. In due course, Vivendi struggled with its leveraged balance sheet and the stock fell hard.
- *Jerks.* In April 2001 Enron held a conference call to announce results for the first quarter. Jeffrey Skilling, the newly installed chief executive officer, had lots of good news to report. But when a fund manager asked to see a balance sheet (a reasonable request, I might add), Skilling used a vulgar word to describe the questioner. Besides shocking everyone who listened to the call, the comment was a revealing insight into the character of the man running the company. Four months later Skilling resigned from the Enron for "personal reasons." That December Enron filed for bankruptcy.

Now that you have ample suggestions for how to pick potential candidates and how to spot those that are likely to cause you trouble, what about *you*? The emphasis thus far has been on the company—its earnings quality, competitive advantage, and valuation. But when it comes to your portfolio, *you* are an integral part.

Here are a baker's dozen other ideas to help make you a better investor.

1. *Get your financial house in order.* Your first step—no ifs, ands, or buts—is to take care of such basics as insurance, savings, wills, guardianships, trustees, estate planning, college tuition, and paying off consumer debt. If you are a procrastinator, get professional help. You'd be surprised how many intelligent, well-educated people neglect this important responsibility.

2. *Save regularly.* Saving and investing regularly is more important than being a good stock picker. Consider two neighbors, Peter Plodder and Hank Hotshot. Peter saves $3000 a year and earns a 10 percent rate of return. Hank, although he books a 15 percent gain every year on his portfolio, because he invests only $1000 per year, has less money. At the end of 25 years Hank has $245,000, Peter $345,000.

If you are like Hank Hotshot and you don't save enough, consider a few cost-saving steps. Take your lunch to work and drive your car for a few more years before trading it in. Also, if your lifestyle is too expensive, meaning you have more financial stress than enjoyment in your life, ask whether you can live in a cheaper and smaller house? Or perhaps you could move to another part of the country with a lower cost of living. Use the savings to build your nest egg.

What Percentage of My Stock Portfolio Should I Manage Myself?

Anyone who buys stocks likes to think that they can choose winners. In fact, beating the market—performing better than a broad market average like the S&P 500—is hard. That's why most investors should probably have most of their assets in professionally managed funds, perhaps even index funds. Index funds give you a broad representation of the stock market, at a low cost.

So what percentage of your stock portfolio should you manage yourself? John C. Bogle, the founder and former CEO of The Vanguard Group and kind author of this book's Foreword, recommends 5 percent. That seems right to me. If after a few years things go well, then maybe you double the allocation to 10 percent.

3. *Formulate an investment strategy.* The poet E.B. White believed if your thinking is clear, then your writing will be clear. The same is true of investing, so formulate a strategy and write it down. This discipline will help you zero in on the kinds of companies you want most and avoid getting distracted by situations that are of peripheral interest. Naturally, your investment strategy should match your personality.

If you're looking for potential Staircases, your blueprint might go something like this:

> *Since I am a long-term cautiously greedy investor, my goal is to find a Staircase company that looks like it still has room to grow. My universe of potential candidates consists of all U.S.-based firms with at least $250 million of revenue and that have been public for at least five years. In addition, these companies will have simple businesses run by honest and competent people that are owner-friendly. Ideally, my holding period is at least five years in order to minimize frictional costs associated with frequent buying and selling activity. Reasons to sell are if the company violates one of my sell criteria (see below).*

If merger arbitrage (don't ask) is more your game, then write a merger arbitrage investment strategy. The point is, commit your plan to paper and it will focus your mind.

4. *Take an accounting class.* Accounting is the language of business, so you need to understand basic concepts such as revenue, depreciation, goodwill, and capital spending. If you don't, investing will be an uphill battle.

5. *Buy the business, not the stock.* One of the benefits of using the earnings power methodology is that it forces you to think about the quality of the *business* rather than just the stock. This will make you a better investor by giving you more insight into what you are buying. Thinking about management, durability of the franchise, and valuation will expand your knowledge of the firm.

6. *View analyst reports skeptically.* On January 8, 2000, that fateful day when Lucent Technologies management announced an earnings shortfall and the stock dropped like a rock, of the 38 analysts that covered it 15 had "strong buy" ratings, 17 "moderate buy" ratings, and 6 "hold" ratings. Incredibly, no one had a "sell" rating. These bright, expensively educated, highly paid analysts either did not or chose not to see the deterioration in Lucent's balance sheet. One analyst even issued a *higher* price target the same day that Lucent announced it was lowering its earnings targets. Of course, if these analysts had used the Earnings Power Chart, they would have known that Lucent's business was deteriorating before management said so publicly.

7. *Keep a list of stocks that you want to own.* Some investors feel compelled to put their loose coin to work immediately. So they buy shares of lower-quality growth companies without knowing whether they possess authentic earnings power as defined in this book. Don't make this mistake. Instead, keep a list of companies that you want to own and buy only when they sell the odds are in your favor.

In addition to notes on valuation, my list of companies to buy also has a short description of what the company does, the source of the idea, and the firm's competitive advantages and shortcomings.

8. *Patience.* Your greatest challenge isn't building defensive and enterprising income statements from scratch (don't worry, you'll get better with practice), but sitting still once you buy the stock. In *One Up on Wall Street*, Peter Lynch says most of the money he made came in the third or fourth year that he owned something.[2]

9. *Don't throw Hail Mary passes.* Control your desire to get rich fast, because it usually leads to taking self-destructive risks. And those risks lead the big losses that are hard to recover from. If you own a stock that drops 50 percent, for example, it needs to gain 100 percent for you to return to break even. (See Table 14.1) And if you own a stock that drops 75 percent, you need a 300 percent return to get back to square one.

By all means don't use margin debt to buy stocks. Ever.

10. *When to sell.* It's tempting to sell when one of your stocks goes down in price (and it will). It takes discipline and conviction to hold on. Still, buy and hold doesn't mean buy and hold *forever*. Eventually the time will come when the company you buy today is not the same company that you own tomorrow. Ideally, you will sell every stock at its peak. Alas, that's easier said than done. In fact, many investors find that selling is devilishly hard, for reasons deeply ingrained in human nature.

If you made a mistake and the stock is down, you may not want to "realize the loss." Selling a stock you lost money on means you made an error along the way, which makes you feel dumb. No one likes feeling dumb. Even if you're selling at a gain, you might be unhappy about the capital gains taxes you'll owe (unless you are using a tax-deferred account) and you might worry about whether you left money on the table if the stock keeps going up after you sell.

To be a better seller, forget what you paid for the stock. The price you pay for a stock determines your return, of course. But once you *own* the stock, your purchase price is irrelevant; it's what economists call a "sunk cost."

Table 14.1

The bigger a stock's decline, the bigger gain you need to recover

Decline	Gain to Recover
10%	11%
25%	33%
50%	100%
75%	300%
90%	900%

Also, if a firm's earnings quality begins to deteriorate, consider selling *gradually*. Just as you don't have to buy a full position all in one day, you do not need to sell all at once. By selling gradually you can mitigate the remorse of missing the boat if the stock keeps climbing. Besides a decline in earnings quality, here are other reasons that might cause you to sell all or part of your holding:

- The debt repayment period is rising
- The return on greenest dollar is falling
- Management misrepresents *anything*
- Earnings get restated
- Accounting irregularities surface
- Management is self-dealing
- Market share declines
- The company embarks on an acquisition spree
- Management buys a business in an industry they know little about
- Customer service declines
- The rate of change in sales growth begins to slow
- A key executive unexpectedly resigns or is fired
- The firm's accountants or lawyers abruptly quit
- Receivables and/or inventory rise sharply while revenue growth slows
- New and better capitalized competitors emerge
- Management, which used to talk freely when things went swimmingly, turns mute when troubles and disappointment occur.
- Insiders start aggressively selling shares
- The company cuts R&D spending or investment in other growth-producing initiatives. (This move may help the company meet its current earnings target but can imperil its long-term viability.)
- A price war erupts. (This tends to happen to commodity businesses, so-called because it is difficult to differentiate products from competition other than by price.)

- The company hires a prominent architect. (Enron's 40-story Houston building, designed by Cesar Pelli, was almost finished when the firm filed for bankruptcy.)
- The CEO buys a yacht with a working fireplace, acquires naming rights for a sports stadium, commissions a work of art, sponsors a golf tournament, or starts appearing in lifestyle magazines with his French chef.

Be sure to incorporate your sell criteria into your investment strategy, which we covered earlier, in point #3.

11. *Learn from your mistakes.* If you habitually lose money in the stock market, don't despair. Recall that even Benjamin Graham was nearly wiped out in the early 1930s, saved only by help from his business partner's cousin. Graham dusted himself off, figured out a strategy that worked for him, and never lost money again.

Jim Cramer, the co-founder of TheStreet.com and a former hedge fund manager, says "almost all of my good moves in the market are made because I have made so many bad ones—but took exquisite notes on the bad ones so they never happened again."[3] This is sensible advice from a man who made his limited partners lots of money.

One of the most efficient ways to learn is by reading articles on investors you admire so that you can learn from their techniques. Then reread these profiles annually. You'll be surprised at how much deeper your understanding of the material will be. Since you will make mistakes, at least make yours original.

12. *Read Philip Fisher.* The patriarch of growth investors, Fisher's motto is that he doesn't want a lot of good investments, he just wants a few outstanding ones. Fisher outlines his modus operandi in *Common Stocks and Uncommon Profits* (which includes his famous 15-point checklist).

13. *Take care of yourself.* Get regular exercise. Physical activity boosts the oxygen flow to your brain, helping you think more quickly and may even speed the production of new brain cells. Also, be positive. Research by the Mayo clinic finds that optimists live about 20 percent longer than pessimists. Last, keep things in perspective. According to a study of 41 nations, money has a *low* correlation with happiness (once basic needs are met), while marriage, friends, community support, free time, and churchgoing correlate highly. Even the joy you'd feel if you won the lottery would last only a few months.[4]

AFTERWORD

From now on, I hope that when you are looking for a stock that will make a difference, that you think about which of the four boxes of the Earnings Power Chart the company resides. If you use the defensive and enterprising income statements, you'll know whether it possesses authentic earnings power. This is where you want to start prospecting for treasure. Moreover, some of these companies will forge steady gains in both defensive and enterprising income. When you see that distinctive staircase pattern, *that's* the sign of profitable growth. With further investigation—calculating earnings power ratios, evaluating the competitive advantage (including the quality of management), and assessing the valuation—you will have the knowledge and confidence to know whether the stock belongs in your portfolio. Is the Earnings Power Chart omniscient? No, of course not. No strategy works all the time. But this two-axis model does fix the four major limitations of accrual income statement.

As you gain experience with the Earnings Power Chart don't expect to see a perfect correlation between defensive and enterprising profits and stock prices. In the short term, stock prices are subject to a variety of influences, including psychology, interest rates, and the direction of the overall market. Over the long term, though, growth in high quality accrual profits matters a lot.

Buying stocks is really a process of elimination, because in truth only a few companies are worthy of your time and money. But that's okay. As Etienne Decroux, the father of modern mime, remarked: "One pearl is better than a whole necklace of potatoes." Perhaps the Earnings Power Chart will help you find your own pearl.

NOTES

FOREWORD

1. *It's Earnings That Count*, Hewitt Heiserman Jr. (McGraw-Hill, 2004).

INTRODUCTION

1. The Buffett quotation is from a videotape made of the panel discussion, which was provided to the author courtesy of Irving Kahn.

CHAPTER 1

1. *Contrarian Investment Strategies*, David Dreman (Simon & Schuster, 1998).
2. Morningstar.com, August 20, 2003

CHAPTER 2

1. Wrigley.com, May 2, 2003

CHAPTER 3

1. *The Intelligent Investor*, Benjamin Graham (Harper & Row, 1973).
2. Biographical information on Graham is from Roger Lowenstein's *Buffett: The Making of an American Capitalist* (Random House, 1995) and John Train's *The Money Masters* (Harper & Row, 1980).

CHAPTER 4

1. Wm. Wrigley Jr. Company 2002 Annual Report.
2. The Speculator, MSN Money, posted 1/9/03, by Victor Niederhoffer and Laurel Kenner. The study is "The Effectiveness of Blue-Ribbon Committee Investigations in Mitigating Financial Restatements: An Empirical Study," by Lawrence J. Abbott, Susan Parker, and Gary Peters.
3. *The Interpretation of Financial Statements*, 1998 reissue of 1937 edition by Benjamin Graham and Spencer Meredith (Harper Business, 1998).
4. Securities and Exchange Commission Web site: www.sec.gov.

CHAPTER 6

1. Wall Street Journal, May 16, 2000.
2. Roger Lowenstein, *Buffett: The Making of an American Capitalist.* (Random House, 1995)

CHAPTER 7

1. *W.C. Fields, His Follies and Fortunes*. Robert Taylor (Doubleday & Company, 1949).
2. Dow Jones Newswires, "Eight Face Charges in Connection With Allou Fraud," August 12, 2003.

CHAPTER 10

1. 2000 edition of Securities Research Company's book of 35-Year Charts.

CHAPTER 12

1. Enron Corporation's 2000 annual report.
2. General Electric.com, April 2, 2003
3. *BusinessWeek*, January 31, 2002, "An Abrupt About-Face by Accountants."
4. *CFO*, May 2002.

CHAPTER 13

1. E-mail to author from Robert L. Rodriguez, August 3, 2003
2. From a videotape courtesy of Irving Kahn.

CHAPTER 14

1. "Be at Risk—and the Market," Zeke Ashton. *The Motley Fool*, May 22, 2003.
2. *One Up on Wall Street*, Peter Lynch (New York: Simon and Schuster, 1989), p.253.
3. RealMoney.com
4. *Money*, Fall 2002.

INDEX

About the Author

Hewitt Heiserman Jr. writes a popular column on earnings power for TheStreet.com's investment website RealMoney.com. A graduate of Kenyon College with Distinction in History, Heiserman conceived the Earnings Power Chart, Earnings Power Box, and Earnings Power Staircase. A financial analyst for the last 15 years, he is a member of the Boston Security Analyst Society and the Association for Investment Management and Research.

(For more information visit www.earningspower.com.)